HOPE FOR TODAY

PREFACE

It was a joy to work with my great friend Peter Marsh on this book *HOPE FOR TODAY*. His mind was stocked with excellent and interesting quotations. We both felt the need for a new book to follow Dorothy M Prescott's inspired daily readings *A NEW DAY*, first published in 1957. We have used her themes for each day throughout and wish to state our indebtedness to her.

Peter, although suffering from cancer, persisted in preparing the book. He had a wonderful spirit and it was a great satisfaction to him that he completed it shortly before he received his 'last posting'.

He prepared a draft Preface in which he wrote:
'... Is not the supreme fulfilment of life to be found only in selfless care for others empowered by the direction of God? To do that it is necessary, as many thousands have found, to make a practice of listening to God for guidance, preferably in the early morning, and writing down the thoughts that come.

'The object of these daily readings is to stimulate the thinking for this purpose, these guidelines providing fulfilment of the purpose for which you have been privileged to be born.'

We hope this book will be helpful to all who read it, and especially to a younger generation looking for something to inspire them in a time of quiet reflection before starting the day. We are indebted to Elizabeth Locke and Michael Hutchinson for their valuable editorial help, criticism and suggestions.

Peter's dedication reads: 'This book is dedicated to Thomas and Katherine and to all great-grandchildren.'

HPE

THE NEW YEAR

THE FIRST HOUR OF THE DAY   January 1

In the early morning, while it was still dark, Jesus got up, left the house and went off to a deserted place and there he prayed.

Mark 1:35

Joy cometh in the morning.   *Psalm 30:5*

The real problem of the Christian life comes where people do not usually look for it. It comes the very moment you wake up each morning. All your wishes and hopes for the day rush at you like wild animals. And the first job each morning consists simply in shoving them all back; in listening to that other voice, taking that other point of view, letting that other larger, stronger, quieter life come flowing in. And so on, all day.

C S Lewis

In the calmness of the morning, before the mind is heated and weary by the turmoil of the day, you have a season of unusual importance for communing with God and with yourself.

William Wilberforce

I found that when I began to spend an hour daily in quiet that, far from taking up precious time and adding to an already heavy programme, that hour became the simplifying, unifying, time-saving key to the whole day.

Rev Cecil Rose, describing the experience of a busy housewife

LAUNCH OUT!   January 2

It is important that we go forward in the light of such truth as we have already learned.   *Philippians 3:16*

Jesus said: The Father has never left me alone for I always do what pleases him.   *John 6:29*

Every life should have a purpose to which it can give the energies of its mind and the enthusiasms of its heart.

Neil C Strait

7

A youthful gang leader was dared to go into the cathedral and make the most startling confession, then do whatever penance the priest suggested. At the end of the confession the priest told the lad to kneel before the crucifix and say: 'You died for me and I don't care a damn.' The lad knelt down and repeated, 'You died for me,' but he couldn't look at the crucifix and complete the sentence. (Archbishop Montini added: 'I know the story is true because I was the gang leader.')

This is the secret of joy. We shall no longer strive for our own way; but commit ourselves, easily and simply, to God's way, acquiesce in his will and in so doing find our peace.

Evelyn Underhill

Our task as laymen is to live our personal communion with Christ with such intensity as to make it contagious.

Dr Paul Tournier

PIONEERS   January 3

When I have completed this task... I shall come to you en route for Spain. I feel sure that in this visit I shall bring with me the full blessing of Christ.   *Romans 15:27-8*

What makes life dreary is absence of motive. What makes life complicated is multiplicity of motive. What makes life victorious is singleness of motive.   *George Eliot*

Here is what frightens me: to see the sense of this life dissipated; to see the reason for our existence disappear. That is what is intolerable. People cannot live without meaning.

Albert Camus

Someone without purpose is like a ship without a rudder.

Thomas Carlyle

Each man and each woman counts. Part of our trouble is that we think the individual is powerless. That is a lie. He is not powerless. Your vote counts. Your voice counts. Each man and woman is needed if the drift towards chaos is to stop. Your country needs you.   *Archbishop Donald Coggan*

And the Lord said unto Joshua, Get thee up; wherefore liest thou thus upon thy face?   *Joshua 7:10*

THE NEW WORLD   January 4

In my opinion whatever we may have to go through now is less than nothing compared with the magnificent future God has in store for us. The whole creation is on tiptoe to see the wonderful sight of the children of God coming into their own.

Romans 8:18-19

Islam means to yield to the will of God, and to believe in the unity of mankind.   *Dr A Bazoz, one-time Prime Minister of Iraq*

The only ultimate disaster that can befall us is to feel at home on this earth.   *Malcolm Muggeridge*

Someone has worked out a recipe for a country's ruin, and here are a few ingredients for it: affirm man's animal origin, nature and functions to the exclusion of everything else and ridicule all reference to his spiritual qualities... Soft-pedal all discussion of loyalty, responsibility, patriotism, duty and sacrifice in order that freedom of dissent may be established. Discourage the practice of prayer and Bible reading by forbidding it in schools... A recipe for a country's healing is contained in the verse: If my people... will humble themselves and pray and seek my face, then I will hear from heaven and will forgive their sin and will heal their land (*2 Chronicles 7:14*).

Canon David Watson

The future belongs to those who belong to God. This is hope.

W T Purkiser

HOW THE WORLD CAN   January 5
BE REGENERATED

For God has allowed us to know the secret of his plan, and it is this: he purposed long ago in his sovereign will that all human history should be consummated in Christ, that everything that exists in heaven or earth find its perfection and fulfilment in him.   *Ephesians 1:9-10*

God is the power-house of the world. Yet so few who fight for power pay attention to him. It is like living next to a power-station and yet insisting on groping and stumbling round your house in darkness, because you are too proud to turn the switch from which illumination is constantly and instantly available.

Peter Howard

We must aim above all at a spiritual renewal, a liberation from the mere following of conventions, a new departure in our way of thinking. More than anything else we must lament our short-comings before God and the community of our brethren. We must renew the self-understanding each must have of himself or herself as a child of God, as a Christian, as a member of the Church.

Pope Paul VI

Mere outward reformation differs as much from regeneration as white-washing an old rotten house differs from pulling it down and building a new one in its place.

A M Toplady

GOD'S INSTRUMENTS

January 6

I send you to open their eyes, to turn them from darkness to light, from the power of Satan to God so that they may know forgiveness of their sins and take their place with all those who are made holy by their faith in me.

Acts 26:18

When a person turns to God desiring to serve him, God directs that person to the world and its need.

Emil Brunner

O Lord convert the world – and begin with me.

Chinese student

If he stood by Paul saying 'Fear not', just as really and maybe as evidently will he stand by you. If he guided Paul in his work, restraining him from preaching here and calling him to service there, he will give you leadings just as certain and maybe as distinct.

J Rendel Harris

The Lord does not shine upon us except when we take his word as our light.

John Calvin

I heard the voice of the Lord saying, 'Whom shall I send, and who will go for us?' Then I said, 'Here am I, send me.'

Isaiah 6:8

COMMISSIONED BY GOD   January 7

He saved us and called us to be his own people, not because of
what we have done, but because of his own purpose and grace.
                                                    2 Timothy 1:9 GNB

Amiable agnostics will talk cheerfully about the search for God.
For me they might as well talk about the mouse's search for a
cat... God closed in on me.   *C S Lewis*

The meanest work for Jesus is a grander thing than the dignity
of an emperor.   *C H Spurgeon*

When I respond to God's call, the call is God's and the response
is mine; and yet the response is God's too; for not only does he
call me but also by his grace brings the response to birth within
my soul.   *Professor John Baillie*

Since my heart was touched at 17, I believe I have never wa-
kened from sleep, in sickness or in health, by day or by night,
without my first waking thought being how best I might serve
my Lord.   *Elizabeth Fry, English Quaker prison reformer*

Vocation is not the exceptional prerogative of a few specially
good or gifted people... All men and women are called to serve
God.   *Bishop F R Barry*

He never asked us to join a movement, nor just to change and
become good. He gave us the breath-taking challenge to give
our lives to the building of the new world that God wants.
                                    Oxford student on Frank Buchman

FELLOW-WORKERS WITH HIM   January 8

We told you from our own experience how to live lives worthy
of the God who is calling you to share the splendour of his own
kingdom.   *1 Thessalonians 2:12*

I used to ask God to help me. Then I asked if I might help him. I
ended by asking him to do his work through me.
                                            Dr J Hudson Taylor

My first step was to buy an alarm clock to wake up early each
morning; my second to listen to God to see what I should do

that day; my third step took much longer: to sense what God was doing and to gear all my plans to become a fellow-worker with him. *University student*

Sometimes talents, unknown or long-hidden, blossom as they are used to advance God's kingdom. In this way Alan Thornhill, whom I first knew when he was Fellow and Chaplain of an Oxford College and a lecturer in theology, became an outstanding playwright, giving God's truth to people round the world through his plays and films. *K D Belden*

WHAT IS GOD LIKE? January 9

God's divine power has given us everything we need to live a truly religious life through our knowledge of the one who has called us to share in his own glory and goodness. In this way he has given us the very great and precious gifts he promised, so that by means of these gifts you may escape from the destructive lust that is in the world, and may come to share the divine nature. For this very reason do your best to add goodness to your faith. *2 Peter 1:3-5 GNB*

The presence of a superior reasoning power revealed in the incomprehensible universe, forms my idea of God.

Albert Einstein

As soon as we realise that God takes an interest in all we do, we can bring it all to him. About our religious problems, of course, we can talk with him as with a God; about moral questions, as with the One who alone knows where good and evil lie; but about scientific questions as well, as with a scientist, about professional problems as with a colleague, about family problems as with a father, about technical matters as with an expert, about philosophy as with a professor, about law as with a jurist, about painting as with an artist, about city planning as with an architect, about finance as with an economist. *Dr Paul Tournier*

We cannot make too sure of this – that religion, communion with God, is not luxury, but necessity for the soul. We must have God. *G A Studdert-Kennedy*

THE SEARCH FOR GOD

When you seek me with all your heart, I will be found by you, says the Lord. *Jeremiah 29:13 RSV*

He who goes after what he likes, that is temptation, instinct, gain and self-interest, is treading a false path. We must, on the contrary, listen to the voice of the Lord, not because we like it... but because it is the voice of God with its authority... The desires of the heart come after the absolute primacy of the conversation with God. *Pope Paul VI*

It has been the universal opinion of mankind from ancient times that there is one God, the maker of heaven and earth... For nature reveals the author, the work suggests the artist, and the world manifests its designer. But the whole Church throughout the world has received this tradition from the apostles. *St Irenaeus*

The search for meaning and purpose for life goes on. There is a passion for justice, a hatred of war, a desire to respect the dignified rights of each person and a determination not to go along with the false even if the right is not clearly seen. Deep in their hearts most people want to know if they are wanted, and if they can be of service in playing an effective part in righting what is wrong in our civilisation and in shaping a worthwhile future. *Roger Hicks*

Bestow upon me, O Lord my God, understanding to know thee, diligence to seek thee, wisdom to find thee and a faithfulness that may finally embrace thee. *St Thomas Aquinas*

SEARCH FOR GOD II

Seek ye the Lord while he may be found; call ye upon him while he is near. *Isaiah 55:6*

What is the purpose of it all? I felt desperate as I looked at this riddle without an answer.

Then I began to think about God. Did God exist then?

Suddenly I cried out. Or rather, something inside me cried

out, something powerful enough to reach the furthest limits of the universe, 'Give me an answer, Lord. Show me the Truth, and I will consecrate my whole life to it.'

Immediately I knew that I had not cried in vain. I felt that there was an answer to the riddle, and that it would be given to me. I had come out of my despair. I knew that truth existed, and that I would come to know it and give all my life to it.

Père Alphonse Gratry

The trouble with many people today is that they have not found a God big enough for modern needs. While their experience of life has grown in a score of directions and their mental horizons have been expanded to the point of bewilderment by world events and by scientific discoveries, their ideas of God have remained largely static. *Canon J B Phillips*

> To see a World in a grain of sand,
> And a Heaven in a wild flower,
> Hold Infinity in the palm of your hand,
> And Eternity in an hour. *William Blake*

AWE AND WONDER January 12

And his name shall be called Wonderful, Counsellor, The mighty God, The everlasting Father, The Prince of Peace.

Isaiah 9:6

The first great epoch in a Christian's life, after the awe and wonder of its dawn, is when there breaks into his mind some sense that Christ has a purpose for mankind, a purpose beyond him and his needs, beyond the churches and their creeds, beyond heaven and its saints – a purpose which embraces every man and every woman born, every kindred and nation formed, which regards not their spiritual good alone but their welfare in every part, their progress, their health, their work, their wages, their happiness in this present world.

Professor Henry Drummond

The learning of the Christian ought to begin with the fear of God. *Archbishop Thomas Cranmer*

The person who cannot wonder is but a pair of spectacles behind which there is no eye. *Thomas Carlyle*

I have known clever scientists as well as people of the highest calibre in literature or the arts who regard God with the deepest awe and at the same time know him through Christ as a personal friend. *Canon J B Phillips*

I never had any difficulty in believing in miracles since I experienced the miracle of change in my own heart. *St Augustine*

SEEK GOD, NOT HIS GIFTS   January 13

So then, my brothers and sisters, because of God's great mercy to us I appeal to you: Offer yourselves a living sacrifice to God, dedicated to his service and pleasing to him. This is the true worship you should offer. Do not conform yourselves to the standards of this world, but let God transform you inwardly by a complete change of your mind... So we are to use our different gifts in accordance with the grace that God has given us... Whoever shares with others should do it generously.
Romans 12:1-2,6 and 8 GNB

God has a gift for every member of his Church. He will not give it to you nor show you what it is unless you ask him to and want the gift. If you do not use your gift you are making God sad and robbing others of the blessing he wants to give them through you. Gifts are always and only for using to glorify God and build up his Church. *Canon David Watson*

God looks at the intentions of the heart rather than the gifts he is offered. *Bishop Jean-Pierre Camus*

There are three kinds of giving: grudge giving, duty giving and thanksgiving. Grudge giving says 'I have to' ; duty giving says 'I ought to' ; thanksgiving says 'I want to' . *Robert Rodenmayer*

> Thou art coming to a king;
> Large petitions with thee bring;
> For his grace and power are such,
> None can ever ask too much. *John Newton*

When we have given God all we have and are, we have simply given him his own. *William S Plumer*

WORSHIP

Jesus said: the time is coming and is already here, when by the power of God's Spirit, people will worship the Father as he really is, offering him the true worship that he wants.

John 4:23 GNB

Worship is the submission of all our nature to God. It is the quickening of conscience by his holiness, the nourishment of mind into his truth, the purifying of imagination by his beauty, the opening of heart to love, the surrender of will to his purposes. *Archbishop William Temple*

A man can no more diminish God's glory by refusing to worship him than a lunatic can put out the sun by scribbling 'darkness' on the walls of his cell. *C S Lewis*

What is the chief end of man?
The chief end of man is to glorify God and enjoy him forever.

Westminster Catechism

> The dearest idol I have known,
> Whate'er that idol be;
> Help me to tear it from thy throne,
> And worship only thee. *William Cowper*

POWER OF GOD

This is my prayer: That the God of our Lord Jesus Christ, the all-glorious Father, will give you the spiritual wisdom and the insight to know more of him; that you may receive that inner illumination of the Spirit which will make you realise how great is the hope to which he is calling you... and how tremendous is the power available to us who believe in God. That power is the same divine energy which was demonstrated in Christ when he raised him from the dead. *Ephesians 1:17-20*

We are the wire, God is the current. Our only power is to let the current pass through us. *Carlo Carretto*

There is one source of power that is stronger than every disappointment, bitterness or ingrained mistrust and that power is

Jesus Christ who brought forgiveness and reconciliation to the world. *Pope John Paul II*

Does God's power change character? Does his spirit provide strength to resist and overcome? Does it restore after failure? Does it purify? Does it satisfy? Is it something bigger than us all, that must be followed at any cost? We must give a clear affirmation on each of these points because this is where people's minds and desires really are. *Dr Margaret Mewton*

THE ETERNAL CHANGELESSNESS   January 16

Every good endowment and every complete gift must come from the Father of all lights, with whom there is never the slightest variation or shadow of inconsistency. *James 1:17*

I am the Lord, I change not. *Malachi 3:6*

Whatever may happen to you, God is your Father and he is interested in you and that is his attitude towards you.
Dr Martyn Lloyd-Jones

Soli Gloria Deo (to God alone be the glory) was inscribed on every musical score, sacred or secular, that Johann Sebastian Bach composed.

> Change and decay in all around I see;
> O Thou who changest not, abide with me.
> *Henry Francis Lyte*

'If you approach someone with their best interests at heart and they reject you, you'll feel a stab of pain,' said Julie. 'But you've got to keep going even if they reject you ten or 20 times.' At such times, she says, it is her faith in Christ that gives her the strength to keep going. *Quoted by Kenneth Noble*

Here below to live is to change, and to be perfect is to have changed often. *Cardinal J H Newman*

> Faint not nor fear, his arms are near;
> He changeth not, and thou art dear.
> *J S B Monsell*

ALL-GREAT, ALL-LOVING January 17

Thine, O Lord, is the greatness, the power, the glory, the splendour and the majesty; for everything in heaven and on earth is thine. *1 Chronicles 29:11*

I have become absolutely convinced that neither death nor life, neither messenger of heaven nor monarch of earth, neither what happens today nor what may happen tomorrow, neither a power from on high nor a power from below, nor anything else in God's world has any power to separate us from the love of God in Christ Jesus our Lord. *Romans 8:38-39*

This is the fundamental thing, the most serious thing of all, that we are always in the presence of God. *Dr Martyn Lloyd-Jones*

Don't give people a thimbleful of the Gospel.
Professor Henry Drummond

Until a man has found God he begins at no beginning and ends at no end. *H G Wells*

So to the king of all the ages, the immortal, invisible, and only God, be honour and glory, for ever and ever. *1 Timothy 1:17*

PEACE OF GOD January 18

Try to be at peace with everyone, and try to live a holy life, because no one will see the Lord without it. *Hebrews 12:14 GNB*

Peace flows from purity. *Thomas Watson*

I am a man of peace. I believe in peace. But I do not want peace at any price. I do not want peace that you can find in stone; I do not want peace that you find in the grave; but I do want the peace which you find embedded in the human breast, which is exposed to the arrows of the whole world, but which is protected from all harm by the power of Almighty God.
Mahatma Gandhi

The peace of the soul consists in an absolute resignation to the will of God. *Archbishop François Fénelon*

If we wish to have true peace, we must give it a soul. The soul of peace is love. It is love that gives life to peace, more than victory or defeat, more than self-interest or fear or weariness or need. The soul of peace is love, which for us believers comes from the love of God and expresses itself in love for men.

Pope Paul VI

You will never find peace and happiness until you are ready to commit yourself to something worth dying for. *Jean-Paul Sartre*

FRIENDSHIP WITH GOD   January 19

There is no greater love than this – that a man should lay down his life for his friends. You are my friends if you do what I tell you to do. *John 15:13-14*

Those who fear God will come by true friendship.

Ecclesiasticus 6:17

If we address him as children it is because he tells us he is our Father. If we unbosom ourselves to him as a Friend, it is because he calls us friends. *William Cowper*

A friend should bear his friends' infirmities. *Shakespeare*

A friend is someone who knows all about you and still likes you. *Schoolboy's definition*

When once we get intimate with Jesus we are never lonely, we never need sympathy, we can pour out all the time without being pathetic. The saint who is intimate with Jesus will never leave impressions of himself, but only the impression that Jesus is having unhindered way, because the last abyss of his nature has been satisfied by him. *Oswald Chambers*

KNOWING GOD – THE CONDITIONS   January 20

No longer need they teach one another to know the Lord; all of them, high and low alike, shall know me, says the Lord, for I will forgive their wrongdoing and remember their sin no more.

Jeremiah 31:34 NEB

The fear of the Lord is the beginning of knowledge. *Proverbs 1:7*

Do that much of the will of God which is plain to you, and you shall know of the doctrine, whether it be of God. *F W Robertson*

The knowledge of God without that of our wretchedness creates pride. The knowledge of our wretchedness without that of God creates despair. The knowledge of Jesus Christ is the middle way because in him we find both God and our wretchedness. *Blaise Pascal*

My parents were devoted Christians... Yet it never took with me. By the time I reached Oxford I had no faith at all... What transformed my life was meeting people to whom God was a vivid reality in a more definite and practical way that I had ever seen before. *K D Belden*

There is one thing in the world really worth pursuing – the knowledge of God. *Monsignor R Hugh Benson*

How blest are those whose hearts are pure; they shall know God. *Matthew 5:8*

KEEPING THE LINE OPEN   January 21

Happy are those who reject the advice of evil people, who do not follow the example of sinners or join those who have no use for God. Instead they find joy in obeying the law of the Lord, and they study it day and night. *Psalms 1:1-2 GNB*

Be sure you do not refuse to hear the voice that speaks.
Hebrews 12:25

Obey exactly and immediately the commands of the inner still voice. It can be recognised by the fact that it never alters, never asks questions but is always direct and explicit. *Rev F B Meyer*

For the early Christians 'koinonia' was not... tea, biscuits and sophisticated small talk in the Fellowship Hall after the sermon. It was an unconditional sharing of their lives with the other members of Christ's body. *Ronald J Sider*

O let me hear thee speaking
In accents clear and still,
Above the storms of passion,
The murmurs of self-will.

J E Bode

WHAT PASSES KNOWLEDGE January 22

It is true of course that 'all of us have knowledge' , as they say.
Such knowledge, however, puffs a person up with pride; but
love builds up. Those who think they know something really
don't know as they ought to know. But the person who loves
God is known by him.   *1 Corinthians 8:1-3 GNB*

I stand amazed at the fathomless wealth of God's wisdom and
God's knowledge. How could man ever understand his reasons
for action, or explain his methods of working?... For everything
began with him, continues its existence because of him and
ends in him. To him be the glory for ever, Amen.

Romans 11:33 and 36

Once you become aware that the main business that you are
here for is to know God, most of life's problems fall into place
of their own accord.   *J I Packer*

Knowledge is power. But it is not a power great enough to
make us live unselfishly. That power lies in action based on
faith. Do we all have a father in God and therefore are we the
object of a love that will not let us go? A love that has a plan for
each of our lives and a meaning for our existence? A love that
has a work for each of us to do in caring for the needs of the human family and has the strategy for doing it? A love that has
the power to enable each of us to live forgetful of self?

Dr Paul Campbell

GIVE GOD TIME January 23

To everything there is a season, and a time to every purpose
under heaven: a time to be born and a time to die; a time to
plant and a time to pluck up that which is planted... I know that

whatsoever God doeth, it shall be for ever; nothing can be put to it, nor anything taken from it; and God doeth it that men should fear before him. *Ecclesiastes 3:1-2 and 14*

Time is not a commodity that can be stored for future use. It must be invested hour by hour or else it is gone for ever.
Thomas Edison

The year is made up of minutes. Let these be watched as having been dedicated to God. It is by the sanctification of the small that the hallowing of the large is secure. *Dr G Campbell Morgan*

To please Christ is to live in such fellowship with him that our walk is characterised by an eagerness to explore his every wish.
Dr Graham Scroggie

You have to give the other person unhurried time. If you have any impatience or stress, you can do nothing to help him express his deepest fears or anger or sense of injustice. And give God time – to let him do it his way. *Peter Hannon*

QUIET TIME   January 24

And he said, Go forth and stand upon the mount before the Lord. And behold, the Lord passed by, and a great and strong wind rent the mountains, and brake in pieces the rocks before the Lord; but the Lord was not in the wind: and after the wind an earthquake, but the Lord was not in the earthquake: and after the earthquake a fire; but the Lord was not in the fire: and after the fire a still small voice. *1 Kings 19:11-12*

The 'immediate' person thinks and imagines that when he prays, the important thing, the thing he must concentrate upon, is that God should hear what he is praying for. Yet in the true, eternal sense it is just the reverse; the true relation in prayer is not when God hears what is prayed for, but when the person praying continues to pray until he is the one who hears, who hears what God wills. The 'immediate' person ... makes demands in his prayers; the true man of prayer only attends.
Søren Kierkegaard

Think oftener of God than you breathe. *Epictetus*

The sound of our words strikes the ear, but the Master is within you. Outward teaching is but a kind of help and prompting. The teacher of hearts and minds has his chair in heaven. Let him then speak to you within, when no one else is there.

St Augustine

There are many hearts in which I (God) would gladly speak but the world makes so much noise inside them that my voice cannot be heard. *St Teresa of Avila*

THE GUIDANCE OF GOD   January 25

He will draw on my truth and reveal it to you.   *John 16:14*

Again and again, we must clear out the channel to God and to others. That is the point of the 'quiet time' and of being honest with each other. It means always being open to God, looking away from yourself, listening to God, giving God time to spread his light through every part of every day. It means always being open to the next person, clearing away whatever gets in the way, even the smallest dishonesty, the slightest grudge... When a channel is clear and open, the wind of God can blow through. *Dr Theophil Spoerri*

The question of how to balance family and professional life is a problem. The real question is how to do God's will in all these areas of life. Finding out how to do God's will also takes time – how to reserve enough time to be alone with God every day. How to live in such a way that all the demands on me do not stop me finding divine direction.

Paula Snellman, Helsinki consultant –
with family of husband, three-year-old son and stepchildren

So live that God can speak to you at any time of the day or night. *Dr Frank N D Buchman*

GUIDED WHERE I GO   January 26

He leadeth me in the paths of righteousness.   *Psalms 23:3*

Keep thy heart with all diligence; for out of it are the issues of life... Let thine eyes look right on... Turn not to the right hand nor to the left: remove thy foot from evil.

Proverbs 4:23, 25 and 27

I feel myself a man of many frailties and much weakness. I hope that before I die I shall have changed out of all recognition... But I tell you that as I begin each day by listening to God, it is a time of enthralment. It is like a great shoal of silver fish flashing through your heart and mind – new ideas for people, fresh approaches to problems – deeper insight into the mood of the times, costly daily personal decisions. I am not much of a fisherman, but I try and snatch one or two of those silvery fish as they fly from the mind of God into the mind of men and women and children like ourselves. *Peter Howard*

There are certain practical directions which we must attend to in order that we may be led into the mind of the Lord:

1. Our motives must be pure. When thine eye is single, thy whole body is also full of light. *Luke 11:34*

2. Our will must be surrendered. My judgment is just because I seek not mine own will, but the will of the Father. *John 5:30*

3. The mind must be given reliable information.

4. We must be much in prayer for guidance.

5. We must wait the gradual unfolding of God's plan in providence. *Rev F B Meyer*

NEED FOR GOD'S GUIDANCE   January 27

Your Father knows your needs before you ask him. *Matthew 6:8*

They that wait upon the Lord shall renew their strength; they shall mount up with wings as eagles; they shall run and not be weary; and they shall walk and not faint. *Isaiah 40:31*

The best and most wonderful thing that can happen to you in this life is that you should be silent and let God work and speak. *Dag Hammarskjöld, formerly U N Secretary General*

To go up alone into the mountain and come back as an ambassador to the world, has ever been the method of humanity's best friends. *Evelyn Underhill*

God's promises of guidance are not given to us to save us the bother of thinking. *Rev John R W Stott*

I can say from experience that 95 per cent of knowing the will of God consists in being prepared to do it before you know what it is. *Donald G Barnhouse*

The prayer that has become common to the heart of humanity says: 'Give us this day our daily bread;' and 'thy will be done.' The first is a need; the second a purpose. *Peter Howard*

THE SECRET OF SILENCE   January 28

Silence, all mankind, in the presence of the Lord! For he has bestirred himself out of his holy dwelling-place.
Zechariah 2:13 NEB

Unto thee will I cry, O Lord, my rock; be not silent to me.
Psalms 28:1

Mere silence is not wisdom, for wisdom consists in knowing when and how to speak and when and where to keep silent.
Bishop J P Camus

Be silent about great things; let them grow inside you. Never discuss them; discussion is so limiting and distracting. It makes things grow smaller. You think you swallow things when they ought to swallow you. Before all greatness be silent – in art, in music, in religion, silence. *Baron Friedrich von Hügel*

God is a tranquil being, and abides in a tranquil eternity. So must thy spirit become a tranquil and clear little pool, wherein the serene light of God can be mirrored. *Gerhard Tersteegen*

Enter into the inner chamber of your mind. Shut out all things save God; and having barred the door of your chamber, seek him. *St Anselm of Canterbury*

Some of you are guilty of talking too much. We need to listen more and talk less. *Dr Frank N D Buchman*

TWO-WAY PRAYER   January 29

Hear, O Lord, when I cry with my voice; have mercy also on me
and answer me. Wait on the Lord... wait, I say, on the Lord.
Psalms 27:7 and 14

And if in the process any of you does not know how to meet
any particular problem, he has only to ask God... and he may be
quite sure that the necessary wisdom will be given to him.
James 1:5

If we spend 16 hours a day dealing with tangible things and
only five minutes a day dealing with God, is it any wonder that
tangible things are 200 times more real to us than God?
Dean William R Inge

Take away everything I have but do not take away the sweetness of walking and talking with the King of Glory.   *John Stam*

Adequate time for daily waiting on God ... is the only way I can
escape the tyranny of the urgent.   *Charles Hummel*

> More things are wrought by prayer
> Than this world dreams of. Wherefore, let thy voice
> Rise like a fountain for me night and day.
> *Alfred, Lord Tennyson*

THE LISTENING EAR   January 30

I love the Lord, because he hath heard my voice and my suppli-
cations. Because he hath inclined his ear unto me, therefore will
I call upon him as long as I live.   *Psalms 116:1-2*

For the word that God speaks is alive and active.   *Hebrews 4:12*

I am amazed at the number of Christians I have spoken with
who give no time to the listening side of prayer. I sometimes
wonder if the reason some Christians don't take time to listen to
God is because they are afraid what God might say to them
about some unsurrendered habit or sin, if they stopped talking
long enough to listen to his voice.   *Rev Selwyn Hughes © CWR*

> I have just hung up, why did he telephone?
> I don't know... Oh! I get it...

I talked a lot and listened very little.
Forgive me Lord, it was a monologue and not a dialogue.
I explained my idea and did not get his;
Since I didn't listen, I learned nothing,
Since I didn't listen, we didn't communicate.
Forgive me Lord, for we were connected
And now we are cut off;

If we knew how to listen to God, we should hear him speaking to us, for God does speak. He speaks in his gospel! He speaks also through life – that new gospel in which we ourselves add a page each day. *Abbé Michel Quoist*

WRITE IT DOWN   January 31

And the Lord said unto Moses, Write thou these words... And he wrote upon the tables the words of the covenant, the ten commandments. *Exodus 34:27-28*

We have decided to try and lead our lives as God wants us to live them. We have found that if we listen to him each morning and write down the thoughts which come to us, we get a clear plan and direction for the day. We have discovered, too, that God will tell us exactly what he wants us to do in any situation, whether it be hard or easy, if we really aim to discover his wishes instead of being constantly guided by our own.
Peter Howard

As we take time every day to listen and to write down our thoughts, we find we are beginning to think more clearly than ever before. Whenever self-interest is mastered we are free to consider other people and national issues with a perspective previously denied. *Dr Paul Campbell*

The Spirit of Truth will guide you into all truth. *John 16:13*

GOD'S PROGRAMME

How can any man learn what is God's plan? How can he apprehend what the Lord's will is? *Wisdom 9:13 NEB*

Now to him who is able to set you firmly on your feet – according to my gospel, according to the preaching of Jesus Christ himself, and in accordance with the disclosing of that secret purpose which, after long ages of silence, has now been made known... by the command of the everlasting God.

Romans 16:25-26

God has a life plan for every human life. In the eternal counsels of his will, when he arranged the destiny of every star... the Creator had a thought for you and me... It was a thought of what we were to be, or what we might become, or what he would have us do with our days and years, our influence and our lives. *Professor Henry Drummond*

I can hardly recollect a single plan of mine, of which I have not since seen reason to be satisfied that, had it taken place in season and circumstances just as I had proposed, it would, humanly speaking, have proved my ruin; or at least it would have deprived me of the greater good that the Lord had designed for me. *John Newton*

It is important to have a big enough aim in life. 'Thy kingdom come, thy will be done' could become a commitment. There may be also 'a call within a call' – a call to serve God in a certain ministry or field of life. *Brian Boobbyer*

GOVERNED BY GOD

This is the word of the Lord unto Zerubbabel, saying, Not by might, nor by power, but by my spirit, saith the Lord of hosts.

Zechariah 4:6

If therefore it is natural for men to live in the society of many, it is necessary that there exist among men some means by which the group may be governed. For where there are many men together and each one is looking after his own interest, the group would be broken up and scattered unless there were also

perfectly certain that no really effective way of dealing with evil will be found apart from the rediscovery of true religion.

Canon J B Phillips

Arthur Kanodereka was a man who hated the white regime in Rhodesia. Although a Methodist minister he supported the guerrillas in the bush war. He was arrested by the white-led security forces and suffered brutality. At a conference in Salisbury he heard the son of Prime Minister Ian Smith, Alec, describe his own change and his commitment to building a new Rhodesia. They became friends and worked together to fight what was wrong by changing people. Kanodereka became a force in the country in the fight against evil. It led to his assassination, but raised many new fighters. *H P E*

FIGHTERS EVER   February 12

Fight the worthwhile battle of the faith, keep your grip on that life eternal to which you have been called, and to which you boldly professed your loyalty. *1 Timothy 6:12*

The battle line runs not between certain nations nor between certain classes but it runs through every nation and class, through every organisation or community, through every home and every heart. It is the battle against 'I want', whether limited to purely personal matters or projected out through the channels of power of an organisation, an industry or a nation to create a tyranny to others. This battle will be won in my heart first of all and then in others. *Edward T Perry*

The battle is fought out on that one word of the 'will'. Will you obey the voice of God and do as he commands you? No man can obey for you any more than he can eat and drink for you. You must obey God for yourself. *Dwight L Moody*

Help us, O Lord Christ, to stand for the hard right against the easy wrong. Help us not to lower our standards to win favours from others. Help us to do battle royally and to the end against all that thou dost condemn in us. *John Hunter*

SIN THE DISEASE

The soul that sinneth, it shall die. *Ezekiel 18:4*

Sin is essentially a departure from God. *Martin Luther*

Sin is an old-fashioned word, which most shrink from nowadays. Psychologists like Freud, scientists like Bertrand Russell and Huxley, aided by writers like Wells, have done their best to abolish sin for us. It would have been splendid for us all if they had succeeded. But alas and alack, in fact all that these fellows have managed to do is to offer to themselves and other humans, excuses for behaving exactly as they want to behave, rather than behaving as their conscience tells them they should behave. *Peter Howard*

No sin is small. No grain of sand is small in the mechanism of a watch. *Bishop Jeremy Taylor*

Mrs Stanley Baldwin once said to Frank Buchman in a friend's house in the 'thirties, 'Dr Buchman, I don't like that word "sin" you keep using.' 'Well,' said Buchman affably, 'let's call it something else. How about calling it "rheumatism"?' 'Oh no!' cried Lucy Baldwin, 'I'm full of rheumatism.' *K D Belden*

God loves us in our sin and through our sin and goes on loving us, looking for a response. *Archbishop Donald Coggan*

CHRIST THE CURE

This statement is completely reliable and should be universally accepted: 'Christ Jesus entered the world to rescue sinners.'
1 Timothy 1:15

I went to Africa that I might be able to sin to my heart's content. I was a wild beast on the coast of Africa till the Lord came and tamed me.
John Newton, slave trader – and later, author of 'How sweet the name of Jesus sounds in a believer's ear'

Christ cannot live his life today in this world without our mouth, without our eyes, without our going and coming,

without our heart. When we love it is Christ loving through us.
This is Christianity.   *Cardinal Leon J Suenens*

Decide every morning: *out* of self, *into* Christ, *for* others.
                                          Dr Frank N D Buchman

THE RESULT, A MIRACLE   February 15

You had wandered away like so many sheep, but now you have
returned to the shepherd and guardian of your souls.
                                          1 Peter 2:25

He came into his own world, and his own people would not
accept him. Yet wherever men did accept him he gave them the
power to become sons of God.   *John 1:11-12*

One woman changed so much through knowing Jesus, that
when she sent in her passport with a new photograph of herself
asking if that could be substituted for the old one, the officials
wrote back saying, 'We cannot believe that the two photo-
graphs are of the same person.'   *Canon David Watson*

He who shall introduce into public affairs the principles of
primitive Christianity will change the face of the world.
                                          Benjamin Franklin

Our God does not need noble characters as the groundwork of
his masterpieces. He can raise up stones as children. He can
turn thorns into fir trees, briars into myrtle trees. He can take
fishermen from their nets and publicans from their toll-booths
making them into evangelists, apostles and martyrs.
                                          Rev F B Meyer

Fredrik Ramm, the Norwegian journalist who accompanied
Amundsen in his daring flight across the North Pole, was in-
vited to attend a conference of the Oxford Group in Norway.
Travelling up to it, he asked his companion, 'What is going to
happen there?' 'Miracles – and you'll be one of them,' was the
reply. Ramm, sceptical at first, began to think of the articles he
had been writing of hate and criticism, attacking the Danes. He
decided to go to Denmark and he apologised publicly. A reconciliation began between Norway and Denmark.
                                          Reginald Holme

CAUSE AND EFFECT

Having made known unto us the mystery of his will, according to his good pleasure, which he hath purposed in himself: that in the dispensation of the fullness of times, he might gather in one all things in Christ, both which are in heaven and which are on earth. *Ephesians 1:9-10 AV*

How do we have the mystery of his will unfolded to us? ...it is by absorbing into our beings the inspiration of the New Testament, as it unfolds the person of our Lord, Jesus Christ. As we do, we obtain God's wisdom as expressed in the life of his Son, a wisdom that knows how to think, how to feel, how to act, how to be. For too long we in the church of Jesus Christ have been concentrating on belief to the exclusion of behaviour. The result is we have a generation of Christians who think the Christian life is just believing a set of principles. It is more – it is behaving by those principles. *Rev Selwyn Hughes © CWR*

In the name of God, most gracious, most merciful ...master of the Day of Judgment ...Show us the straight way.
From the Opening Prayer daily of every Muslim

> Be Thou my vision, O Lord of my heart;
> Naught be all else to me, save that thou art,
> Thou my best thought, by day or by night,
> Waking or sleeping, thy presence my light. *Irish hymn*

CALLING A SPADE A SPADE

Search me, O God, and know my heart; try me and know my thoughts; and see if there is any wicked way in me, and lead me in the way everlasting. *Psalms 139:23-24*

Jesus said: be on your guard against the yeast of the Pharisees – I mean their hypocrisy. Whatever is covered up will be uncovered, and every secret will be made known. *Luke 12:1-2*

It is not for me to decide whether you should confess your sins to a priest or not... but if you do not, you should at least make a list on a piece of paper and make a serious act of penance about each one of them... It is essential to use the plain, simple, old-fashioned words like theft or fornication or hatred, instead of 'I did not mean to be dishonest' or 'I was only a boy then' or 'I lost my temper'. I think that this steady facing of what one does know and bringing it before God, without excuses, and seriously asking for forgiveness and grace, and resolving as far as in one lies to do better, is the only way.   *C S Lewis*

The evil must be called by its right and ugly name when it is discovered. Judas missed salvation because he never called his avarice by its right name – he disguised it by a love for the poor.   *Archbishop Fulton Sheen*

ABSOLUTE OR RELATIVE   February 18

The Lord says, 'Now let's settle the matter. You are stained red with sin, but I will wash you as clean as snow. Although your stains are deep red, you will be as white as wool.'
                                                    Isaiah 1:18 GNB

You are the salt of the earth. But if the salt has lost its taste how shall its saltiness be restored?   *Matthew 5:13 GNB*

I thought I was pretty good. But it was only when I measured my life against absolute moral standards that I started to take practical steps in change and realised my total dependence on God.   *University student*

To live by absolute standards is not a rigid rule laying burdens on men too great for human weakness to bear. It is an entry into a life of release and freedom in which God himself imparts moral powers of which we know ourselves wholly incapable. Dedication to the one increasing purpose of bringing his kingdom on earth and obeying his guidance in every detail produces the 'integrated personality' of the psychologists.
                                                    Rev Hallen Viney

I am not interested in moderate honesty. Who wants to draw most of his salary? to eat an egg that is moderately fresh? to live in a house that keeps out most of the rain? The kind of honesty I am interested is absolute honesty, honesty upon two legs – and may I remind you that you have two legs!   *Daw Nyein Tha*

BE YE PERFECT   February 19

I do not consider myself to have 'arrived' spiritually, nor do I consider myself already perfect. But I keep going on, grasping ever more firmly that purpose for which Christ grasped me.

Philippians 3:12

You must be perfect – just as your Father in heaven is perfect!

Matt 5:48 GNB

The word (perfect) implies full development, growth into maturity of godliness, not sinless perfection. In this passage the Father's kindness, not his sinlessness is the point in question.

Rev C I Scofield

And passing on I went among the professors at... Manchester where I stayed awhile and declared truth among them. And there were some convinced, who received the Lord's teaching, by which they were confirmed and stood in the truth... But the Lord's power was over all.

George Fox

The divine nature is perfection; and to be nearest to the divine nature is to be nearest in perfection.

Xenophon

What is Christian perfection? Loving God with all our heart, mind, soul and strength.

John Wesley

A practical way of keeping personal purity unsullied in relation to other people is to say to yourself, 'That man, that woman, perfect in Christ Jesus! that friend, that relative: perfect in Christ Jesus!'

Oswald Chambers

HOPE FOR ALL   February 20

Abraham, when hope was dead within him, went on hoping in faith, believing that he would become 'the father of many nations'. He relied on the word of God which definitely referred to 'thy seed'. With undaunted faith he looked at the facts – his own impotence... and his wife Sarah's apparent barrenness. Yet he refused to allow any distrust of a definite pronouncement of God to make him waver.

Romans 4:18-20

> Hope springs eternal in the human breast;
> Man never is, but always to be blessed.   *Alexander Pope*

The most unfounded hope is much more founded than the most founded despair. I know it from my own experience. I was sentenced to 25 years of hard labour. I had been deathly sick in prison, and doctors had abandoned any hope that I would recover. Under those circumstances I had a completely unfounded hope of ever leading a world-wide mission, having as its purpose the helping of persecuted Christians in communist countries. Despair and suicide would have been logically justified. There seemed no hope that I would see my son again. Now I have my grandson on my lap.

Pastor Richard Wurmbrand

WE CAN WIN   February 21

The eternal God is thy refuge, and underneath are the everlasting arms.   *Deuteronomy 33:27*

For this reason we never become discouraged. Even though our physical being is gradually decaying, yet our spiritual being is renewed day after day.   *2 Corinthians 4:16 GNB*

Not long after landing on the mainland of China, the father (of a missionary family) contracted an infection which left him blind. The mother soon died of cancer after a long and painful illness. One son died of an oriental disease while studying in college and not long after another son died from an infection. In addition to this the daughter was struck down with infantile paralysis... The father, with the help of a guide-dog, went about his pastoral duties and the daughter, hobbling on crutches, kept home for him. Together they went on unbeaten, radiating the love of God to everyone they met. They looked beyond the wreckage of their circumstances to the author of abundant life and from him received such victory in their spirits they were able to say: 'This is the victory that overcometh the world, even our faith.'   *Rev Selwyn Hughes © CWR*

We will win if we live convinced that God means us to win.

Peter Howard

HONESTY   February 22

We are taking care not to stir up any complaints about the way
we handle this generous gift. Our purpose is to do what is right,
not only in the sight of the Lord, but also in the sight of others.

Corinthians 8:20-21 GNB

When I preach to my people about the love of God and the
beauties of nature and the moonlight on the water, they all
think it's wonderful. But when I preach to them about chicken
stealing, a kind of coolness comes over the congregation.

A country preacher in Southern USA

Honesty is an essential ingredient of marriage because your
partner is inevitably different from yourself. She looks at everything from a woman's point of view.   *Brian Boobbyer*

A beginner once asked, 'But what is absolute honesty?' 'Something a lot different from the way you and I behave, wouldn't
you think? If we put right what we see now to be wrong, we'll
probably find out more about it' was the reply... You cannot
have a Russian honesty or a French honesty or British honesty;
there is only honesty. Unless a standard is absolute it is not a
standard. Absolute moral standards are yardsticks by which to
measure our behaviour. Like the whole life lived in surrender
and obedience to God's will, they are not an attitude attained
but an attitude maintained.   *Rev Hallen Viney*

BRIDGING THE GAP   February 23

How can young people keep their lives pure? By obeying your
commands.   *Psalms 119:9 GNB*

Christ asks of us the purity of heart which matches our state
and our calling. He demands it absolutely; but much more he
leads us to values which are revealed only to pure eyes and
hearts. You do not gain this purity without giving up yourself,
without inner battles against our own weakness, but once it is
gained, you are rewarded a hundred times over for your effort
with a maturity of thought and heart. It leads to a new sponta-
neity of feelings, acts and behaviour which eases relationships
with people.   *Pope John Paul II*

I hope I shall possess firmness and virtue enough to maintain what I consider to be the most enviable of all titles, the character of an honest man.   *President George Washington*

MOTIVES   **February 24**

If you have these qualities [of faith, goodness, knowledge, self-control, ability to endure, devotion to God, brotherliness, Christian love] existing and growing in you then it means that knowing our Lord Jesus has not made our lives either complacent or unproductive.   *2 Peter 1:8*

How many of the Peace Corps men and women are great idealists who really want to do something for the world? But frankly it isn't enough today to go and teach nations in Asia and Africa a language, scientific or political techniques or methods of sanitation, important though these are. What is absolutely essential is to produce men and women in those nations who can lead their people, who will be dependable, whose work can be trusted, who will work hard, who will be solid leaders. You can't actually do a job in those nations if you don't know how to deal with the character of people.   *Rajmohan Gandhi*

How happy is a pure heart. With a living faith it sees God. You see him in everything and at every moment, working within you and without. In everything you are his subject and his tool. In everything he controls you and to everything he brings you.
J P de Caussade

THE TRUTH   **February 25**

For yourself concentrate on winning God's approval, on being a workman with nothing to be ashamed of, and who knows how to use the word of truth to the best advantage.   *2 Timothy 2:15*

Truth is incontrovertible. Panic may resent it; ignorance may deride it; malice may distort it. But there it is.
Sir Winston S Churchill

Truth is the foundation of all knowledge; and the cement of all societies.   *John Dryden*

Truth is the perfect correlation of mind and reality; and this is actualised in the Lord's person. If the gospel is true and God is, as the Bible declares, a living God, the ultimate truth is not a system of propositions grasped by a perfect intelligence, but is a personal being apprehended in the only way in which persons are ever fully comprehended, that is by love.

Archbishop William Temple

Peace if possible, but truth at any rate.   *Martin Luther*

Lord, give us light, thy truth to see.

SELF-KNOWLEDGE   February 26

Examine me, O God, and know my mind;... and guide me in the everlasting way.   *Psalms 139:1-2 GNB*

I may have the gift of inspired preaching; I may have all knowledge and understand all secrets; I may have all the faith needed to move mountains – but if I have no love, I am nothing.

1 Corinthians 13:2 GNB

A humble knowledge of yourself is a surer way to God than a deep search after learning.   *Thomas à Kempis*

A man has many skins in himself, covering the depths of his heart. Man knows so many things; he does not know himself... Go into your own ground and learn to know yourself there.

Meister Eckhart

I thank thee, Lord, for knowing me better than I know myself and for letting me know myself better than others know me.

Abu Bekr

Most of us do not like to look inside ourselves for the same reason we don't like to open a letter that has bad news... There is a definite correlation between knowing God and knowing oneself; God cannot be known unless we know ourselves as we really are.   *Archbishop Fulton J Sheen*

Knowledge without integrity is dangerous and dreadful.

Samuel Johnson

TAKING ALL THE BLAME   February 27

And you yourselves, who were strangers to God and, in fact,
through the evil you had done, his spiritual enemies, he has
now reconciled through the death of Christ's body on the cross,
so that he might welcome you to his presence clean and pure,
without blame or reproach.   *Colossians 1:21-22*

We blame someone else's influence for the mistakes we have
made or for the trouble in which we have found ourselves...
Burns wrote:
> Thou knowest thou hast formed me
> With passions wild and strong,
> And listening to their witching voice
> Has often led me wrong.

As if to say that if God had made him differently, he would not
have made the mistakes he did make. But a man is not so much
what God made him as he is what he has made himself. The
way to forgiveness and to betterment begins when we learn to
say, 'God be merciful to me a sinner.'   *Dr William Barclay*

The camel never sees its own hump; but its neighbour's hump
is ever before its eyes.   *Arab Proverb*

TRUE AND FALSE VALUES   February 28

The time will come when people will not listen to sound doctrine, but will follow their own desires and will collect for themselves more and more teachers who will tell them what they
are itching to hear. They will turn away from listening to the
truth, and give their attention to legends.

                                        2 Timothy 4:3-4 GNB

My philosophy was to pursue truth, beauty and goodness. On
truth I was far from wholly honest; on beauty I was expert – my
chief enjoyment was chasing girls; on goodness, I regarded that
as an optional extra. I met men who were living faster and more
effectively than I was. My life was revolutionised when I faced
absolute moral standards and gave my life to God and started
to put things right.   *University student*

45

Men proud of their intellectual maturity are moral embryos. They are spiritually undeveloped. They miss the truth that a civilisation that has grown up intellectually and industrially must grow up morally and spiritually or perish.   *Peter Howard*

Let us remember when we are inclined to be disheartened that the private soldier is a poor judge of the fortunes of a great battle.   *Dean W R Inge*

SPIRITUAL BLINDNESS   **February 29**

The unspiritual man simply cannot accept the matters which the Spirit deals with – they just don't make sense to him for, after all, you must be spiritual to see spiritual things. The spiritual man, on the other hand, has an insight into the meaning of everything, though his insight may baffle the man of the world.
1 Corinthians 2:14-15

If there is anything in your life more demanding than your longing after God, then you will never be a Spirit-filled Christian.   *A W Tozer*

There must be a real giving up of the self. You must throw it away 'blindly' so to speak. Christ will indeed give you a real personality; but you must not go to him for the sake of that... The very first step is to try to forget about the self altogether. Your real, new self... will not come as long as you are looking for it. It will come when you are looking for him.   *C S Lewis*

The best measure of a spiritual life is not its ecstasies but its obedience.   *Oswald Chambers*

Shame on us for being paupers, when we were meant to be princes.   *Dr Martyn Lloyd-Jones*

> Isn't it, isn't it terribly sad
> That I'm so good and the world so bad?
> *Song by the Colwell Brothers*

A SANE ESTIMATE   March 1

Everything that belongs to the world – what the sinful self de-sires, what people see and want, and everything in this world that people are so proud of – none of this comes from the Fa-ther; it all comes from the world. The world and everything in it that people desire is passing away; but those that do the will of God live for ever.   *1 John 2:16–17 GNB*

If I truly want to see the world fundamentally different, there is (sadly) no other logical place to begin than with myself... Make no mistake. For many of us, it would mean the complete up-turning of the pattern of our lives and the values by which we have lived. It meant for one wife being told to love her unfaith-ful husband more, not less. It meant for one employer deciding to set up a new business in order to create jobs for everyone he had to make redundant. For one French woman after the war, it meant forgiving the Germans who had tortured her son and pouring out her life to help rebuild her former enemy's country. These are some of the ways God cultivates that greatness of the human spirit which lies dormant beneath our pigmy existences.
Authors of The Secret*

You may get to the very top of the ladder and then find it has not been leaning against the right wall.   *A Raine*

ON 'BEING RIGHT'   March 2

Even then many of the Jewish authorities believed in Jesus, but... they loved human approval rather then the approval of God.   *John 12:42–43 GNB*

I keep going on, trying to grasp that purpose for which Christ Jesus grasped me... I do concentrate on this: I forget all that lies behind me and with hands outstretched to whatever lies ahead, I go straight for the goal – my reward the honour of my high calling by God in Christ Jesus.   *Philippians 3:12–14*

I am now free from that driving deadly feeling that my own success is the most important thing in life, that everything

* Juliet Boobbyer, Sydney Cook, James Hore-Ruthven, John Lester, Graham and Jean Turner

depends on our own efforts and that I must claw my own way upward, striking out right and left around me as I go. I have come to the realisation that my own exertions are a very small part of the future of mankind – and that the future of mankind is more important than my own exertions... The thing that I have discovered, the truth about the meaning of life, the very heart of the whole body of creation was there all the time – like the force of gravity or steam power. But I, I have got at the secret... I have been touched by a hand which I know is there, even if others deny it or refuse to see it.   *Peter Howard*

> Batter my heart, three person'd God; for you
> As yet but knock, breathe, shine and seek to mend;
> That I may rise and stand, o'erthrow me and bend
> Your force to break, blow, burn and make me new.
>   *John Donne*

AS FREE AS WE WANT TO BE   March 3

Hate what is evil, and love what is right, and see that justice prevails in the courts.   *Amos 5:15*

Jesus said: If you are faithful to what I have said, you are truly my disciples. And you will know the truth, and the truth will set you free.   *John 8:31–32*

There are two freedoms – the false where a man is free to do what he likes; the true where a man is free to do as he ought.
                                                    Charles Kingsley

It daily becomes more apparent that God's respect for the freedom of our affections, thoughts and purposes is complete. It is part of that respect for our freedom that he never forces upon us his own gifts. He offers them but unless we actually accept them, they remain ineffective as far as we are concerned. Behold I stand at the door and knock – that is always the relation of God our Redeemer to our souls.   *Archbishop William Temple*

Do you hate sin? Today is a time for drastic decisions. What some of you need is not a feather duster but a rotary street broom.   *Dr Frank N D Buchman*

Fire of love, burn in us, burn evermore
Till we burn out for thee.

O for a passionate passion for souls,
O for a pity that yearns,
O for a love that loves unto death,
O for the fire that burns;

O for the pure prayer power that prevails,
That pours itself out for the lost,
Victorious prayer in the Conqueror's name:
The Lord of Pentecost.

Amy Carmichael

ULTIMATE CLEANSING   **March 7**

What you learned was to fling off the dirty clothes of the old
way of living, which were rotted through and through with
lust's illusions, and with yourselves mentally and spiritually
re-made, to put on the clean, fresh clothes of the new life which
was made by God's design for righteousness and the holiness
which is no illusion.   *Ephesians 4:22–24*

Set your heart on integrity, true piety, faithfulness, love, endurance and gentleness.   *1 Timothy 6:11*

All God's giants have been weak men who did great things for
God because they reckoned on his being with them. They
counted on God's faithfulness.   *Dr Hudson Taylor*

Redemption means buying-back, so that if I belong to him
either I have to be a thief and keep what is not mine, or else I
have to give up everything to him. When I came to see that
Jesus Christ had died for me, it did not mean I had to give up
everything for him. It was just common ordinary honesty.

C T Studd

It is right that you should begin again every day. There is no
better way to finish the spiritual life than to be ever beginning it
all over again and never to think that you have done enough.

St Francis de Sales

51

The six greatest words in the English language: Make and keep me pure within. *Dr Frank N D Buchman*

CLEAN AS A WHISTLE   March 8

Here and now, my dear friends, we are God's children. We don't know what we shall become in the future. We only know that when he appears we shall be like him, for we shall see him as he is! Everyone who has at heart a hope like that keeps himself pure, as Christ is pure. *1 John 3:2–3*

When we are in the light, walking in the light, we are cleansed from all sin. All God's revelations are sealed until they are opened to us by obedience. You will never get them open by philosophy or thinking. Immediately you obey, a flash of light comes. Let God's truth work in you by soaking in it, not by worrying into it. *Oswald Chambers*

Very earnestly I would say to anyone who is responsible for the purity of a spiritual work, at all costs keep it pure. It may be costly, but do not falter. To falter is to sap the very foundations of that which it was committed to you to guard. Cost what it may resolve to build only with precious stones what you are building. *Amy Carmichael*

> A humble, lowly, contrite heart,
> Believing, true and clean,
> Which neither death nor life can part
> From him that dwells therein.

Charles Wesley

A POSITIVE, VIBRANT FORCE   March 9

Christ Jesus our Saviour... he gave himself for us, that he might set us free from all our evil ways and make for himself a people of his own, clean and pure, with our hearts set upon living a life that is good. *Titus 2:13–14*

'Mind that which is pure in you to guide you to God,' George have no faith in God – their very minds and consciences are diseased. They profess to know God but their behaviour contradicts their profession. *Titus 1:15–16*

The price of purity is high but impurity is dirt cheap.
John Blanchard

> You are the light of the world;
> But the tallest candlestick
> Ain't much good without a wick.
> You gotta live right to be the light of the world.
> *S Schwartz in the musical* Godspell

A victorious Christian life is not a superior brand of Christianity reserved for the elite of the elect. It is the normal Christian life for every Christian. *Ronald Dunn*

Absolute purity is the secret of the power that God gives.
A young man whose whole life was altered
after meeting Frank Buchman

We must become so pure in heart... and it needs much practice... that we shall see God. That explains life – why God puts man in the crucible and makes him pure by fire.
Professor Henry Drummond

DAILY RENEWAL   March 13

Encourage each other every day, while it is still called 'today', and beware that none of you becomes deaf and blind to God through the delusive glamour of sin. *Hebrews 3:13*

Wisdom speaks: Listen to what you are taught. Be wise; do not neglect it. Those who listen to me will be happy – those who stay at my door every day, waiting at the entrance to my home.
Proverbs 8:33–34 GNB

Every day a messenger of God. *Russian proverb*

Life is a hard fight, a struggle, a wrestling with the principle of evil, hand to hand, foot to foot. Every inch of the way is disputed. The night is given to us to take breath and to pray, to drink deep at the fountain of power; the day, to use the strength which has been given us, to go forth to work with it till the evening. *Florence Nightingale*

Strive to be like a well-regulated watch, of pure gold, with open face, busy hands, full of good works. *David Newquist*

Write it on your heart that every day is the best day of the year. No man has learnt anything rightly until he knows that every day is doomsday. *Ralph Waldo Emerson*

HABITS   March 14

They found me in the temple ritually purified and engaged in this service. I had no crowd with me, and there was no disturbance. *Acts 24:18 NEB*

Have you forgotten that your body is the temple of the Holy Spirit, who lives in you and is God's gift to you and that you are not the owner of your own body? You have been bought and at what a price! *1 Corinthians 6:19–20*

I do know from experience that if you really want to help people gripped by some bad habit, you have to be free of habit yourself. When I began to do things in my life that I could do, like putting things right with my brother... I found that people around me began to change. I also found that habits which for years had gripped me were broken. *Peter Howard*

I had certain habits which I knew stood in the way of full effectiveness for God. Because they were not very bad ones, I argued and postponed change. One day I had a clear thought to cut them clean out. That very day I was able to use this experience with a friend who was in need of a decision to change on worse habits. *University student*

NEW HABITS FOR OLD   March 15

Anyone who is joined to Christ is a new being; the old is gone, the new has come. *2 Corinthians 5:17 GNB*

Then Jesus said to his disciples, 'If anyone wants to follow in my footsteps he must give up all right to himself, take up his cross and follow me.   *Matthew 16:24*

There is no room for God in him who is full of himself.
                                          Jewish Service of the Heart

Let us take the difference between ourselves and Christ as regards our conduct, our attitudes, manner, judgments and feelings toward others... Self-love shows itself in the love of praise and popularity and social success... We develop what we are pleased to call sensitiveness, but which we can better call touchiness. Then self-pity creeps in. We feel inferior, we positively hug failure and point to previous defeats as evidence of our limitations. Then self-importance often gives rise to jealousy and makes us run on our position and reputation, though inwardly defeated.   *Loudon Hamilton*

Our calling is to offer such selfless friendship to others, with care and vision for them, that they become what they are meant to be.   *Gordon Wise*

It is indeed great joy that the pearl of great price is found; but take notice that it is not yours; you can have no possession of it till, like the merchant did, you sell all you have and buy it.
                                          William Law

LIVING TO MAKE OTHERS GREAT   March 19

Jesus said: Give to others, and God will give to you. Indeed, you will receive a full measure, a generous helping, poured into your hands – all that you can hold.   *Luke 6:38 GNB*

So we preach Christ to everyone. With all possible wisdom we warn and teach them in order to bring each one into God's presence as a mature individual in union with Christ. To get this done I toil and struggle, using the mighty strength which Christ supplies and which is at work in me.
                                          Colossians 1:28-29 GNB

I live only to obey God's slightest commands. In his presence I stand like the meanest soldier, ready to do all. This must be my task my whole life long, because I was born for this. I am a servant. I must always look on myself as a servant. Therefore I shall not have one single moment free for serving my own interests, my own pleasures, etc. If I were to do so, I should be no better than a thief because I should be stealing time that is not my own.   *Pope John XXIII*

One of the marks of true greatness is the ability to develop greatness in others.   *J C Macauley*

In our work we are not concerned to promote ourselves, but to live to make the other fellow great.   *Dr Frank N D Buchman*

UNDEMANDING   March 20

Live together in harmony, live together in love as though you had only one mind and one spirit between you. Never act from motives of rivalry or personal vanity, but in humility think more of each other than you do of yourselves. None of you should think only of his own affairs but consider other people's interests also.   *Philippians 2:2–4*

For Frank Buchman the cross was the starting point of his life work. For many of us it seems to be the end point of our experience... the cross means we stop living inside ourselves and think for the world... For a great many, their idea is no greater than their own personal experience, and that becomes, nine times out of ten, the only thing they talk about... If we dealt with the chief sin against our nations and the Holy Ghost, these minor sins would be dealt with as we went along. But that would end the luxury of talking about ourselves all the time – a terrible fate to contemplate. Some of us would have nothing left.   *Dr Paul Campbell*

(Jean Valjean, ex–convict, whom the bishop had welcomed in his house, had stolen money and silver from him and was brought back by the police.) The bishop went up to him and said in a low voice: 'Don't forget, never forget, that you promised me to use this money to become an honest man.' Jean Valjean remained speechless. He had no memory of having promised anything. The bishop, who had spoken with great emphasis, continued very seriously: 'Jean Valjean, my brother,

you belong to evil no longer; you belong to good. It's your soul I'm buying for you. I am rescuing it from black thoughts and from the spirit of destruction, and I give it to God.' *Victor Hugo*

BEARING WITH OTHERS   March 21

Help to carry one another's burdens, and in this way you will obey the law of Christ. Those who are being taught the Christian message should share all the good things they have with their teachers.   *Galatians 6:2 and 6 GNB*

The most godlike thing in the world is the passion to help others... In many ways selfishness and self-centredness are the essential human sins. Maybe something might happen if we remembered that we are never nearer God, and we are never more kin to God than when we are sharing someone's trouble, bearing someone's burden and helping someone's need.

Dr William Barclay

I have read in Plato and Cicero sayings that are very wise and very beautiful; but I never read in either of them: 'Come unto me all ye that labour and are heavy laden.'   *St Augustine*

The world is full of difficult people. The question is – how do we deal with them? ...Only the person who can change, and can change others is relevant to the national needs.

Paul Cambell and Peter Howard

I do not pray for a lighter load, but for a stronger back.

Phillips Brooks

SPRING   March 22

While the earth remaineth, seedtime and harvest, and cold and heat, and summer and winter, and day and night shall not cease.   *Genesis 8:22*

Consider how the wild flowers grow. They neither work nor weave, but I tell you that even Solomon in all his glory was not arrayed like one of these! Now if God so clothes the flowers of the field, which are alive today and burnt in the stove tomorrow, is he not much more likely to clothe you, you 'little-faiths'? *Matthew 6:28–30*

Mungo Park, the great explorer, had been journeying for days and miles in the wilds of China, in the most desolate surroundings. Then quite suddenly he saw on the ground at his feet, a little blue flower. And as he saw it, he said gently, 'God has been here.' ...(Beauty) should move us to the memory of God, the awareness that this is God's world and that not even the sin and thoughtlessness and the selfishness of people can entirely obliterate the beauty of God. *Dr William Barclay*

Almighty One, in the woods I am blessed. Happy is everyone in the woods. Every tree speaks through thee. O God! What glory in the woodland! On the heights is peace – peace to serve him. *Ludwig van Beethoven*

THE ART OF SENSITIVE FRIENDSHIP   March 23

There is no greater love than this – that a man should lay down his life for his friends. You are my friends if you do what I tell you to do. *John 15:13–14*

Never cease loving a person, and never give up hope for him, for even the Prodigal Son, who had fallen most low, could still be saved. The bitterest enemy... could again be your friend. Love that has grown cold can kindle again. *Søren Kierkegaard*

Love seeks one thing only: the good of the one loved. It leaves all the other secondary efforts to take care of themselves. *Thomas Merton*

A judicious friend, into whose bosom we may pour out our souls and tell our corruptions as well as our comforts, is a very great privilege. *George Whitefield*

Though we do not have our Lord with us in bodily presence, we have our neighbour, who, for the ends of love and loving service, is as good as our Lord himself. *St Teresa of Avila*

What was it that got me started? I had a friend who had obviously found something, but he never pressed his views on me. He just gave me his friendship. *University student*

EACH A ROYAL SOUL   March 24

For thou art an holy people unto the Lord thy God; the Lord thy God hath chosen thee to be a special people unto himself, above all people that are on the face of the earth. *Deuteronomy 7:6*

You are God's 'chosen generation', his 'royal priesthood' – all the old titles of God's people now belong to you. It is for you now to demonstrate the goodness of him who has called you out of darkness into his amazing light. *1 Peter 2:9*

Every Christian has the potential to be a first-class disciple... When I finally surrendered to Christ I did not lose my individuality – I found it. *Rev Selwyn Hughes © CWR*

Tommy was 45 and a tough old lag with four convictions, a burglar. He still thieved for a living. What had we in common? All I could do was to tell Tommy about my recent change... I had stolen money from my brother's drawer. Tommy was fascinated. We were a pair. Beginning to know myself, I could understand him. *Garth Lean*

Friendship is in loving rather than in being loved.
Robert Bridges

HE DOETH MUCH   March 25
THAT LOVETH MUCH

Dear friends, let us love one another, because love comes from God. Whoever loves is a child of God. Whoever does not love does not know God, for God is love. *1 John 4:7–8 GNB*

C F Andrews used to have a story of true friendship. In the 1914–18 war there were two men who were close friends. One was left wounded in no-man's land between the trenches. His friend waited until darkness came, and then at the peril of his life crawled out to help him. The first words which the wounded man said were, 'I knew you would come.'

In all ups and downs of life, in the chances and the changes, when the light shines and the darkness falls, true friendship remains the same. The writer of Proverbs 18:24 said a wonderful thing: there are friends who pretend to be friends; but there is a friend who sticks closer than a brother.   *Dr William Barclay*

The surest evidence of our love to Christ is obedience to the laws of Christ... Love is the root, obedience the fruit.

Matthew Henry

WHAT IS MY PASSION?   March 26

Now that you have, by obeying the truth, made your souls clean enough for a genuine love of your fellows, see that you do love each other fervently and from the heart.   *1 Peter 1:22*

A patient consulted the psychoanalyst Jung. The man, by hard work and application had built up a big business; but, when he retired, he began to go to pieces. His purpose had been success. He had been successful. His purpose achieved, he had nothing left to live for... Jung listened and then said,'You can be shown a greater thing to live for.' Jesus himself told us to pray regularly, thy kingdom come and thy will be done on earth, and bade us seek first the kingdom of God and his righteousness. Men sustained by faith in that purpose have been a profound constructive influence in the world.   *Rev Hallen Viney*

'Anything short of passion has no place today' was Buchman's conviction. 'No heart is pure that is not passionate.' And he would pray, 'Lord come with thy trumpet call and awaken our sense of destiny.' Whether or not they were on fire was the first thing he noticed about people. 'Shed every secondary allegiance for ever,' he once said. 'To do so is the mark of a normal personality.'   *Dr Paul Campbell*

Go for gold. Go all out – for God's sake and for others. If you are tepid, where has your passion gone?   *Brian Boobbyer*

NEIGHBOURLINESS March 27

For after all, the whole law towards others is summed up by this one command, 'Thou shalt love thy neighbour as thyself.'
Galatians 5:14

Love of God is the root, love of our neighbour is the fruit of the tree of life. Neither can exist without the other, but the one is cause the other effect. *Archbishop William Temple*

The fact that the infinite God focused himself in a man is the best proof that God cares about people. In the teachings of that man, Jesus Christ, we find repeated again and again, an insistence on love to God and love to men being inseparably linked. He violently denounced those who divorced religion from life. He had no use at all for those who put up a screen of elaborate ceremonial and long prayers, and exploited their fellow-men behind it. *Canon J B Phillips*

He alone loves the Creator perfectly who manifests a pure love for his neighbour. *The Venerable Bede*

> When I needed a neighbour were you there,
> were you there?
> And the creed and the colour and the name won't matter,
> were you there? *Sydney Carter*

PEACEMAKERS March 28

Peace I leave with you; my peace I give to you; not as the world gives it do I give to you. Let not your hearts be troubled; neither let them be afraid. *John 14:27 RSV*

> Lord, make me an instrument of your peace.
> Where there is hatred, may I bring love;
> Where there is malice, may I bring pardon;
> Where there is discord, may I bring harmony.
> *St Francis of Assisi*

Father and son differences are commonplace enough. For me it became an excuse not to heed the promptings of my heart to seek forgiveness for my petty generational superiority. Yet the thought to act with a spirit of apology always came alive in a moment of quiet prayer... The letter written and despatched. Then later, a meeting and then the discovery from the doctor that my father had less than six months left in this world. Then the gratitude to God for personal proof of his mercy and divinity. This personal experience of reconciliation has led me to accept that acts of forgiveness, however miniature, demonstrate the divine at work in human affairs, forgiveness carried the power of healing – personal and social.   *Allan Griffith*

Let me now show you, my son, the way of peace and inner freedom:
>Genuinely want to do another's will more than your own;
>Always choose to have less rather than more;
>Always look for the lowest place, below everybody;
>Always want and pray that God's will may be wholly
>fulfilled in you.   *Thomas à Kempis*

THE PRIZE OF LEARNING LOVE   March 29

We see real love, not in the fact that we loved God, but that he loved us and sent his son to make personal atonement for our sins. If God loved us as much as that, surely we, in our turn, should love one another.   *1 John 4:10–11*

>For life, with all it yields of joy and woe,
>And hope and fear – believe the aged friend –
>Is just our chance o' the prize of learning love,
>How love might be, hath been indeed, and is;
>And that we hold thenceforth to the uttermost
>Such prize despite the envy of the world,
>And, having gained truth, keep truth: that is all.
>   *Robert Browning*

The prize of learning love is that love provides the only way of approach to God. We cannot reach him through human understanding alone – though we are most grateful to God for the great gift of understanding. As Jeremiah 29:13 says, Ye shall seek me and find me when ye shall search for me with your whole heart. In other words it is not possible for me to find God through my mind only; it is possible through my heart and

because of the love he has put there. After all, GOD IS LOVE.

P M

I thought I was pretty good at showing love. But recently I attended a meeting of 25 friends, Bridge-Builders, black and white, Jamaican and Indian. I became more and more impatient as the meeting dragged on. Some people talked and talked. I thought 'Not her again!', increasingly irritated. After 2½ hours I was glad to go. My friend, who was driving me, said, 'Yes, but people will never grow unless you let them express themselves.' I had been totally without love. I asked God to forgive me. *H P E*

REMORSE OR REPENTANCE   March 30

Turn back all of you, by God's help.   *Hosea 12:6 NEB*

Victor (a schoolboy in rebellion) said he was sorry.

'How much are you sorry? Do you know what remorse is?'

'Oh yes, I know. That's sorrow for sin when you go ahead and do it again.'

'Then what do you think you need?'

'Repentance.'

'What's that?'

'Oh, that's when a fellow is sorry enough to quit!' ...(Frank Buchman) began to talk to Victor about finding a companion who would always understand, a friend he would never wish to run away from. 'I know who that is,' said the boy. 'That's Christ. I'd like to be a Christian.'   *Professor Theophil Spoerri*

Repentance means an about-turn. It means being willing, with the help of Christ, to turn away from all that is wrong in our lives and to go with Jesus instead... Often certain practical consequences of repentance will have to be faced: a young couple sleeping together must either separate or get married; dishonest business deals or fiddling the income tax returns will have to be put right; resentment and bitterness must be handed over immediately to Christ... (Repentance) is a turning towards a life of sacrificial love as a true follower of Christ. *Canon David Watson*

BECAUSE I KNEW NOT March 31

So foolish was I, and ignorant... Nevertheless I am continually with thee; thou hast holden me by my right hand. Thou shalt guide me with thy counsel. *Psalms 73:22–23*

Most of us don't know the evil we do; we're blind; we're afraid; we're preoccupied. To the African Americans I ask, 'Forgive us our blindness; forgive us our fear; forgive us our preoccupation.' *Mrs Margaret Palmer, Chicago lawyer*

Mr Keble used to quote the words of the Psalm: 'I will guide thee with mine *eye*. Be ye not like to horse and mule, which have no understanding; whose mouths must be held with bit and bridle, lest they fall upon thee.' This is the very difference, he used to say, between slaves and friends or children. Friends do not ask for literal commands; but, from their knowledge of the speaker, they understand his half words, and from love of him they anticipate his wishes... We are treated as sons, not as servants; not subjected to a code of formal commandments, but addressed as those who love God, and wish to please him.

John Henry Newman

Because I knew no real repentance for my sins, I argued with that man and failed him. If I had told him where I was wrong, and had to change, I might have helped him. *University student*

The greatest charity in the world is the communication of divine truth to the ignorant. *Alex Maclaren*

Conviction of ignorance is the doorstep to the temple of wisdom. *Charges H Spurgeon*

GOD'S FORGIVENESS   April 1

Jesus said: That is why I tell you, Simon, that her sins, many as they are, are forgiven; for she has so much love. But the man who has little to be forgiven has only a little love to give.

Luke 7:47

Suddenly Corrie ten Boom caught sight of him in the congregation at Munich – the former SS man who had been their guard at Ravensbruck camp. Somehow she managed to go on speaking, but scenes of horror and anguish from those past days crowded into her mind. It was not for herself she cared – she remembered poor Betsie, ill, frail, yet made to strip while those mocking guards examined their helpless prisoners. Now the leader of them was here in the church. After the service he came up the church towards her, smiling broadly and with outstretched hand. 'Thank you for your message,' he said, 'Jesus has washed my sins away.' Corrie looked at him, unable to lift her hand from her side. She had preached forgiveness, but how could she show it to the very person who had humiliated and hurt her beloved sister?... She concluded, 'I discovered that when God tells us to love our enemies, he gives, along with the command, the love itself.'   *Mary Batchelor*

Perhaps the most glorious word in the English language is forgiveness.   *Dr Billy Graham*

AS WE FORGIVE   April 2

As God's picked representatives, purified and beloved, put on that nature which is merciful in action, kindly in heart and humble in mind. Accept life, and be most patient and tolerant with one another, always ready to forgive if you have a difference with anyone. Forgive as freely as the Lord has forgiven you.   *Colossians 3:12–13*

Where I have wronged anyone, please forgive me. Where I have been wronged, I forgive. The past is past. There is room for black and white and brown. We must build this country together.

President Jomo Kenyatta, addressing the white farmers of Kenya

To err is human, to forgive divine. *Alexander Pope*

Forgiveness is our greatest need and highest achievement.
Horace Bushnell

You never so touch the ocean of God's love as when you forgive and love your enemies. *Corrie ten Boom*

EVERY BARRIER DOWN April 3

Who can separate us from the love of Christ? Can trouble, pain or persecution? Can lack of food and clothes, danger to life and limb, the threat of force of arms?... No, in all these things we win an overwhelming victory through him who has proved his love for us. *Romans 8:35 and 37*

The Lord doesn't want the first place in my life; he wants all of my life. *Howard Amerding*

We (American prisoners of the Chinese in Korea) were dead beat. Another terrible day's march lay ahead. The men were lying cold and half-starved in the lousy shacks waiting for the command to get going. Suddenly old Commissioner Lord (Salvation Army) appeared in the doorway of our shack... 'Boys,' he said, 'boys, I've got news for you – great news. Listen!' We all took notice. 'What's with this guy?' That old Commissioner, he just stood among us and said, 'The Lord is my shepherd; I shall not want', and he went right through that psalm like it was God's personal message to us. Chaplain, I'm telling you, you could hear the silence. I never felt so moved in all my life. Then the guards came – it was get going or die. Those men rose like they had new strength. *S J Davies*

Have courage for the great sorrows of life and patience for the small ones. And when you have laboriously accomplished your daily task, go to sleep in peace; God is awake. *Victor Hugo*

AT ANY COST April 4

Only be thou strong and very courageous that thou mayest observe to do according to all the law... Turn not from it to the right hand or to the left that thou mayest prosper wheresoever thou goest. *Joshua 1:7*

To see what is right and not do it, is want of courage. *Confucius*

The communists (in a Soviet labour camp) wished to compel the nuns to abandon their religious habit and to wear the uniform of prisoners. They answered, 'We will not wear the badge of the antichrist.' Because of this they were compelled to walk naked through the snow in freezing temperatures. They walked singing 'Our Father'. Not one of them fell ill. When a communist enquired of the camp's doctor, Mrs Bravermann, herself an atheist, how this was possible from a medical point of view, she replied: 'Did you not hear them singing about a father in heaven? Well, this is the scientific explanation.' He is your father too. *Pastor R Wurmbrand*

There may be persons who can glide along like a tramcar on rails without a solitary jerk. But I find I have a vile nature to contend with, and spiritual life is a struggle with me. I have to fight from day to day with inbred corruption, coldness, deadness, barrenness and if it were not for my Lord Jesus Christ, my heart would be as dry as the heart of the damned. *Charles B Spurgeon*

CHOOSING THE HARD WAY April 5

Obey my voice, and I will be your God, and ye shall be my people; and walk ye in all the ways I have commanded you, that it may be well with you. *Jeremiah 7:23*

'Herr Pastor' (said three Nazi officials, visiting a huge hospital for epileptics and the mentally disturbed in 1940), 'the Fuehrer has decided that all these people must be gassed.' Von Bodelschwingh looked at them calmly. 'You can put me into a concentration camp, if you want; that is your affair. But as long as I am free, you do not touch one of my patients. I cannot change to fit the times or the wishes of the Fuehrer. I stand under orders from our Lord Jesus Christ.'   *John Foster*

Christ has given us an example, that we may follow in his steps. He went through far more, infinitely more than we can be called to suffer. Our brethren have gone through much more; and they seem to encourage us by their success. Now it is our turn.   *Cardinal J H Newman*

There are no loopholes for anybody who wants to be honest. On any given day, any of us will be confronted with one of the choices: either truth or falsehood, either a choice towards spiritual independence or a choice towards spiritual submission or servitude.   *Alexander Solzhenitsyn*

THE CROSS   April 6

Then Jesus said to his disciples, 'If anyone wants come with me, he must forget self, carry his cross, and follow me. For whoever wants to save his own life will lose it, but whoever loses his life for my sake will find it.   *Matthew 16:24–25 GNB*

The cross is not a real cross if it is only something on a hill 2,000 years ago. It is an aweful and devastating contact with the holiness of God, which breaks but remakes, which condemns but cures, which hates the sin but loves the best in us, which shatters but makes whole, which is the end but also the beginning and which leads to the death of self and to the newness and the power of the resurrection life of Jesus Christ. ... (The doctrine of the cross), which I knew as a boy, which my church believed, which I had always taught, that day became a great reality for me. I had entered the little church with a divided will nursing pride, selfishness, ill-will. The woman's simple talk personalised the cross for me that day and suddenly I had a poignant vision of the crucified one.   *Dr Frank N D Buchman*

The cross is 'I' crossed out.   *Anon*

The cross of Christ is the most revolutionary thing ever to appear among men.   *A T Tozer*

NO OTHER GOOD ENOUGH April 7

For Christ suffered for you and left you a permanent example, so that you might follow in his footsteps. He was guilty of no sin nor of the slightest prevarication. Yet when he was insulted he offered no insult in return. When he suffered he made no threats of revenge. He simply committed his cause to the one who judges fairly. *1 Peter 2:24–25*

> There was no other good enough
> To pay the price of sin.
> He only could unlock the gate
> Of heaven and let us in. *C F Alexander*

The cross is where history and life, legend and reality, time and eternity intersect. There Jesus is nailed for ever, to show how God could become a man and a man become God.

Malcolm Muggeridge

You will never, never come into this experience until you know the cross of Christ. Some of you have heard about it Sunday by Sunday, but it is not an experience. If it were an experience you would not shrink from anything. *Dr Frank N D Buchman*

THE STUMBLING BLOCK OF THE CROSS April 8

It is to you who believe in him that he is 'precious', but to those who disobey God, it is true that... he is to them a 'stone of stumbling and a rock of offence'. *1 Peter 2:7–8*

To us today the cross is an offence. We tend to say, 'Why should this man have to die such an agonising death?' It is because we have lost the sense of the heinousness of sin. *Anon*

The cross of Christ will always be an offence to the natural man.

John Blanchard

The cross is the key. If I lose this key, I fumble. The universe will not open to me. But with the key in my hand I know I hold its secret. *Rev E Stanley Jones*

I realise now that I have to choose between my will and God's will. When I choose God's will, that is the cross for me.

Tolon Na, a Muslim leader in northern Ghana

The cross comes into my life when Christ's aim – thy kingdom come, thy will be done on earth – crosses my aim and I choose his aim. My will is the real ME. It is the big 'I' crossed out.

Dr Paul Campbell

HEART OF FLAME, SPIRIT OF STEEL   April 9

I will give them a different heart and put a new spirit into them; I will take the heart of stone out of their bodies and give them a heart of flesh. Then they will confirm to my statutes and keep my laws. They will become my people and I will become their God.   *Ezekiel 11:19–20 NEB*

Did not our hearts burn within us, while he talked with us by the way?   *Luke 24:32*

To my God a heart of flame; to my fellowmen a heart of love; to myself a heart of steel.   *St Augustine*

I realised that there was softness in me that made me avoid some people. I thought of a man, a leader, whom I had avoided. The thought came, as I began to 'listen' for God's guidance that I should apologise to him for criticising him behind his back. With thumping heart I did so. He swung round and asked me to sit down. We had a marvellously honest talk. I walked back to college thinking, 'This thing really works.'

Oxford undergraduate

The 'heart' in the Biblical sense is not the inward life but the whole man in relation to God.   *Dietrich Bonhoeffer*

Christ speaks:
    It is all so very much simpler than you think:
    Give me the greedy heart and the little creeping treasons,
    Give me the proud heart and the blind, obstinate eyes;
    Give me the shallow heart, and the vain lust and the folly;
    Give me the coward heart and the spiritless refusals;
    Give me the confused self that you can do nothing with;
    I can do something.

Dorothy L Sayers in The Just Vengeance

THE SECRET OF LIFE   April 10

Jesus said: I am come that they might have life, and that they might have it more abundantly.   *John 10:10*

The probability of life originating from accident is comparable to the probability of the unabridged dictionary resulting from an explosion in a printing shop.   *Edward Conklin, biologist*

The man who regards his own life and that of his fellow creatures as meaningless is not merely unfortunate but almost disqualified for life.   *Albert Einstein*

He only is advancing in life whose heart is getting softer, whose blood warmer, whose brain quicker, whose spirit is entering into living peace.   *John Ruskin*

Some day you will read in the papers that D L Moody of East Northfield is dead. Don't you believe a word of it! At that moment I shall be more alive than I am now.   *Dwight L Moody*

What intrigued me about these men was their joy in life, the depth of their friendships, their bold aims for a new Britain and new world, combined with their care for others and their fearless sharp challenges delivered to anyone, starting with themselves.   *A student on first meeting the Oxford Group*

HE IS RISEN   April 11

'I am the resurrection and the life,' Jesus told Martha (sister of Lazarus); 'those who believe in me will live even though they die; and all those who live and believe in me will never die. Can you believe this?'   *John 11:25–26 GNB*

By virtue of the resurrection, nothing any longer kills inevitably, but everything is capable of becoming the blessed touch of the divine hands, the blessed influence of the will of God upon our lives.   *Teilhard de Chardin*

Mary Magdalene was deeply sad because she thought she'd lost for ever the person whom she loved so deeply and who had transformed her life. She stood outside the grave weeping (*John 20:10–18*). But the Lord came to her, called her by name and showed her that he was still alive and would be with her always. She was filled with joy... The risen Christ still comes to us, however we may be feeling, and says, I am with you always.   *Canon David Watson*

> And I hope and trust most fully
> In that manhood crucified;
> And each thought and deed unruly
> Do to death, as he has died.

Cardinal J H Newman

VICTORY   April 12

It is sin which gives death its sting... All thanks to God, then, who gives us the victory over these things through our Lord, Jesus Christ. And so, brothers of mine, stand firm! Let nothing move you as you busy yourselves in the Lord's work. Be sure that nothing you do for him is ever lost or ever wasted.

1 Corinthians 15:56–58

A committed Christian learns to forgive those who react wrongly to him. He follows a man who saw his attempts to build a new kingdom end up on a cross, and yet who, before he died, uttered a prayer of forgiveness for his murderers knowing that, out of the seeming defeat, God would bring a resounding victory. We too can enter into that victory.

Rev Selwyn Hughes © CWR

In daily life you find Jesus through prayer. Teresa of Avila wrote, 'The devil knows that he has lost the soul that perseveringly practises mental prayer'... We have to remain in contact with Jesus the whole day, through short prayers and meditations about everything which occurs. Be aware that in all circumstances God is present and discuss with him, your best friend, what would be the best thing to do.

Pastor Richard Wurmbrand

CHAIN OF FATE   April 13

The hope is that in the end the whole of created life will be rescued from the tyranny of change and decay, and have its share
in that magnificent liberty which can only belong to the children of God.   *Romans 8:21*

We must wait for God, long, meekly, in the wind and wet, in
the thunder and lightning, in the cold and the dark. Wait and
he will come. He never comes to those who do not wait... When
he quickens his pace, be sure of it before you quicken yours. But
when he slackens, slacken at once; and do not be slow only, but
silent, very silent, for he is God.   *Frederick W Faber*

God Almighty has set before me two great objectives, the suppression of the slave trade and the reformation of manners.
      *William Wilberforce (1759–1833); written in his early morning
            journal, shortly after asking God to direct his life*

My parents were separated. As a boy at school many years ago
I felt it keenly when happy parents collected happy boys at half
term and I was left. For years I felt bound into a hereditary dis-
advantage. But I did break that chain. I cared for both and in
the end, after 25 years separation, they became reunited and at
peace.   *H P E*

CHOICE   April 14

I offer you the choice of life or death, blessing or curse. Choose
life and then you and your descendents will live; love the Lord
your God, obey him and hold fast to him.
                              Deuteronomy 30:19–20 NEB

Plant your feet firmly therefore within the freedom that Christ
has won for us, and do not let yourselves be caught again in the
shackles of slavery.   *Galatians 5:1*

When you have to make a choice and don't make it, that is in
itself a choice.   *William James*

Jesus has many lovers of his heavenly kingdom these days, but
few of them carry his cross. He has many who desire comfort,

but few who desire affliction. He has many friends to share his meals, but few to share his fasts. Everyone is eager to rejoice with him, but few are willing to endure anything for him. Many follow Jesus up to the breaking of the bread, but few as far as drinking from the chalice of his Passion... Those who love Jesus for himself and not for their own comfort bless him in every trial and heart-felt anguish, just as they do in moments of great comfort. And even if he should never give them comfort, they would still always praise him and always want to thank him. Oh, how powerful is a pure love of Jesus, untainted by self-interest or self-love! *Thomas à Kempis*

No man or woman oozes into the kingdom of God. In the final analysis, all enlist and every soldier knows that he is enlisted.
Professor Henry B Wright

GIVING ALL... April 15

None of you can be my disciple unless you give up everything you have. *Luke 14:33 GNB*

Teach me to do thy will for thou art my God; in thy gracious kindness show me the level road. *Psalms 143:10 NEB*

I will place no value on anything I have or may possess except in relation to the kingdom of God. *David Livingstone*

Christianity is the total commitment of all I know of me to all I know of Jesus Christ. *Archbishop William Temple*

God is the master of the scenes; we must not choose what part we shall act; it concerns us only to be careful that we do it well, always saying, 'If this please God let it be as it is'.
Bishop Jeremy Taylor

God creates out of nothing, therefore until a man is nothing God can make nothing out of him. *Martin Luther*

In the early days of the Oxford Group, Frank Buchman challenged us to give all. It sifted us. Some wanted to give vague, genial support. Others went the whole way. It meant in some cases giving up career prospects, sometimes the bitter opposition of parents and family. But those who came through the fire

became the nucleus that continued after Frank Buchman's death.   *H P E*

FOR SOMETHING GREAT   April 16

Indeed we want to prove ourselves genuine ministers of God... with sincerity, with insight and patience; by sheer kindness and the Holy Spirit; with genuine love, speaking the plain truth and living by the power of God.   *2 Corinthians 6:4 and 6*

The price of greatness is responsibility.   *Sir Winston S Churchill*

(President Jomo Kenyatta, speaking to a crowd of 50,000 Kenyans, said): 'We want to build a great country. But can we do this if the men go out womanising?' A few bold souls said 'No.' Kenyatta pursued the point. 'Do you really mean it?... I want you to stop stealing and to start working.' I believe Kenyatta has the right view. If a man is to lead a nation today, the moral life of that nation is his responsibility, and his leadership cannot be effective unless he tackles it.   *Bremer Hofmeyr*

As statesmen we must learn to look less for popularity and make our first aim that the other fellow and the other nation become great.
           Ole Bjorn Kraft, formerly Foreign Minister of Denmark

> Were the whole realm of nature mine,
> That were an offering far too small;
> Love so amazing, so divine,
> Demands my soul, my life, my all.   *Isaac Watts*

DECISION   April 17

Choose you this day whom ye will serve; whether the gods which your fathers served... or the gods of the Amorites in whose land ye dwell; but as for me and my house we will serve the Lord.   *Joshua 24:15*

Turning to the third evil spirit the devil asked, 'And what about you?' 'I shall tell people that there is a God and a judgment to come,' answered the third evil spirit, 'but I shall add that there's no hurry.' 'Excellent!' said the devil. 'Many will believe that.' I believe that the devil does try to persuade people that there's no hurry about turning to God or putting things right in the world, whereas the truth is that time is running out fast and the right time to respond to God's voice is always now – as soon as we hear it.   *Canon David Watson*

Some people are very decisive when it comes to avoiding decisions.   *Brendon Francis*

I wanted in theory to give my life to God, but thought that I was fairly good as I was. I used to go and see the chaplain of my college and argue with him about the Oxford Group. Finally he said, 'I shall always be glad to see you, but from now on I will not talk with you any more on this subject. You must decide.' This gave me the shock I needed. I got up early one morning and seriously asked God to show me where I needed to change and put things right.   *H P E*

GREAT GIVING IS GREAT LIVING   April 18

Jesus said: Believe me, this poor widow has put more (into the Temple almsbox) than all the others. For they have put in what they can easily afford, but she in her poverty who needs so much, has given away everything, her whole living.
Mark 12:43–44

Whosoever shall compel thee to go a mile, go with him twain, said Jesus, Matthew 5:41. This was the most practical advice in the world, for it is the extras of life which make all the difference. It makes all the difference to a thing whether it is done with a smile or with bad grace. There is no reason why efficiency and courtesy should not go hand in hand. And there is no sphere in life – in the home, at business, in study, in our pleasure – when the spirit in which a thing is done, does not make all the difference... Every time Jesus gave he gave nothing less than himself. Every time he gave his help, virtue went out of him, but yet we never find a case where Jesus gave ungraciously or unwillingly.   *Dr William Barclay*

The best thing to give:
>to your enemy is forgiveness;
>to an opponent, tolerance;
>to a friend, your heart;
>to your child, a good example;
>to a father, deference;
>to your mother, conduct that will make her proud of you;
>to yourself, respect;
>to all men charity.   *Lord Balfour*

HOW MUCH DO YOU WANT IT?   April 19

The kingdom of heaven is like a merchant searching for fine pearls. When he has found a single pearl of great price, he goes and sells all his possessions and buys it.   *Matthew 13:45–46*

When we have given God all we have and are, we have simply given him his own.   *William S Plumer*

For what pay would you procure men to do this service? – to be always ready to go to prison and death?   *John Wesley*

For Wesley's Christian helpers 'no weather was too inclement, no ford too swollen, no community too degraded, no privation too severe'.   *J W Bready*

The young mother was all for letting her child do what she wanted – a modern idea with which her mother was not wholly in sympathy... Grannie, who had been quietly sewing, was asked, 'And what do you think, Grannie?' For a moment she did not reply. Then without raising her eyes from her needle, she said: 'Well, I've always believed the right time to start teaching a child about right and wrong is 20 years before it's born!' Precept is all very well – but example's the thing.
                              Francis Gay

He wanted to do God's will, but he also wanted certain things for himself. A friend said to him, 'You must choose. How much do you want to put God's will first?'   *Rev Alan Thornhill*

81

UNCONDITIONAL SURRENDER   April 20

Commit thy way unto the Lord; trust also in him, and he shall bring it to pass.   *Psalms 37:5*

The world has yet to see what Jesus Christ can do in, by, for and through someone who is wholly given up to the will of God.   *Dwight L Moody*

Several hundred people from many different countries and backgrounds come to a city to bring it a revolution. They are no fanatics. They are people of the world – from business, politics, universities, and the world of sports. They live together at one and the same time like a large family, a disciplined army. Even more remarkable, they are not out for personal aims or personal gain from the success of their enterprise... They have discovered that God can actually change people's lives from the roots up. They have experienced it themselves... If God can change people he can change the world.   *Dr Theophil Spoerri*

Before we can pray 'thy kingdom come', we must be willing to pray 'my kingdom go'.   *Alan Redpath*

I do not want merely to possess a faith. I want a faith that possesses me.   *Charles Kingsley*

I offer myself to thee, O God, this day, to do in me, and with me as to thee seems most meet.   *Bishop Thomas Wilson*

TOTAL COMMITMENT   April 21

Don't let the world around you squeeze you into its own mould but let God remake you so that your whole attitude of mind is changed.   *Romans 12:2*

This total commitment of ourselves to the God who loves us is central to our effectiveness and to our experience of his presence in our lives. But although in the Church of England, for instance, we regularly commit and offer 'our souls and bodies to be a living sacrifice' in the post-communion prayer, we may not always fully grasp the implications of these mighty phrases.

'Commitment' has far-reaching consequences: it is commitment to the God who demands everything and drives us out to fulfil his strategy in the world; the God whose power can destroy our dearest idols, free us from our most cherished indulgences, separate us from our over-ruling ambitions, deliver us from our entrenched prejudices and set us apart for his service only.

K D Belden

Teach us, good Lord, to serve thee as thou deservest; to give and not to count the cost, to fight and not to heed the wounds, to toil and not to ask for rest, to labour and not to ask for any reward save that of knowing that we do thy will.

St Ignatius of Loyola

TO LIVE WITH ALL MY MIGHT April 22

This one thing I do: forgetting what lies behind and straining forward to what lies ahead, I press onward towards the goal for the prize of the upward call of God in Jesus Christ.

Philippians 3:13–14

Resolved: to live with all my might while I do live.
Resolved: never to lose one moment of time; but improve it in
  the most profitable way I can.
Resolved: that I will live so as I shall wish I had done when I
  come to die. *Jonathan Edwards*

Next to grace, time is the most precious gift of God. Yet how much of both we waste. We say that time does many things: it teaches us many lessons, weans us from our follies, strengthens us in our good resolves and heals many wounds. And yet it does none of these things. Time does nothing. But time is the condition of all these things which God does in time. Time is full of eternity. As we use it so shall we be. Every day has its opportunities, every hour has its offer of grace.

Cardinal Henry E Manning

That daily quarter of an hour, for now 40 years or more, I am sure has been one of the greatest sustenances and sources of calm for my life. *Baron Friedrich von Hügel*

Our only real education comes from what God says directly to us. Books and historical research do not make us learned in the knowledge of God; by themselves they make for confusion and conceit. Moment by moment we must listen to God.

J P de Caussade

THE HUNGER FOR GREAT LIVING   April 23

Now that you have, by obeying the truth, made your souls clean enough for a genuine love of your fellows, see that you do love each other fervently and from the heart. For you are not just mortals now but sons of God; the live, permanent word of the living God has given you his own indestructible heredity.

1 Peter 1:22–23

It is not enough to wish to be good unless we hunger after it.

St Jerome

Are you going all out? If I am not all out, the devil gets in.

Peter Howard

Nothing great was ever achieved without enthusiasm.

R W Emerson

We need to heed the words of Richard Foster, 'Something more than good intentions and will-power is needed to transform our egocentric, greed-captivated personalities into an all-inclusive community of living, sharing persons.' I believe that the 'something more' is obedience to God, from whom, if we listen, we will receive both correction and direction. Modern technology and man's wisdom have failed to answer poverty and hunger in the world. Is it not time to seek from God his inspired plan?

Stanley Barnes

USE OF ALL WE HAVE   April 24

In everything we do, we show that we are God's servants by patiently enduring troubles, hardships and difficulties. By our purity, knowledge, patience and kindness we have shown ourselves to be God's servants.   *2 Corinthians 6:4 and 6 GNB* down and really work at it.'... The second necessity is prayer. There can be no work without prayer and there can be no prayer without work. Teilhard de Chardin, mystic and scientist, always insisted that adoration and research are one and the same thing... The third necessity is vision... To work to the limit of one's strength; to pray with all the intensity of one's being; to lift up one's eyes and to see the harvest to be reaped – these are the things which will make a congregation a real power-house for Christ.   *Dr William Barclay*

Do I know the power of my risen Lord's indwelling Spirit? Do I have boundless confidence in him? If I take up any other method, I depart altogether from the method laid down by him – 'All power is given unto me... therefore go ye.'
                                           Oswald Chambers

IDEAS ON TWO LEGS   February 6

The kingdom of God is within you.   *Luke 17:21*

Those in whom the seed has been sown are changed from within... They have seen evidence of the light of the absolute and moved by this evidence, they become capable of over-throwing the barriers which separate them from themselves and from each other. At the same time these men and women become radiant and in a certain sense radio-active. Anyone who has come into direct contact with them is immediately aware of this.   *Gabriel Marcel*

British builder and property developer, Bob Woodward, had a son Robert, aged 8, who was diagnosed as having cancer. The treatment shocked Bob by the weight he was losing. While he was bathing him, Robert said: 'Dad, why are you crying? I'm not scared. You said you would always be there.' Later, Bob said that a dark period in his life was transformed. 'I have learnt to trust God as Robert trusted me. If I can be there for my son, how can I possibly doubt that God can be there for me?' The idea came to him to launch the Cancer and Leukaemia Childhood Trust in 1976. It has become a thriving charity, CLIC, with international recognition for its contribution to re-search.   *News Letter*

AFTER COMMUNISM – WHAT? February 7

This faith of ours is the only way in which the world can be conquered.   *1 John 5:4*

Communism was an ideology which demanded total devotion and deeply attracted me as a student. For 75 years it ruled Russia. Now it has collapsed. What will take its place? The alternatives seem to be nationalism – leading to wars or threats of war in many places – or the selfish free-market capitalism we practise in the West. What is the positive devotion which can take over and replace these false alternatives? I came to the conclusion that it is the decision to let God rule in personal affairs to the point where any man or woman can be used to play their part in rebuilding the world according to his plan.   *H P E*

In the struggle for Africa today manpower, munitions, money and military strength, important though these are, are not by themselves an answer. Without an ideology all these things will be in vain. We need an aim fundamental enough to deal with the problems raised and roused by hate, fear, greed – both in individuals and nations... The answer is a commitment to the greatest revolution of all time, whereby the cross of Christ will transform the world.

Vice-president of 10,000 African teachers of South Africa

There is one source that is stronger than every disappointment, bitterness or ingrained mistrust and that power is Jesus Christ who brought forgiveness and reconciliation to the world.

Pope John Paul II

A FAITH TO CONQUER THE WORLD February 8

And there was given him dominion, and glory and a kingdom, that all people, nations and languages should serve him; his dominion is an everlasting dominion, which shall not pass away, and his kingdom which shall not be destroyed.   *Daniel 7:14*

The past century has seen the rise of ideologies. Marx launched a world-wide concept for universal human society with the thesis 'One class shall rule'. Hitler countered with an even more divisive thesis, 'One race shall rule'. But Jesus had long since someone to take care of what appertains to the common weal.

St Thomas Aquinas

That government is best which governs the least, because its people discipline themselves.

John Adams, second President of the United States

To surrender my own will is like giving up life itself. It is a dying to self. One great revolutionary said of his experience, 'I die daily.' It has been called taking up the Cross. It means a fundamental decision once taken and then renewed day by day by a superior will, not our own.   *Paul Campbell and Peter Howard*

YOU CAN'T LEGISLATE IT   February 3

The statutes of the Lord are right, rejoicing the heart; the commandment of the Lord is pure, enlightening the eyes. The fear of the Lord is clean, enduring for ever; the judgments of the Lord are true and righteous altogether.   *Psalms 19:8-9*

If you obey the royal law, expressed by the scripture, 'Thou shalt love thy neighbour as thyself', all is well. But once you allow any invidious distinctions to creep in, you are sinning, you stand condemned by that law.   *James 2:8-9*

There is a universal moral law, as distinct from a moral code, which consists of certain statements of fact about the nature of man; and by behaving in conformity with which, man enjoys his true freedom.   *Dorothy L Sayers*

There is nothing more necessary for the national or international community than respect for the majesty of the law and the salutary thought that the law is also sacred and protected, so that whoever breaks it is punishable and will be punished.

Pope Pius XII

When the law of God is written in our hearts, our duty will be to our delight.   *William Henry*

People make excuses for not keeping the law of God, which is proof how deeply they believe in the law.   *C S Lewis*

THE GOLDEN AGE   February 4

And the ransomed of the Lord shall return and come to Zion with singing; everlasting joy shall be upon their heads; they shall obtain joy and gladness, and sorrow and sighing shall flee away.   *Isaiah 35:10 RSV*

There arose loud voices in heaven and they were saying: 'The kingship of the world now belongs to our Lord and to his Christ and he shall be king for timeless ages.'   *Revelation 11:15*

Trying to find happiness from this world is like trying to light up a dark room by lighting a succession of matches. You strike one, it flickers for a moment and then it goes out. But when you find Jesus Christ, it's as though the whole room is suddenly flooded with light.   *Professor C E M Joad*

Jesus Christ himself began the vast project of establishing the kingdom of God upon earth by calling together a handful of men. Before his own departure from the visible human scene, he entrusted to these few the awe-inspiring task of telling the world about God and his kingdom... The movement proved unconquerable, and still proves unconquerable; because its unseen roots are in the eternal God.   *Canon J B Phillips*

If you do not wish for his kingdom don't pray for it. But if you do, you must do more than pray for it; you must work for it.
                                                    John Ruskin

MORE POWERFUL THAN THE ATOM   February 5

How can a human being win a case against God?   *Job 9:2 GNB*

The Christ you have to deal with is not a weak person outside you, but a tremendous power within you. He was 'weak' enough to be crucified, yes, but he lives now by the power of God.   *2 Corinthians 13:3-4*

How is a church to be a Christian power-station? The first necessity is, quite simply, work. It could be said that work is the most underrated activity in the world. There is a kind of delusion that things can happen without work... Sir William Walton, the great composer, says, 'Nothing occurs to me unless I sit

30

posed his thesis, 'One God shall rule'. He called his ideology 'The kingdom of God'. In this lies the answer to all the 'isms' if we will obey it. *Rev Hallen Viney*

Seek ye first the kingdom of God. We argue in exactly the opposite way, even the most spiritually minded of us. 'But I must live; I must make so much money; I must be clothed; I must be fed.' The great concern of our lives is not the kingdom of God, but how we are to fit ourselves to live. Jesus reverses this order: get rightly related to God first, maintain that as the great care of your life and never put the concern of your care in the other things. *Oswald Chambers*

THE COST OF CIVILISATION   February 9

Righteousness exalteth a nation; but sin is a reproach to any people. *Proverbs 14:34*

In the world ye shall have tribulation; but be of good cheer, I have overcome the world. *John 16:33 AV*

Neither civilisation nor Christianity can be promoted alone. In fact they are inseparable. *David Livingstone*

The truth is that civilisation collapses when that essential reverence for absolute values which religion gives disappears. Rome had discovered that in the days of her decadence. Men live on the accumulated self-disciplines. Overthrow these and nothing seems to happen at first... But something has gone as well, the mortar which held society together, the integrity of the individual soul; then the rats come out of their holes and begin burrowing under the foundations and there is nothing to withstand them. *Dr Monk Gibbon*

Religion is a main determining factor in the formation of a culture or a civilisation. *Arnold Toynbee*

The true test of civilisation is not the census nor the size of cities... but the kind of people that the country turns out.
R Waldo Emerson

MORAL AND MATERIAL VALUES   February 10

Tell those who are rich in this present world not to be contemptuous of others, and not to rest the weight of their confidence on
the transitory power of wealth but on the living God, who generously gives us everything for our enjoyment.

1 Timothy 6:17

Right is right even if everyone is against it; and wrong is wrong
even if everyone is for it.   *William Penn*

We forget the eternal struggle between Evil and Good, victory
in which brings the blessings of security and prosperity. But
defeat in this struggle, and even ignorance of it, brings poverty,
hunger, slavery and death... An extreme of evil must be met
with an extreme of good. A fanatical following of evil by a passionate pursuit of good. Only a passion can cure a passion.

Dr Frank N D Buchman

Even a cursory glance at the revolutionary trends in modern
science is sufficient to show that the strictly materialistic world,
which is still dominant in sociology, the behavioural sciences
and among educated laymen, has in fact no leg to stand on; it is
a Victorian anachronism.   *Arthur Koestler*

Strive we then to think aright, that is the first principle of moral
life.   *Blaise Pascal*

THE FIGHT BETWEEN GOOD   February 11
AND EVIL

Here is my advice. Live your whole life in the Spirit and you
will not satisfy the desires of your lower nature. For the whole
energy of the lower nature is set against the Spirit, while the
whole power of the Spirit is contrary to the lower nature.

Galatians 5:16-17

For evil to triumph, it is only necessary for good men to do
nothing.   *Edmund Burke*

I do not believe that we take the question of 'evil' seriously
enough in modern days, so that we are continually being disap-
pointed, shocked or horrified by its manifestations... I am

34

God forces no one, for love cannot compel, and God's service, therefore, is a thing of perfect freedom. *Hans Denk*

God creates us with freedom to choose... God doesn't snuff out atheists or agnostics. He doesn't give up on us. At our best and worst moments God is there whispering. He waits courteously with a love which will not let you go. *Archbishop Desmond Tutu*

ROOTS   March 4

There was once a man who went out to sow. In his sowing some of the seeds fell by the roadside and the birds swooped down and gobbled them up. Some fell on stony patches where they had very little soil. They sprang up quickly in the shallow soil, but when the sun came up they were scorched by the heat and withered away because they had no roots. *Matthew 13:4–5*

What other people think of me is becoming less and less important; what they think of Jesus because of me is critical.
Cliff Richard

Self–emptiness prepares for spiritual fitness. *Richard Sibbes*

'I'm a self–made man, you know' explained a certain magnate of modern business to Dr Joseph Parker, who immediately replied, 'Sir, you have lifted a great deal of responsibility from the Almighty.' *Professor John Baillie*

When a man is wrapped up in himself he makes a pretty small package. *John Ruskin*

Big doors swing on little hinges. Sometimes the hinge on which a big door swings is just about the size of a cigarette, sometimes it may be a relationship, sometimes a habit... If you have a 5 per cent or 10 per cent which you still hang on to, that is what runs your life. *Peter Howard*

FULL SATISFACTION   March 5

The Lord is my light and my salvation; whom should I fear? The Lord is the refuge of my life; of whom then should I go in dread? *Psalms 27:1 NEB*

God through Christ is able to do for you
all that you ask or think,
above all that you ask or think,
abundantly above all that you ask or think,
exceeding abundantly above all that you ask or think.

Ephesians 3:20–21

Full satisfaction: to help someone to find God... simple care for people, sharing our own spiritual needs to help others to become open to God, may be the most important and rewarding work. *John Lester and Pierre Spoerri*

That man is perfect in faith who can come to God in the utter dearth of his feelings and desires, without a glow or an aspiration, with the weight of low thoughts, failures, neglects and wandering forgetfulness, and say to him, 'Thou art my refuge.'

George Macdonald

A PASSION TO CURE A PASSION March 6

The calling of God is not to impurity but to the most thorough purity. *1 Thessalonians 4:7*

Don't begin by arguing with yourself whether absolute purity is possible; nor by assuming that because you want to be pure, this standard holds no further challenge for you. Think of the purity of Jesus Christ – joyous, free, unrepressed – and write down the things God tells you about yourself. Absolute purity in actions? In thoughts? In motives?... Think of the time, the energy, the thought and the planning of a nation in which the creative energies of all its people were liberated by positive purity and directed into constructive channels! *Edward T Perry*

Father, forgive the cold love of the years,
While here in the silence we bow,
Perish our cowardice, perish our fears,
Kindle us, kindle us now.

Lord, we believe, we accept, we adore,
Less than the least though we be;

Then I will sprinkle clean water upon you, and ye shall be clean; from all your filthiness and from all your idols will I cleanse you. A new heart also will I give you and a new spirit will I put within you. *Ezekiel 36:25–26*

We have to get into the habit of hearkening to God about everything, to form the habit of finding out what God says. If, when a crisis comes, we instinctively turn to God, we know that the habit has been formed. We have to take the initiative where we are, not where we are not. *Oswald Chambers*

My life does not belong to myself. I have no preconceptions of any kind, any day, for the rest of my life: where I will go, what I will do or not do, what I will say or not say. I want to be used by God, if he will use me. *Peter Howard*

THE REWARD OF PURITY   March 16

For thou, Lord, wilt bless the righteous; with favour wilt thou compass him, as with a shield. *Psalms 5:12*

Don't worry over anything whatever; whenever you pray tell God every detail of your needs in thankful prayer, and the peace of God, which passes human understanding, will keep constant guard over your hearts and minds, as they rest in Christ Jesus. *Philippians 4:7*

In reading the lives of great men, I found that the first victory they won was over themselves and their carnal urges.
Harry S Truman

Every victory over impurity and selfishness clears the spiritual vision... deny self, give no quarter to sin, resist the devil and thou shalt see God. *Rev F B Meyer*

God wants us to be victors, not victims; to grow, not grovel; to soar, not sink; to overcome, not to be overwhelmed.
William A Ward

The world passes away and its lusts but he who does the will of God abides for ever. *1 John 2:17*

Thanks be to God who gives us the victory.

1 Corinthians 15:57 AV

TWO COMMON WAYS –
AND A THIRD

Have you forgotten that the kingdom of God will never belong
to the wicked? Don't be under any illusion – neither the impure,
the idolater or the adulterer; neither the effeminate, the pervert
or the thief; neither the swindler, the drunkard, the foul-
mouthed or the rapacious shall have any share in the kingdom
of God. *1 Corinthians 6:9–10*

A man and a woman... can be taken over by instinct into indulgence... or they can try to contain that boisterous energy by
their own wills... These are the common ways – indulgence and
repression. The third way is rare, but valuable beyond any
price. It is the redirection of this energy into creative caring for
people and a fight for a decent world. *Kenaston Twitchell*

God thought of sex before people did, and when people leave
God out of their sexual thinking they are in trouble.

J Blanchard

As he returned from a victorious battle, the Prophet said: 'We
have come from the lesser Jihad to the greater Jihad.' He meant
the struggle with one's own passions. *Sheikh Ahmed Surur*

He was a great help to me during my time at Oxford. They
were difficult days... Garth Lean offered support and battled to
help me find what I felt was right, not what he thought was
right, or his point of view. *A 1970s Oxford student*

UNSELFISHNESS

Let no man, then, set his own advantage as his objective, but
rather the good of his neighbour. *1 Corinthians 10:24*

Fox would say. Even in childhood, he tells us, he had been taught how to walk to keep pure; and he had kept his childhood's vow not to be wanton when he grew to manhood. If he could be kept pure, so could others. He claimed no special grace for himself, no gift that was not for all men to receive who would. Nor did he pretend that it was possible to live in purity without persistent watchfulness, in utter dependence on the power of God.   *Dr G F Nuttall*

It is inconceivable that the God who created the human mind has left himself with no means of communicating with it. It is not reasonable to suppose that the God who expects us to do his will, should have no way of letting us know what that will is, except in broad generalities... It is certainly right to pray, to talk to God. But we need even more to listen to him.
                                    Edward T Perry

If you want to be fully effective, you must give God that first hour of the day.   *Rev F B Meyer*

WIDE MARGINS   March 10

Those who think they are standing firm had better be careful that they do not fall. Every test that you have experienced is the kind that normally comes to people. But God keeps his promise and he will not allow you to be tested beyond your power to remain firm; at the time you are put to the test, he will give you the strength to endure it, and to provide you with a way out.
                                    1 Corinthians 10:12–13 GNB

Can you walk on hot coals without burning your feet?
                                    Proverbs 6:28 GNB

Ask the Lord to make your life a glory to him, a menace to the devil, a strength to your church and a witness to the world.
                                    Frederick P Wood

A simple thought comes to the mind, and then a vivid picture takes shape; afterwards comes delight, then a small mental concession, and finally ready acceptance. Thus, little by little, the malignant enemy gains full entrance when he is not resisted at the beginning. And the longer one puts off resisting, the weaker he becomes each day and the stronger the enemy grows.

Thomas à Kempis

Guard your eyes, since they are the windows through which sin enters into the soul. Never look curiously on those things which are contrary to modesty, even slightly.   *St John Bosco*

Be such a person and live such a life that if every person were such as you and every life a life like yours, this earth would be God's paradise.   *Phillips Brooks*

ABC OF HUMAN HAPPINESS   March 11

Whoso trusteth in the Lord, happy is he.   *Proverbs 16:20*

Thou wilt shew me the path of life; in thy presence is fulness of joy; at thy right hand are pleasures for evermore.   *Psalms 16:11*

There is no happiness out of God.   *Charles Wesley*

The Greater Jihad is fighting one's animal tendencies. It is internal rather than external, striving in the path of God to overcome one's animal side... To bring those passions under control, that is what Jihad means.   *Professor Yusuf Ibish of Beirut*

I come from the joy of Christ in prison to the joy of Christ with my family.   *Pastor Richard Wurmbrand,*
after 14 years of brutal treatment in prison

> Fear is a liar. Truth is that God moulds
> Our days in love and with the same precision
> As he makes wings for flight or petal folds
> Within a sheath, or shapes an eye for vision.
> He hands us strength to welcome what is right –
> Then, swift and sudden, hurls us our delight.   *Garth Lean*

PATH TO PURITY   March 12

Everything is clean to those who have clean minds. But nothing is wholesome to those who are themselves corrupt and who

Commit your fortunes to the Lord and he will sustain you; he will never let the righteous be shaken.   *Psalms 55:22 NEB*

True commitment means that all our resources – income, capital, possessions, prospects – are given to God as he directs. This may make us reconsider what we spend our money on if it all now belongs to God: the size of our house, the size of our car, what kind of holidays we take or where we send our children to school, whether we spend God's money on tobacco or alcohol... God is generous, but he also has the needs of the world and the advance of the Kingdom in mind.   *K D Belden*

I am afraid of saying 'yes', Lord. Where will you take me?
Abbé Michel Quoist

When I have learned to do God's will, I shall have fully realised my vocation on earth.   *Carlo Carretto*

Take my life and let it be
Consecrated, Lord, to thee.   *Frances Ridley Havergal*

INTO HIS HAND WENT MINE   April 25

Noah was a just man and perfect in his generation; and Noah walked with God.   *Genesis 6:9*

The one who is coming to stand by you, the Holy Spirit whom the Father will send in my name, will be your teacher and will bring to mind all that I have said to you.   *John 14:26*

Meditate daily on the words of your Creator. Learn the heart of God in the words of God, that your souls may be kindled with greater longings for heavenly joys.   *Pope St Gregory I*

Lionel Jardine had to make a choice. He had a promising career in front of him in the Indian Civil Service, or he could risk his prospects and live differently as Frank Buchman had suggested and pass on what he had found to others. He did so and found the satisfaction of God leading him to build friendship between an amazing group of British and Indians at a critical point in the history of India.   *H P E*

The first mark (of a Christian) is a deep reverence for persons as destined for eternity with God. The second is a kind of heavenly serenity which is able to draw the sting of suffering. And the third is the humility of a man or woman who has known authentically the presence of God. *Archbishop A M Ramsey*

GOD'S WILL FOR MY CAREER   April 26

Work as servants of Christ, conscientiously doing what you believe to be the will of God. Work cheerfully as if it were for the Lord and not for a man. You may be sure the Lord will reward each man for good work. *Ephesians 6:7–8*

My life has been ruled by duty. Innumerable things I had to do kept me so busy I hardly had time to think. When I put remaking the world first, I began to choose priorities and leave out irrelevancies. I decided to make the guidance of God the ruling factor of my life. *Wall Street banker*

If you want to have the time of your life, come with me and run a hospital next summer for the orphans. There will not be a cent of money in it for you and you will have to pay your own expenses. But I'll guarantee you will feel a love for life you have never before experienced. It's having the time of anyone's life to be in the service of Christ.

Sir Wilfred Grenfell, in America,
looking for a nurse to help with work in Labrador

His father, a colonel in the army, had planned a career for his son of which he could be proud. John decided that he was called to enlisting others to build a hate-free world. His father was furious. But John stuck to his calling and eventually his father stood by him.   *H P E*

ULTIMATE RESPONSIBILITY   April 27

Now get up and stand on your feet for I have shown myself to you for a reason – you are chosen to be my servant and a witness to me. *Acts 26:16*

The condition for a life that is led by the Spirit is commitment, the surrender of all we have and are into the hands of God. It is a condition to seek and obey his will before every other consideration. The second condition, naturally enough, is to set aside enough time every day to be in the presence of God, with wills and minds open to the thoughts he gives us and, if we are wise, to write them down. He can and will speak to us at any time, but the least we can do is to be unhurriedly available every morning.   *K D Belden*

Has it ever dawned on you that you are responsible for other souls before God? For instance, if I allow any private deflection from God in my life, everyone about me suffers. When once you allow physical selfishness, mental slovenliness, moral obtuseness, spiritual density, everyone belonging to your crowd will suffer. 'But', you will say, 'who is sufficient for these things if you erect a standard like that?' Our sufficiency is of God, and of him alone.   *Oswald Chambers*

WHO DARE TO LIVE   April 28

God has given us eternal life, and this life has its source in his Son. Whoever has the Son has this life.   *1 John 5:11–12*

Wherever there is life, there is danger; but the danger of rejecting the call of God, and so lacking the guidance of his Spirit, is far greater than that of being occasionally self-deceived. Life is action; and we have to choose whether or no we will habitually act with or without that Spirit. And it is in action that we find it.
                                                          Canon B H Streeter

'Brave Men Choose' was the theme of Frank Buchman's last public message before he died. He gave many examples of those who had taken daring action in critical situations to cure hatred and bring healing. He ended: 'There is no neutrality in the battle between good and evil.'   *P M and H P E*

> Then it is the brave man chooses
> While the coward stands aside,

And the multitude make virtue
Of the faith they had denied.   *J R Lowell*

Life is designed to show us that God is enough for us.
                    Catherine Bramwell Booth, at the age of 100

THE DISCIPLINED WILL   April 29

I run the race then with determination.   *1 Corinthians 9:26*

Pray then like this: Our heavenly father, may your name be honoured; may your kingdom come, and your will be done on earth as it is in heaven.   *Matthew 6:9–10*

Where God loves, he afflicts in love, and wherever God afflicts in love there he will, first or last, teach such souls such lessons as shall do them good to all eternity.   *Thomas Brooks*

The whole duty of man is summed up in obedience to God's will.   *George Washington*

God will always reveal his will to one who is willing to do it.
                    Hilys Jasper

Every day I know not what God will ask of me. I have to be ready for anything, to go anywhere, to see anybody – flexible to his command.   *Peter Howard*

> Hear me, O God!
> A broken heart
> Is my best part;
> Use still thy rod,
> That I may prove
> Therein, thy love.   *Ben Jonson*

THE UNSHIELDED HEART   April 30

I do not judge as people judge. They look at the outward appearance but I look at the heart.   *1 Samuel 16:7 GNB*

By this we shall know that we are of the truth, and reassure our hearts before him whenever our hearts condemn us. For God is greater than our hearts, and he knows everything.

1 John 3:19 RSV

Perhaps few among you have so many dealings with men of different races, different religions, different beliefs and different cultures as I – unworthily – have. In all these dealings I have found that a great love, a wide open heart, always opens the heart of others. This great love must be not mere diplomacy, but the result of an inner conviction that we are all children of one God, who has created mankind, who has created each one of us, and whose children we all are.   *Cardinal Augustin Bea*

There was only one way to stop Chief Buthelezi from boycotting the elections in South Africa – by 'the African Way' – by the friendship of the heart. It worked. God gave a miracle.

Professor Washington Okumu

God be in my head
And in my understanding;
God be in myne eyes,
And in my looking;
God be in my mouth,
And in my speaking;
God be in my heart,
And in my thynking;
God be at my end.
And at my departing.   *Sarum Missal*

PASS IT ON   May 1

So open your hearts to one another as Christ has opened his
heart to you, and God will be glorified.   *Romans 15:7*

On the liner from Bombay to London in the summer of 1934 he
(the Most Reverend Dr Foss Westcott, Metropolitan of India,
Burma and Ceylon) was a dignified but solitary figure and during the voyage he failed to achieve a single talk with anyone
which vitally affected that person's life. On the voyage back to
India a few months later, having faced fresh truth about himself, he had deep personal talks with 18 people who committed
their lives to God as a result. To the end of his life he never
stopped winning people.   *K D Belden*

If Christ lives in us, controlling our personalities, we will leave
glorious marks on the lives we touch. Not because of our lovely
characters, but because of his.   *Eugenia Price*

I want to see opening up all over Britain, groups of men and
women of all denominations who will sit down and face these
two questions: 'What sort of society do we want?' and 'What
sort of people do we need to be in order to achieve it?'... Perhaps this is England's greatest need today – a band of men and
women whose patriotism goes so deep that it leads them to
pray, to criticise, to agonise; and out of that prayer, that criticism and that agony, to bear their witness to the truth of God as
it has been revealed to them in Christ.

Archbishop Donald Coggan

COURTESY   May 2

If anybody forces you to go a mile with him, do more – go two
miles with him. Give to the man who asks anything from you,
and don't turn away from the man who wants to borrow.
Matthew 5:41–42 GNB

Let us flee to our Lord, and we shall be comforted. Let us touch
him, and we shall be made clean. Let us cleave to him, and we
shall be sure and safe from every kind of peril. For our courteous Lord wants us to be as familiar with him as heart may
think or soul desire; but let us beware that we do not accept this

familiarity so carelessly as to forsake courtesy. For our Lord himself is supreme familiarity, and he is as courteous as he is familiar, for he is true courtesy. *Mother Julian of Norwich*

We never find a case where Jesus gave ungraciously and unwillingly. There are many people in this world to whom we hesitate to go if we need anything... But we have only to read the gospel story to see how easy it was to approach Jesus, how no-one was ever afraid to ask him for help, how none was met with ungraciousness and how all went happier away.

Dr William Barclay

There is a grace of kind listening as well as a grace of kind speaking. *F W Faber*

> That best portion of a good man's life!
> His little, nameless, unremembered acts
> Of kindness and of love. *William Wordsworth*

If a man be gracious and courteous to strangers, it shows that he is a citizen of the world and that his heart is no island cut off from other lands, but a continent that joins to them.

Francis Bacon

INTERCESSION   May 3

In all your petitions pray at all times with every kind of spiritual prayer, keeping alert and persistent as you pray for all Christ's men and women. *Ephesians 6:18*

If any of you lacks wisdom, you should pray to God who will give it to you; because God gives generously and graciously to all. *James 1:5 RSV*

When I pray coincidences happen; when I don't, they don't.
Archbishop William Temple

I can take my telescope and look millions of miles into space; but I can go to my room and in prayer get nearer to God and heaven than I can when assisted by all the telescopes on earth.

Sir Isaac Newton

I have decided that I am meant not to go rushing about, but to spend many hours in prayer for others.   *H W 'Bunny' Austin*

God says 'Open your mouth and I will fill it.' ...We have not to fill our mouths after we have opened them wide; that is, we have not by our own power and ability and skilfulness to bring about the fulfilment of the promise. We have to leave this to God. He will do it.   *George Müller*

CRITICISM OR APPRECIATION   May 4

You fraud, take the plank out of your own eye first and then you can see clearly how to remove the speck out of your brother's eye.   *Luke 6:42*

There is nothing that makes us love someone so much as praying for them.   *William Law*

We are made in the image of God who has a bias to those on the margins of life. So it is holy to leave part of the harvest for those he favours. Sin alienates, splits, divides. Love includes and embraces.   *Archbishop Desmond Tutu*

Let gratitude for the past inspire us with trust for the future.
    Archbishop François Fénelon

If I long to improve my brother, the first step toward doing so is to improve myself.   *Christina Rossetti*

WORKING FOR PEOPLE   May 5

It is to freedom you have been called... You should be free to serve each other in love. For after all, the whole law towards others is summed up by this one command, 'Thou shalt love thy neighbour as thyself.'   *Galatians 5:13-14*

The fact that the Infinite God focused himself in a man is the best proof that God cares about people. In the teachings of that man, Jesus Christ, we find repeated again and again, an insistence on love to God and love to men being inseparably linked. He violently denounced those who divorced religion from life. He had no use at all for those who put up a screen of elaborate ceremonial and long prayers, and exploited their fellows behind it. *Canon J B Phillips*

Ready service, according to our ability, even in very small things... is acceptable to God. *St Basil*

You have not done enough, you have never done enough so long as it is possible that you have something to contribute. *Dag Hammarskjöld*

THE SACRAMENT OF WORK   May 6

You shall gain your bread by the sweat of your brow until you return to the ground; for from it you were taken. *Genesis 3:19 NEB*

Whatsoever thy hand findeth to do, do it with all thy might. *Ecclesiastes 9:10*

John Wesley travelled 250,000 miles on horseback, averaging 20 miles a day for 40 years; preached 40,000 sermons; produced 400 books; knew ten languages. At 83, he was annoyed that he could not write more than 15 hours a day without hurting his eyes; and at 86, he was ashamed he could not preach more than twice a day. He complained in his diary that there was an increasing tendency to lie in bed until 5.30 in the morning. *The Arkansas Baptist*

God never imposes a duty without giving time to do it. *John Ruskin*

O God, who hast ordained that whatever is to be desired, should be sought by labour, and who, by thy blessing, bringest honest labour to good effect; look with mercy upon my studies and my endeavours. *Samuel Johnson*

TO THE GLORY OF GOD   May 7

You fool! Do you want to be shown that faith without actions is useless?... You see, then, that it is by people's actions that they are put right with God and not by their faith alone.

James 2:20 and 24 GNB

Ask the Lord to make your life a glory to him, a menace to the devil, a strength to your church and a witness to the world.

Frederick P Wood

Perfect work expresses our total commitment to God's will. If we are not giving perfect work in everything we do, we are not living up to our calling.   *Rev Roland Hill*

In 1910, 260 English Trades Union leaders representing 500,000 workmen carried processional banners which read: 'We proclaim the Fatherhood of God and the brotherhood of man'; 'Jesus Christ Leads and Inspires'.   *Anon*

O Lord God, when thou givest to thy servants to endeavour any great matter, grant us to know that it is not the beginning but the continuing of the same until it be thoroughly finished, which yieldeth the true glory.   *Sir Francis Drake*

THREE WAYS OF WORKING   May 8

I do not live to please myself but to do the will of the Father who sent me.   *John 5:30*

We may make the best plans we can, and then carry them out to the best of our ability. Or, having laid our plans, we may ask God to help us. There is yet another mode of working: to begin with God, to ask his plans, and to offer ourselves to carry out his purposes.   *Dr Hudson Taylor*

I like work, it fascinates me; I can sit and look at it for hours.

Jerome K Jerome

'My doctrine,' Christ said, 'is not mine but his that sent me. If any man will do his will, he shall know of the doctrine whether it be of God.' The abandonment of our own interests and our surrender to his guidance must be the first step. After that our trust will grow. Evelyn Underhill has a good illustration of the situation. She supposes someone looking at a great cathedral, a mass of grey stone with the windows showing a dark, dusty colour. It does not look very cheerful. But if we push open the doors and go in, we suddenly see that all the windows are really brightly coloured glass... You cannot see the glory if you stand outside, asking sneeringly what proof there is that the inside is beautiful. You have to go in yourself.   *John Bagot Glubb*

Sometimes I think the church would be better off if we would call a moratorium on activity and just waited on God to see what he is waiting to do for us.   *A W Tozer*

THE DAY'S WORK   May 9

Those who listen to me (wisdom) will be happy – those who stay at my door every day, waiting at the entrance to my house.
Proverbs 8:34 GNB

Encourage each other every day, while it is still called 'today', and beware that none of you becomes deaf and blind to God through the delusive glamour of sin.   *Hebrews 3:13*

If a man cannot be a Christian where he is, he cannot be a Christian anywhere.   *Henry Ward Beecher*

Vocation is not the exceptional prerogative of a few especially good or gifted people... All are called to serve God.
Bishop F R Barry

Relying on God has to begin again every day as if nothing had yet been done.   *C S Lewis*

You always knew when he came into the office that he would bring good cheer. Hard work, yes – but with a sense of fun, fellowship and bold aims.
Alan Thornhill on a friend he worked with

If you want to be fully effective, you must give God that first hour of the day.   *Rev F B Meyer*

RIGHT AND WRONG WAYS OF WORKING   May 10

Commit your work to the Lord and your plans will be established.   *Proverbs 16:3 RSV*

In the same way, your light should shine before people so that they will see the good things you do and praise your Father in heaven.   *Matthew 5:16 GNB*

We must begin in the beginning with the Holy Spirit. This means humbly watching in any situation in which we find ourselves in order to learn what God is trying to do, and then doing it with him.   *Bishop John Taylor*

The only basis for real fellowship with God and man is to live out in the open with both.   *Roy Hessian*

Grant that this day we fall into no sin, neither run into any kind of danger; but that all our doings may be ordered by thy governance, to do always that which is righteous in thy sight.

Book of Common Prayer

DRUDGERY IS GRUDGERY   May 11

Love one another warmly as Christian brothers and sisters and be eager to show respect for one another.   *Romans 12:10 GNB*

If any of you has a servant looking after the sheep, are you likely to say to him when he comes in from the fields, 'Come straight in and sit down to your meal'? Aren't you more likely to say to him, 'Get my supper ready'?... It is the same with yourselves – when you have done everything that you are told to do, you can say, 'We are not much good as servants; we have only done what we ought to do.'   *Luke 17:7-10*

The race of mankind would perish from the earth did they cease to aid each other.   *Sir Walter Scott*

As a boy, my worst drudgery was to be told to help my aunt to weed the flower beds. I resented it. Years later it helped me to hear a woman guest, staying with my wife and me, say, 'I love weeding! It is so satisfying!'   *H P E*

O Jesus I have promised
To serve thee to the end;
Be thou for ever near me,
My master and my friend;
I shall not fear the battle,
If thou art by my side,
Nor wander from the pathway,
If thou wilt be my guide.   *John Ernest Bode*

TWO SIDES OF LIFE   May 12

Martha asked Jesus: 'Lord, don't you mind that my sister
(Mary) has left me to do everything by myself?...' But the Lord
answered her, 'Martha, my dear, you are worried and bothered
about providing so many things. Only one thing is really
needed. Mary has chosen the best part!'   *Luke 10:40-42*

I am called to live in perfect relation to God so that my life produces a longing after God in other lives, not admiration for myself. Thoughts about myself hinder my usefulness to God. God
is not after perfecting me to be a specimen in his show-room; he
is getting me to the place where he can use me. Let him do
what he likes.   *Professor Henry Drummond*

Christ be with me, Christ within me,
Christ behind me, Christ before me,
Christ beside me, Christ to win me,
Christ to comfort and restore me,
Christ beneath me, Christ above me,
Christ in quiet, Christ in danger,
Christ in hearts of all that love me,
Christ in mouth of friend and stranger.   *St Patrick*

THE GLOW WITHIN   May 13

God is light and no shadow of darkness can exist in him.
Consequently if we were to say that we enjoyed fellowship with
him and still went on living in darkness, we should be both telling and living a lie. But if we are living in the same light in

which he eternally exists, then we have true fellowship with each other, and the blood which his son Jesus shed for us keeps us clean from all sin.   *1 John 1:5-7*

You know how things look when the sun's beams are on them, the very air then appears full of impurities which, before it came out, were not seen. So it is with our souls. We are full of stains and corruptions, we see them not; but though we see them not, God sees them. He pervades us as the sunbeam.
Cardinal J H Newman

'Normal living' as *Frank Buchman* used to put it, 'is to be in touch with God day and night.' That gives the 'glow within'.

Make every effort to walk in the presence of God, to see God in everyone you meet, and to live your morning meditation throughout the day. In the streets in particular, radiate the joy of belonging to God, of living with him and being his.
Mother Teresa

WHOSE GLORY   May 14

For the earth shall be filled with the knowledge of the glory of the Lord, as the waters cover the sea.   *Habakkuk 2:14*

All of us, then, reflect the glory of the Lord with uncovered faces; and that same glory, coming from the Lord, who is the Spirit, transforms us into his likeness in an ever greater degree of glory.   *2 Corinthians 3:18 GNB*

We can no more diminish God's glory by refusing to worship him than a lunatic can put out the sun by scribbling the word 'darkness' on the walls of his cell.   *C S Lewis*

Praise I call the product of a singing heart. It is the inner being responding – the moment you begin to delight in beauty, your heart and mind are raised.   *Cardinal Basil Hume*

> Direct, control, suggest this day,
> All I design, or do, or say,
> That all my powers, with all their might,
> In thy sole glory may unite.   *Bishop Thomas Ken*

FRIENDSHIP   May 15

Those who fear God will come by true friendship.

Ecclesiasticus 6:17

There must be a care which expresses itself, not in seeking to please, but in so living that others want to be their best. It is a care which... always puts the needs of the other fellow first... It is the art of expert friendship.

Paul Campbell and Peter Howard

We take care of our health, we lay up our money, we make our roof tight and our clothing sufficient, but who provides wisely that he shall not be wanting in the best property of all – friends?

R W Emerson

Nothing is more stimulating than friends who speak the truth in love.   *Os Guiness*

St Francis heard the Lord speaking with him by night, as with a friend.   *St Bonaventura*

The friends I find most 'difficult' are the friendships I most need to cultivate and treasure.   *H P E*

FREE FROM DESIRE TO PLEASE   May 16

They loved human approval rather than the approval of God.

John 12:43 GNB

Never act from motives of rivalry or personal vanity, but in humility think more of each other than you do of yourselves. None of you should think only of his own affairs, but consider other people's interests also.   *Philippians 2:3-4*

All my activities and energies were directed by the prospects of more fame, of pleasing my employers, of increasing my own comforts or of getting a rise in pay. I was governed by prejudice and temper or by predilection and desire. I was swayed by the swirl of a skirt or the softness of a lip – even by a mere appetite for food or flagon. Make no mistake. I enjoyed that sort of life. But in my secret heart I knew, without putting it into words or fully thinking it through, that a man ruled by desires for tobacco or money or fame or drink or a woman to that extent is a prisoner. He is not a free man... I speak of what I know. I have lived both ways, in darkness and in light... God has a plan for the re-thinking of men and nations. Be still and know that I am God. In a quiet time of listening he makes clear to you your part in that plan.   *Peter Howard*

A TEACHABLE SPIRIT   May 17

Jesus said: Remember this! Whoever does not receive the kingdom of God like a child will never enter it.   *Luke 18:17 GNB*

Do you hear the voice of the Lord which calls, inspires, counsels, directs and consoles – the true promise and hope of the destiny that awaits us?... How can we distinguish the voice of the Lord?... He speaks to those who want to listen.
Pope Paul VI

My life has turned out to be totally different from the one I had planned for myself... It has been beyond anything I deserved or anticipated. To me the most satisfying thing in life is to see the Spirit of God at work in the life of another person and to see that person develop into a potential leader for his or her nation.
Dr Paul Campbell

I have found that there are two great stages in learning to live by the guidance of God. The first is when we say, 'I will do anything that God tells me.' The second, much more searching, comes when we say: 'I will do only what God tells me.'
K D Belden

LIKE A MIGHTY ARMY   May 18

Fight the worthwhile battle of the faith, keep your grip on that life eternal to which you have been called, and to which you boldly professed your loyalty before many witnesses. I charge you in the sight of God... to keep your commission clean and above reproach until the final coming of Christ.

1 Timothy 6:12–14

The battle line runs not between certain nations nor between certain classes but it runs through every nation and class, through every organisation or community, through every home and every heart. It is the battle against I WANT, whether limited to my purely personal matters or projected out through the channels of power of an organisation, an industry or a nation to create a tyranny to others. This battle will be won in my heart first of all and then in others.

Edward T Perry

You are but a poor soldier of Christ if you think you can overcome without fighting and suppose you can have the crown without the conflict.

St John Chrysostom

A noble army, men and boys,
The matron and the maid...
They climbed the steep ascent of heaven,
Through peril, toil and pain.
O God to us may grace be given
To follow in their train.

Bishop Reginald Heber

The battle is fought on that one word of the 'will'. Will you obey the voice of God and do as he commands you? No one else can obey for you any more than he can eat and drink for you. You must obey God for yourself.

Dwight L Moody

THE NEW SOCIETY   May 19

Neither by force of arms nor by brute strength, but by my Spirit! says the Lord of Hosts.

Zechariah 4:6 NEB

These men and women had a quality of life which we were lacking; they had succeeded in forgetting their own egos, they were always eager to help and to serve, they could talk quite openly and naturally about things which we had stored away in the secret places of the heart until we could not find them. They could openly make restitution if they had wronged anybody. They were liberated and no longer besieged by the forces of selfishness; people who were living in a new spirit of fellowship and in complete freedom from fear because they had nothing to hide.

The Hon C J Hambro, President of the Norwegian Parliament, after the visit of the Oxford Group to Norway in 1934

Our task together is to liquidate hunger and hate, want and waste, poverty and pride, bitterness and bloodshed, from the face of the earth and to revolutionise the whole world. In this large task the races of Britain will learn to heal every division in our land – in our home, heart, industry, education – and by our exertions and by our example kindle others to do the same in nation after nation.

Conrad Hunte, formerly Vice-Captain of the West Indies Cricket team

ALL THINGS COMMON   May 20

All the believers joined together and shared everything in common; they sold their possessions and divided the proceeds among the fellowship according to their needs.   *Acts 2:44-45*

These men (ie the believers in Acts 2:44–46) who joined together and shared everything in common, did not make acts of faith, they believed. They did not say their prayers, they really prayed. They did not hold conferences on psychosomatic medicine, they simply healed the sick... The Spirit of God found what he must always be seeking – a fellowship of men and women so united in love and faith that he can work in and through them with the minimum of hindrance.

Canon J B Phillips

When a high official from an East European country came to an evening gathering that had been arranged in Geneva, she asked one of those present who was the 'chief ideologist'. Upon receiving the answer that (in this Christian group) such a position did not exist, she said in amazement: 'Do you mean to say you have real collective leadership – all races, men and women, young and old?' The possibility of such teamwork opened up prospects she had never thought possible until then.

Pierre Spoerri

RELATIONSHIPS   May 21

Let us love not merely in theory or words – let us love in sincerity and in practice! This is how we shall know we are children of the truth.   *1 John 3:18–19*

An African cabinet minister asked me if I was aware that a fellow countryman of mine, sent out to negotiate his nation's independence, was temporarily living with his secretary. He went on: 'If this man's wife can't trust him,' said the minister, 'why should I? And if my cabinet colleagues consider him untrustworthy, why should they trust the government that chose him as negotiator?' This made sense.   *A Cultural Attaché*

Consider the mistresses and adulteries which are accepted as normal in the ranks of political and industrial and labour leadership. People who cannot say 'no' to themselves in this selfishness can hardly expect the rank and file to say 'yes' to their pious call for production, unity and sacrifice. An individual's selfishness has everything to do with his public relationship.
                                                        Dr Paul Campbell

It is a wonderful experience to let the hand of God transform all one's personal life. Some leave it there. But the crucial next step is to let him transform all one's personal relationships.
                                                        P M and H P E

IDOLS OR STEPPING STONES   May 22

And there they will set up 'the abominable thing that causes desolation'.   *Daniel 11:31*

Be on your guard, my dear children, against every false god!
                                                        1 John 5:21

Idolatry is anything which cooleth thy desires after Christ.
                                                        Oliver Cromwell

I worship a Rolls Royce sports model, brother. All my days, I give it offerings of oil and polish... I worship my house beautiful, sister. Long and long meditation have I spent on it. I worship my comfort; after all, isn't enjoyment the goal of life?.. I worship myself... What shape is your idol?... If we are to be saved, it must be by the one power that is built into a man at his beginning and that he does not have to make with his hands – the power of the Holy Spirit, which is God.   *Joy Davidman*

> The dearest idol I have known,
> Whate'er that idol be,
> Help me to tear it from thy throne,
> And worship only thee.   *William Cowper*

Whatever someone seeks, honours or exalts more than God, this is the god of idolatry.   *Bishop William Ullathorne*

'SALTY'   May 23

Be wise in the way you act towards outsiders; make the most of every opportunity. Let your conversation be always full of grace, seasoned with salt, so that you may know how to answer everyone.   *Colossians 4:5–6 NIV*

After a meeting, Peter Howard was approached by a woman who said: 'I am all for what you are doing, but I do not feel able to bring people to an experience of change. How can I?' Howard replied: 'If you have a cold codfish and pour tepid water over it, you won't have a very good cooked meal.'
        Dr Paul Campbell

A lady who got to know my mother at the conference, came up to me and said, 'Have you ever been really honest with your mother?' 'Certainly,' I replied. 'Well then,' she persisted, 'if you have, why does she still think you are such a wonderful fellow?' I got the point. I took mother for a walk and told her.
        H P E

A man entered a barber shop and sat in the chair next to me. Every word that he uttered... showed a personal and vital interest in the man who was serving him... The barbers did not know his name but they knew that something had elevated their thought. The man was Dwight L Moody who, early in life, had decided never to let a day go by without speaking to someone about eternal values.
        Woodrow Wilson, 28th President of the United States

PATIENCE   May 24

The seeds that fell in good soil stand for those who hear the message and retain it in a good and obedient heart, and they persist until they bear fruit.   *Luke 8:15 GNB*

When trials come endure them patiently; steadfastly maintain the habit of prayer.   *Romans 12:12*

Take pains to be patient in bearing all the faults and weaknesses of others, for you too have many flaws that others must put up with.   *Thomas à Kempis*

Patience is the companion of wisdom.   *St Augustine*

Patient waiting is often the highest way of doing God's will.
Jeremy Collier

Patience with ourselves is a duty for Christians and the only humility. For it means patience with a growing creature whom God has taken in hand and whose completion he will effect in his own time and way.   *Evelyn Underhill*

Patience and endurance, like faith, remove mountains.
William Penn

APOLOGY   May 25

For if you forgive other people their failures, your heavenly Father will also forgive you. But if you will not forgive other people, neither will your Father forgive you your failures.
Matthew 6:14–15

You should get into the habit of admitting your sins to each other and praying for each other, so that you may be healed.
James 5:16

A pastor was led by the spirit of God to make public confession of his failure as a minister of the gospel. There and then he walked across the meeting hall toward one of the elders of his church, with whom he had not been on good terms for a long period of seven years, and asked him for forgiveness. He declared that while there was wrong on both sides, his was the greater.   *H A Walter*

The old Puritans used to pray for 'the gift of tears'. If ever you cease to know the virtue of repentance, you are in darkness. Examine yourself and see if you have forgotten how to be sorry.

Oswald Chambers

An apology so often can start surprising adventures in life with God.

P M and H P E

CAUGHT NOT TAUGHT   May 26

They were fishermen, so Jesus said to them: 'Follow me and I will teach you to catch men!'

Matthew 4:19

If we really are living in the same light in which he eternally exists, then we have true fellowship with each other.

1 John 1:7

Religion is imparted by contagion, not taught by words.

Henry B Wright

When I have learned to do the Father's will I shall have fully realised my vocation on earth.

Carlo Carretto

To change people is an art as different from preaching and moralising as an operation to save a person's life differs from a classroom lecture on anatomy.

Dr Paul Campbell

What's important is that God is so much part and parcel of life that spontaneous chat becomes second nature.

Cliff Richard

If it is possible for your closest contacts to be neutral about Christ, then there is something wrong with your Christianity.

Alan Redpath

LIVING WITH SINNERS   May 27

The truth is that we neither live nor die as self-contained units.

Romans 14:7

The greatest saint in the world... is he who is always thankful to God; who receives everything as an instance of God's goodness and has a heart always ready to praise God for it. If anyone would tell you the shortest, surest way to all happiness and perfection, he must tell you to make a rule to thank and praise God for everything that happens to you   *William Law*

The New Testament... gives us a pretty clear idea of what a fully Christian society would be like... We have all departed from that total plan in different ways, and each of us wants to make out that his own modification of the original plan is the plan itself. You will find this again and again about anything that is really Christian; everyone is attracted to bits of it and wants to pick out those bits and leave the rest.   *C S Lewis*

A fellow who has the guts to come and share his weaknesses – it shows that somehow or other he trusts you enough to tell you all the things in his life he does not like. It's a tremendous thing. I would do anything for a fellow like that. He can have my shirt or anything I have any day.   *Dr Frank N D Buchman*

LEADERSHIP   May 28

'If I, your teacher and Lord, have washed your feet, you must be ready to wash one another's feet. I have given you this as an example so that you may do as I have done.'   *John 13:13–15*

It is quite true to say that a man who sets his heart on leadership has laudable ambition.   *1 Timothy 3:1*

Civilisation, says Arnold Toynbee, moves forward on the basis of challenge and leadership... My own concept of leadership was turned round, reading about Jesus washing the feet of the disciples after the Last Supper. It was a story I had read often but that winter morning it suddenly became alive. 'Is this my order of leadership?' I asked myself.   *R M Lala*

We all at different times want the limelight or recognition of leadership or the appreciation of other people, even for our work for God and we can have hard feelings towards anyone who belittles it or, worse, takes it from us. God's work can become my work and if someone else tries to move in on it, there is trouble. Each humbly considering each other the better person, to use St Paul's words, is a text I have often found hard to live up to. But 'living to make the other fellow great' as someone put it, is so much more rewarding than trying to make sure my own spiritual qualities and selfless work are fully recognised.   *K D Belden*

ON THE GET OR ON THE GIVE   May 29

For everything comes from thee, and it is only of thy gifts that we give to thee.   *1 Chronicles 29:14 NEB*

You should each give, then, as you have decided, not with regret or out of a sense of duty; for God loves the one who gives gladly.   *2 Corinthians 9:7 GNB*

The fellowship of the Holy Spirit... is a revolutionary purpose that takes the whole of God's creation into its concern. Its purpose is to be an instrument in the hand of God to bring each person to full stature as a child of God, to put right what is wrong in the world, to point people and nations to their God-given destiny.   *J M Morrison*

Ultimate responsibility means that in any situation no one is more responsible than I am. And responsibility is not given – it has to be taken.   *Dorothy M Prescott*

Man must cease attributing his problems to his environment and learn again to exercise his will – his personal responsibility in the realm of faith and morals.   *Dr Albert Schweitzer*

SERVICE   May 30

Whoever preaches must preach God's messages; whoever serves must serve with the strength that God gives so that in all things praise may be given to God through Jesus Christ.
                                                      1 Peter 4:11 GNB

Olwen Davies, a middle-aged district nurse served the people of Tregenny for more than 20 years, with fortitude and patience, calmness and cheerfulness. This unconscious selflessness, which above all seemed the keynote of her character, was so poorly rewarded, it worried me. Although she was much beloved by the people, her salary was most inadequate. And late one night, after a particularly strenuous case, I ventured to protest to her as we drank a cup of tea together.

'Nurse,' I said, 'why don't you make them pay you more? It's ridiculous that you should work for so little.'

She raised her eyebrows slightly. But she smiled. 'I have enough to get along.'

'No, really,' I persisted, 'you ought to have an extra pound a week at least. God knows you're worth it.'

There was a pause. Her smile remained, but her gaze held a gravity, an intensity which startled me. 'Doctor,' she said, 'if God knows I'm worth it, that's all that matters to me.'

A J Cronin, when medical officer with a mining community

Teach us, good Lord, to serve thee as thou deservest;
To give and not to count the cost.   *St Ignatius Loyola*

LET GOD TRANSFORM YOU   May 31

Jesus came and spoke these words to them: 'All power in heaven and on earth has been given to me. You, then, are to go and make disciples of all nations and baptise them in the name of the Father and of the Son and of the Holy Spirit. Teach them to observe all that I have commanded you and, remember, I am with you always, even to the end of the world.'

Matthew 28:18–19

In the Holy Land there are two great bodies of water. The Sea of Galilee is full of fish and its shores are fertile; the Dead Sea has no life in it and it is surrounded with barren desert and rocks. Yet both are fed by the same River Jordan. But the Dead Sea has no outlet. Have you?   *Edward T Perry*

The salvation of a single soul is more important than the production or preservation of all the epics and tragedies in the world.   *C S Lewis*

Some like to live within the sound of church or chapel bell; I'd rather run a rescue shop within the sound of hell.
William Booth, Salvation Army

TEAMWORK   June 1

Jesus prayed: I am no longer in the world, but they are in the world. Holy Father! Keep them safe by the power of your name (the name you gave me) that they may be one just as you and I are one.   *John 17:11 GNB*

The way to the union of Christendom does not lie through committee rooms... It lies through personal union with the Lord, so deep and real as to be comparable with his union with the Father.   *Archbishop William Temple*

Teamwork and the life of a community are impossible without absolute moral standards which keep every relationship redemptive. Honesty is one great key – about my own sins, not the other person's. This often calls for honest apology as well, the golden key to teamwork. It also means never harbouring attitudes we know to be less than Christlike... In the same way teamwork and community need purity, so that all relationships are Christ-centred and all motives clear; unselfishness so that we are keener on what others can achieve than on what we can do ourselves... and love, which embraces even the sharpest corners on our friends, and moves closer to our heavenly Father with them.   *K D Belden*

NATIONAL DESTINY   June 2

Happy is the nation whose God is the Lord.   *Psalms 33:12*

And the hope is that in the end, the whole of created life will be rescued from the tyranny of change and decay, and have its share in that magnificent liberty which can only belong to the children of God.   *Romans 8:21*

Whatever bitterness there is in them (the Irish people) we are the cause of it, and whether we can ever undo what we have done, is more that statesmen can say.   *John Henry Newman*

Looking around the world today, how foolish it is to think we can build a peaceful future without healing the wounds of history.   *James Hore-Ruthven*

I confess that I dream of the day when a statesman shall arise with a heart too large for his own country, having courage in the face of his countrymen to assert of some suggested policy: 'This is good for your trade: this is necessary for your domination; but it will vex a people near by, it will hurt a people further off; it will profit nothing to the general humanity; therefore, away with it! – it is not for you or me.'

Elizabeth Barrett Browning

OUR COUNTRY AT ITS BEST June 3

And thou shalt swear 'The Lord liveth' in truth, in judgment and in righteousness; and the nations shall bless themselves in him. *Jeremiah 4:2*

People will never take evil seriously nor even see much need to tap the resources of God until they join in with the costly redemptive purposes of love. *Canon J B Phillips*

Though good laws do well, good men do better. Governments, like clocks, go from the motion that men give them... Let men be good, and the government cannot be bad; if it be ill they will cure it. But if man be bad, let the government be ever so good, they will endeavour to warp and spoil it to their turn... Men must choose to be governed by God, or they condemn themselves to be ruled by tyrants. *William Penn*

MORAL STANDARDS AND NATIONAL LIFE June 4

God's plan is to make you holy, and that means a clean cut with immorality. Every one of you should learn to control his body, keeping it pure and treating it with respect, and never allowing it to fall victim to lust. *1 Thessalonians 4:3–4*

We have a power capable of radically altering our motives; of giving freedom and direction to people once blinded and enslaved by selfishness. Anyone equipped with absolute moral

standards and a source of superior wisdom through guidance
will be a force for transforming the will of men and nations.

Paul Campbell and Peter Howard

No process has been invented which can permanently separate
men from their own hearts and consciences or prevent them
from seeing the results of their own false ideas. You cannot
make men believe that a way of life is good when it spreads
poverty, misery, disease and death. Men cannot be everlast-
ingly loyal unless they are free. *Franklin D Roosevelt*

I have discovered that a life given to God and lived under his
guidance is an adventure – always unexpected, especially if I
steer my ship by the polestar of absolute moral standards. That
attracts others and is what my nation needs. *H P E*

NATIONAL SIN   June 5

You steal, you murder, you commit adultery and perjury, you
burn sacrifices to Baal, you run after other gods whom you
have not known; then you come and stand before me in this
house, which bears my name, and say, 'We are safe'; safe, you
think, to indulge in all these abominations?

Jeremiah 7:9–10 NEB

The strength of a nation is shown in the courage to admit her
own faults. The glory of a nation is to have a creative message
for the world. For this we need not only inspired statesmanship
but daily inspiration in every business, every workshop, every
home. We must teach ourselves to apply practically to conduct
the Christian standards of honesty, purity and love, and to
make fulfilment of the will of God the touchstone of public and
private life. *The Earl of Athlone and others in a letter to*
The Times, 11 November 1938

> God the all-wise! by the fire of thy chastening,
> Earth shall be freedom and truth be restored;
> Through the thick darkness thy kingdom is hastening,
> Thou wilt give peace in thy time, O Lord.
> *Henry Fothergill Chorley*

CHRIST LOOKED AT THE PEOPLE June 6

I am the real vine, my Father is the vine-dresser. He removes any of my branches which is not bearing fruit and he prunes every branch that does bear fruit to increase its yield. Now, you have already been pruned by my words. You must go on growing in me and I will in you. For just as the vine cannot bear any fruit unless it shares the life of the vine, so you can produce nothing unless you go on growing in me. *John 15:1–4*

I am pretty sure that we err in treating these sayings as paradoxes. It would be nearer the truth to say that it is life itself which is paradoxical and that the sayings of Jesus are simply a recognition of the fact. *Sir Thomas Taylor*

The entire New Testament is witness that the real presence of Christ was not withdrawn when the resurrection 'appearances' ceased. The unique and evanescent meetings with the risen Lord triggered off a new kind of relation which proved permanent. *C H Dodd*

Even with the most ordinary decisions and activities, our lives should be so centred on Christ and his glory that our choices and actions contribute to his kingdom. *Canon David Watson*

A NATION'S SECURITY June 7

If only you will now listen to me and keep my covenant, then out of all peoples you shall become my special possession; for the whole earth is mine. *Exodus 19:5–6 NEB*

Nations cannot enjoy stable relationships until they have been inwardly prepared for them. *Chancellor K Adenauer*

Some people regard their country as a place which owes them a living and a luxurious one if possible. They look on it as a great joint of roast beef on which they can gorge if they fight their way to the table... Other people regard their country as a beloved wife or son or mother for whose strength and welfare they would gladly work and save and sacrifice. There is no neutrality in the matter. *Peter Howard*

It is by our own decisions for personal action and also practical action in teamwork with others that our nation can be affected. The security of a nation is grounded in the strength of her people who listen to God.   *Dr Frank N D Buchman*

'PATRIOTISM' IS NOT ENOUGH   June 8

The fruit of the Spirit is an affectionate, loveable disposition, a radiant spirit, a cheerful temper, a tranquil mind, a quiet manner, a forbearing patience in provoking circumstances with trying people, a sympathetic insight and tactful helpfulness, a generous judgment, a big-souled charity, loyalty and reliability under all circumstances, humility that forgets self in the joy of others, in all things self-controlled, which is the final mark of perfection.   *Gilbert Kirby's paraphrase of Galatians 5:22–23*

When my grandfather, the Mahatma, came back to this country from South Africa as a lawyer, his family urged him to continue with his legal practice. Instead, he put aside his private plans in order to free our country. Now there is a bigger job... to save the whole world from dictatorship, corruption and war.

Rajmohan Gandhi

Cursed be that loyalty which reaches so far as to go against the law of God.   *St Teresa of Avila*

He who reforms himself has done more towards reforming the public than a crowd of noisy impotent patriots.   *J C Lavater*

The true patriot gives his life to bring his country under God's control.   *Dr Frank N D Buchman*

THE TRUE PATRIOT   June 9

The whole law towards others is summed up by this one command, 'thou shalt love thy neighbour as thyself.' *Galatians 5:14*

This love... is slow to lose patience, it looks for a way of being constructive. It is not possessive; it is neither anxious to impress... nor does it pursue selfish advantage.

1 Corinthians 13:4

116

During a battle between Muslims and Sikhs, a Sikh water carrier called Ghanaya was seen giving water to wounded Muslim soldiers as they lay suffering from thirst under the hot sun. He was brought to Guru Gobind Singh and accused of being a traitor. The Guru heard the charges and asked Ghanaya to answer them. 'When I walked through the battlefields I saw no Muslims and no Sikhs, only your face in every man,' said Ghanaya. 'You are a true Sikh,' replied the Guru. 'Continue the work; and here is some ointment to put on the wounds.'   *W Owen Cole*

True patriotism does not exclude an understanding of the patriotism of others.   *Queen Elizabeth II*

Love for one's country which is not part of one's love for humanity is not love but idolatrous worship.   *Erich Fromm*

FROM THE INDIVIDUAL TO THE NATION   June 10

The earth is the Lord's and all that is in it, the world and those who dwell therein.   *Psalms 24:1*

Then Jesus said to them, 'You must go out to the whole world and proclaim the gospel to every creature.'   *Mark 16:15*

Amid the failure of human wisdom, there is still one supreme source from whom all can draw new power, new hope, new illumination. God speaks directly to the heart of every man and woman who is prepared to listen and obey. We deeply need the leadership of God-led men and women who base their lives on the Christian principles of honesty, unselfishness and faith.
From the message of civic leaders of 550 cities and towns in the United Kingdom shortly after the outbreak of war in 1939

I needed a miracle to uproot hate from my heart. I hardly believed in God, but he performed that miracle... I went with my husband and son to Germany. There we spoke to ten out of the 11 West German parliaments – and on the radio and at hundreds of meetings and interviews... Can you think what it meant for me to go there? In my heart I had willed the ruins of World War II... I had to ask forgiveness for my hatred from those people who were living in the ruins. Today France and Germany have found each other.   *Irène Laure*

THE FAMILY OF NATIONS   June 11

At the same time, saith the Lord, will I be the God of all the
families of Israel, and they shall be my people.   *Jeremiah 31:1*

For this cause I bow my knees unto the Father of our Lord Jesus
Christ, of whom the whole family in heaven and earth is
named, that he would grant you... to be strengthened with
might by his Spirit.   *Ephesians 3:14–16 AV*

How to have peace of heart? The good way is to tame in yourself the hate and anger. But how to overcome them without a
struggle between anger on one side and love, compassion and
forgiveness on the other? Faith, forgiveness, tolerance require
you to change first before you try to change others.

These are virtues which you can learn only from your enemy.
Your best friend, your teacher, your guru cannot teach them to
you. But when you meet your enemy, you have your best
chance to learn how you practise them. So your enemy will become your teacher.   *Dalai Lama*

To make peace with an enemy one must work with him so that
he becomes your partner.   *Nelson Mandela*

O God, father of all mankind, teach us by thy mercy, how we
thy children can learn to live together in unity, according to thy
holy will. Amen.

THE STRENGTH OF A NATION   June 12

The Lord is their strength, and he is the saving strength of his
anointed. Save thy people and bless thine inheritance.
                                        Psalms 28:8–9

With the prayer out of a purified heart it is important that I
have confessed my sin and have not let any unforgiven sin stay
between God and myself or other people. It means to take the
next step and to cleanse myself wherever God puts his finger
on my life, to ask God and men for forgiveness, and to depart
from this or that – then the way to effective prayer is again free.
                                      Basilea Schlink

Today there is so much trouble in the world and I think that much of it begins at home. The world is suffering so much because there is no peace. There is no peace because there is no peace in the family and we have so many thousands and thousands of broken homes. We must make our homes centres of compassion and forgive endlessly and so bring peace.

Mother Teresa

Nothing is politically right which is morally wrong.

Daniel O'Connell

When you are our strength it is strength indeed; but when our strength is our own it is only weakness.   *St Augustine*

SECURITY IN GOD   June 13

Let us hold on to the hope that we profess without the slightest hesitation – for he is utterly dependable – and let us think of one another and how we can encourage each other to love and do good deeds.   *Hebrews 10:23–24*

Let us keep our eyes fixed on Jesus, on whom our faith depends from beginning to end.   *Hebrews 12:2 GNB*

Do not look at your faith or at your feelings; but look away to the word of promise and, above all, to the promiser. Study the punctuality of his orderings in the starry firmament. Are planets ever overdue? or do the seasons forget to revolve? Consider how he has kept his word with the nations of the past, whose ruined cities attest his judgments! Has he ever failed to keep his word?   *Rev F B Meyer*

The Christian faith has certainty built into it. It was certain of God, certain of man's new relationship with him through the gospel, certain of the living presence of Christ... No one can be certain of God through Christ unless he is willing to do the will of God. In other words, we never know the voice of certainty until we are honestly committed in heart and in mind to following Jesus Christ.   *Canon J B Phillips*

My support is from God alone; in him do I trust and unto him do I turn me.   *The Koran*

SECURITY IN GOD – CONDITIONS   June 14

Trust in the Lord with all thine heart; and lean not unto thine own understanding. In all thy ways acknowledge him, and he shall direct thy paths. Be not wise in thine own eyes; fear the Lord and depart from evil.   *Proverbs 3:5-7*

I had made a start with putting right certain obvious things which could be put right 'at a stroke' – a return of money, some apologies – but to turn away from deeply ingrained greed, pride or self-seeking was another matter. This is where I found the standards of absolute honesty, purity, unselfishness and love – a rough and challenging summary of the Sermon on the Mount – so helpful... I had given what little I knew of myself to the near nothing I knew of God. Knowledge in both spheres grew – and still grow – together... Christ becomes real when one admits one's need.   *Garth Lean*

The more we depend on God, the more dependable we find he is.   *Cliff Richard*

Our confidence in Christ does not make us lazy or negligent, but on the contrary it awakens us, urges us on and makes us active in living righteous lives and doing good.   *Ulrich Zwingli*

The condition for my finding my security in God is that I wait on him and delight in doing his will, whether easy or difficult.
          P M

STABLISHED IN QUIET   June 15

For thus saith the Lord God, the Holy One of Israel: In returning and rest shall ye be saved; in quietness and in confidence shall be your strength.   *Isaiah 30:15*

We beseech you brethren, that ye study to be quiet and to do your own business.   *1 Thessalonians 4:11*

God is a tranquil being and abides in a tranquil eternity. So must thy spirit become a tranquil and clear little pool wherein the serene light of God can be mirrored.   *Gerhard Tersteegen*

Lord, the scripture says: There is a time for silence and a time for speech. Saviour, teach me the silence of humility, the silence of wisdom, the silence of love, the silence of perfection, the silence that speaks without words, the silence of faith. Lord, teach me to silence my own heart that I may listen to the gentle movement of the Holy Spirit within me and sense the depths which are of God.   *Frankfurt Prayer*

If we really want to pray we must first learn to listen, for in the silence of the heart God speaks. And to be able to see that silence, to be able to hear God, we need a clean heart, for a clean heart can see God, can hear God, can listen to God.
                                                              Mother Teresa

AMEN   June 16

Now to him who is able to keep you from falling and to present you before his glory without fault and with unspeakable joy, to the only God, our Saviour, be glory and majesty, power and authority through Jesus Christ our Lord, before time was, now, and in all ages to come. Amen.   *Jude 24*

Materialistic philosophies seek to build the kingdom of heaven on earth. They seek to build a world of prosperity, for some at least. Christianity is simply not about that. It is concerned with creating the kingdom of heaven within the heart of an individual.   *Dr John Lester*

God has never promised to solve our problems. He has not promised to answer our questions... He has promised to go with us.   *Elisabeth Elliott*

We cannot rely on God's promises without obeying his commandments.   *John Calvin*

Really to pray is to stand to attention in the presence of the king and to be prepared to take orders from him.
                                              Archbishop Donald Coggan

THAT WHICH FILLS ALL June 17

It is, remember, the church of the living God, the pillar and the foundation of the truth. No one would deny that this religion of ours is a tremendous mystery, resting as it does on the one who appeared in human flesh, was vindicated in the spirit, seen by angels; proclaimed among the nations, believed in throughout the world, taken back to heaven in glory. *Timothy 3:15–16*

The Christian faith was a way of life long before it became a religion. It still is. You cannot take a certain proportion of life and call that 'religious' any more than you can give God an hour or two on Sunday and consider the rest of your life your own. The way you live, the way you treat others – these are the important things, whether you profess to be a believer or not. For the way in which we behave is an accurate indication of what we really think of God. *Canon J B Phillips*

I ought to spend the best hours of the day in communion with God. It is my noblest and most fruitful employment and is not to be thrust into any corner. *Robert M McCheyne*

Many Christians have enough religion to make them decent but not enough to make them dynamic. *Kenneth Grider*

I know that for the right practice of the presence of God, the heart must be empty of all else, because God wills to possess the heart alone: and as he cannot possess it alone unless it is empty of all else besides, so he cannot work in it what he would unless it be left vacant to him. *Brother Lawrence*

WITH YOU ALWAYS June 18

For God has said: I will never leave you; I will never abandon you. Let us be bold then and say: The Lord is my helper, I will not be afraid. What can anyone do to me? *Hebrews 13:5–6 GNB*

To want all that God wants, always to want it, for all occasions and without reservations; this is the kingdom of God which is all within. *Archbishop François Fénelon*

The kingdom is something within you which has the power of growth like a seed; something that you are searching for, and of whose values you become more confident and excited as the search proceeds and you discover truer, lovelier things which are constantly being surpassed; something for which you have to give everything you have, no less yet no more, including the earlier finds with which you were once so completely delighted. *Bishop George Appleton*

Offer to me all thy works and rest the mind on the supreme. Be free from vain hopes and selfish thoughts, and with inner peace fight thou thy fight. *The Bhagavad Gita c 500 BC*

Whatever you do, begin with God. *Matthew Henry*

Consider every day that you are then for the first time – as it were – beginning; and always act with the same fervour as on the first day you began. *St Anthony of Padua*

WHOSE SERVICE IS PERFECT FREEDOM   June 19

When he made man in the beginning, he left him free to take his own decisions; if you choose you can keep the commandments; whether or not you keep faith is yours to decide.
Ecclesiasticus 14:15 NEB

But those who look closely into the perfect law that sets people free, who keep on paying attention to it and do not simply listen and then forget it, but put it into practice – they will be blessed by God in what they do. *James 1:25 GNB*

True freedom is only to be found when one escapes from oneself and enters into the liberty of the children of God.
Archbishop François Fénelon

A Christian is the most free lord of all, and subject to none; a Christian is the most dutiful servant of all and subject to everyone. *Martin Luther*

True liberty is liberty to do what we ought to do; it is not liberty to do as we like. *Field Marshal Lord Montgomery*

    Lord of all being, I give you my all;
    If e'er I disown you, I stumble and fall;

But sworn in glad service your word to obey,
I walk in your freedom to the end of the way.

Jack C Winslow

JOY OF THE LORD June 20

Those who sow in tears shall reap with songs of joy.

Psalms 126:5

Be happy in your faith at all times. Never stop praying. Be thankful whatever the circumstances may be. For this is the will of God for you in Christ Jesus. *1 Thessalonians 5:16–18*

Joy is never in our power and pleasure is. I doubt whether anyone who has tasted joy would ever, if both were in his power, exchange it for all the pleasures in the world. *C S Lewis*

Those whose sins have perished, whose doubts are destroyed, who are self-restrained and are intent on the welfare of all other beings, these obtain God's everlasting joy.

The Bhagavad Gita

If you have no joy in your religion, there's a leak in your Christianity somewhere. *Bill Sunday*

Joy is for everyone. It does not depend on circumstance or condition; if it did, it could only be for the few. It is not the fruit of good luck, or of fortune, or even of outward success, which everyone cannot have. It is of the soul, or the soul's character; it is the wealth of the soul's whole being when it is filled with the spirit of Jesus, which is the spirit of eternal love.

Horace Bushnell

Joy is prayer – joy is strength – joy is love, joy is a net of love by which you can catch souls. *Mother Teresa*

GOD'S WILL WITH ZEST June 21

Teach me to do thy will; for thou art my God; thy spirit is good; lead me into the land of uprightness. *Psalms 143:10*

This is the secret of joy. We shall no longer strive for our own way; but commit ourselves, easily and simply, to God's way, acquiesce in his will and in so doing find our peace.

Evelyn Underhill

If we would avoid a senseless natural philosophy we must always start with this principle: that everything in nature depends upon the will of God, and that the whole course of nature is only the prompt carrying into effect of his orders.

John Calvin

Lord God Almighty, I charge thee of thy great mercy... that thou guide me to thy will and to my soul's need better than I can myself, that above all things I may inwardly love thee with a clear mind and clean body; for thou art my maker, my help and my hope.   *King Alfred the Great*

At Sunday School I was taught that JOY spells J(esus first), O(thers next), Y(ourself last).   *P M*

GOD IS REQUIRED FOR GAIETY   June 22

Then was our mouth filled with laughter, and our tongue with singing; then said they among the heathen, The Lord hath done great things for them.   *Psalms 126:2*

He will yet fill your mouth with laughter, and shouts of joy shall be on your lips.   *Job 8:21 NEB*

A joyless Christian is a libel on his master.   *Northcote Deck*

It is perfectly true that there is a sense in which preaching must entertain, for the attention of the congregation must be caught. It is quite true, as Jesus so well showed us, that a sunny shaft of humour is often very necessary and very effective. No one would hear Jesus talking about a man with a plank in his own eye trying to take a speck of dust out of another man's eye without a smile or even a roar of laughter... There is something wrong with a sermon of which the jokes are remembered when the message is forgotten. Preaching must leave a man facing his own sin and the holiness of God and the grace of the Lord Jesus Christ.   *Dr William Barclay*

125

I have never understood why it should be considered derogatory to the Creator to suppose that he has a sense of humour.

Dean William R Inge

Keep company with the more cheerful of the godly; there is no mirth like the mirth of believers.

Richard Baxter

HAPPINESS – A BY-PRODUCT   June 23

Where there is no vision, the people perish; but he that keepeth the law, happy is he.

Proverbs 29:18

In everything I have shown you that by such hard work we must help the weak and must remember the words of the Lord Jesus when he said: 'to give is happier than to receive.'

Acts 20:35

God cannot give us happiness and peace apart from himself, because it is not there. There is no such thing.

C S Lewis

I realise I have no right to wake up happy because this world, in anguish and sin, is no place for happiness. Such peace as I have in my heart is because I try to do the will of my Father – that and nothing else. If happiness follows, that is part of his bounty. Meanwhile it is my job to increase the happiness of others and to right the anguish of the world.

Dr Margaret Mewton

Men are made for happiness and anyone who is completely happy has a right to say to himself: 'I am doing God's will on earth.'

Anton Chekhov

> How happy is he born and taught
> That serveth not another's will;
> Whose armour is his honest thought,
> And simple truth his utmost skill.

Sir Henry Wotton

NO DEGREES IN SIN   June 24

Remember that a man who keeps the whole law but for a single exception is none the less a law-breaker.   *James 2:10*

As a very little dust will disorder a clock, and the least grain of sand will obscure our sight, so the least grain of sin which is upon the heart will hinder its right motion towards God.

John Wesley

When Leonardo da Vinci was painting his last masterpiece The Last Supper, he looked for a model for his Christ. At last he located a chorister in one of the churches of Rome who was lovely in life and features, a young man named Pietro Bandinelli. Years passed and the picture was still unfinished. All the disciples had been portrayed but one – Judas Iscariot. Now he started to look for a man whose face was hardened and distorted by sin – and at last he found a beggar on the streets of Rome with a face so villainous that he shuddered when he looked at him. He hired the man to sit for him as he painted the face of Judas on his canvas. When he was about to dismiss the man, he said, 'I have not yet found out your name.' 'My name is Pietro Bandinelli,' he replied; 'I also sat for you as your model of Christ.'   *The Indian Christian*

A slight sore, neglected may prove of fatal consequence, and so may a slight sin slighted and left unrepented of.   *Matthew Henry*

TEMPTATION   June 25

No temptation has come your way that is too hard for flesh and blood to bear. But God can be trusted not to allow you to suffer any temptation beyond your powers of endurance. He will see to it that temptation has its way out, so that it will be possible for you to bear it.   *1 Corinthians 10:13*

> Still let me ever watch and pray,
> And feel that I am frail;
> That if the tempter cross my way,
> Yet he may not prevail.   *J Williams*

Put on the whole armour of God.   *Ephesians 6:1*

Almighty God, who seest that we have no power of ourselves to help ourselves, keep us both outwardly in our bodies and inwardly in our souls; that we may be defended from all adversities which may happen to the body, and from all evil thoughts which may assault and hurt the soul.   *Second Collect for Lent*

Some temptations come to the industrious, but all temptations attack the idle.   *Charles H Spurgeon*

Make and keep me pure within.   *Charles Wesley*

ACTIVISM   June 26

The peace that Christ gives is to guide you in the decisions you make; for it is to this peace that God has called you together in the one body... Everything you do or say, then, should be done in the name of the Lord Jesus.   *Colossians 3:15 and 17 GNB*

One of the greatest dangers in the spiritual life is to live on your own activities. In other words the activity is not in its right place as something which you do, but has become something that keeps you going.   *Dr Martyn Lloyd-Jones*

The essence is stillness – the Sufi way to every believing Muslim.   *Professor Ibish*

A Christian should always remember that the value of his good works is not based on their number and excellence, but on the love of God which prompts him to do these things.
St John of the Cross

We won't get rid of the malady of sin by increasing our activity.
Alan Redpath

The glory of the adventure of life under God's direction lies not in the number of things done, but in the quality of the way they are done.   *H P E*

PRIDE

Pride goeth before destruction, and an haughty spirit before a fall. Better it is to be of an humble spirit with the lowly, than to divide the spoil with the proud.   *Proverbs 16:18–19*

Pride thrust Nebuchadnezzar out of men's society, proud Saul out of his kingdom, proud Adam out of Paradise and proud Lucifer out of heaven.   *Thomas Adams*

According to Christian teachers, the essential vice, the utmost evil, is pride. Unchastity, anger, greed, drunkenness and all that, are mere flea-bites in comparison; it was through pride that the devil became the devil; pride leads to every other vice; it is the complete anti-God state of mind... If you want to find out how proud you are, the easiest way is to ask yourself, 'How much do I dislike it when people snub me, or refuse to take any notice of me, or shove their oar in, or patronise me, or show off?' The point is that each person's pride is in competition with everyone else's pride... Once the element of competition has gone, pride has gone.   *C S Lewis*

If a man must boast of anything as his own, he must boast of his misery and sin, for there is nothing else but this that is his own property.   *William Law*

The proud will not enter the Blissful Abode.
                    The Prophet Mohammed

TRUE HUMILITY

Jesus said: The only 'superior' among you is the one who serves the others. For every man who promotes himself will be humbled, and every man who learns to be humble will find promotion.   *Matthew 23:11–12*

I realise that being seen as a doctor... I was relying on some status or achievement for my life's meaning and purpose... One of my friends asked me 'What do you want for yourself?' I wanted to pull my weight and... a modicum of appreciation and credit. 'Of course,' said my friend, 'you will be like that wherever you are.'   *Dr Paul Campbell*

Humility consists not in thinking meanly of ourselves, but in not thinking of ourselves at all. *Dwight L Moody*

As pride was the beginning of sin, so humility must be the beginning of Christian discipline. *St Augustine*

I desire to humble myself in all sincerity. I implore thee, dear Jesus, to send me a humiliation whensoever I try to set myself above others. *St Thérèse of Lisieux*

SELF-IMPORTANCE June 29

If someone thinks he or she is 'somebody' when really they are nobody, they are only deceiving themselves. You should each judge your own conduct. If it is good then you can be proud of what you yourself have done, without having to compare it with what someone else has done. *Galatians 6:3–4 GNB*

I remember having to give a series of Bible readings at a conference and after the first of these, someone came up to me. Speaking very slowly, he said, 'The greatest Bible study I have ever heard...' 'Give me humility, Lord,' I thought, but the man had not finished and he went on, 'was given by Mr X last week!' So I had a very quick answer to my prayer for humility.
Canon David Watson

The reason why God is so great a lover of humility is because he is the greater lover of truth. For humility is nothing but truth while pride is nothing but lying. *St Vincent de Paul*

Golden deeds kept out of sight are most laudable. *Blaise Pascal*

'MY EXPERIENCE TELLS ME' June 30

Laban said unto Jacob... I have learned by experience that the Lord hath blessed me for thy sake. *Genesis 30:27*

We glory in tribulations also; knowing that tribulation worketh patience; and patience experience; and experience, hope.
Romans 5:3–4 AV

What I like about experience is that it is such an honest thing. You may take any number of wrong turnings, but keep your eyes open and you will not be allowed to go very far before the warnings appear. *C S Lewis*

Thank God there is now at work a world force of people... who know how a moral climate can be produced because of what has happened in their own lives. Workers and soldiers, housewives and statesmen, farmers and industrialists, young and old, they have no paper plans to offer, but they have an experience which cannot be denied. They know that a change of heart is possible. They know that definite, decisive guidance from God is available, today as always. *Dr Frank Buchman*

Every experience God gives us, every person he puts in our lives is the perfect preparation for the future that only he can see. *Corrie ten Boom*

PRIDE AND PREJUDICE – THEIR EFFECT ON FAITH

July 1

He came into the world – the world he had created – and the world failed to recognise him. He came into his own world, and his own people would not accept him. *John 1:10-11*

'Is it because you have seen me that you believe?' Jesus said to Thomas. 'Happy are those who have never seen me and yet have believed!' *John 20:29*

Prejudice is the child of ignorance. *William Hazlitt*

A Lutheran pastor told me, 'I have an emotional complex against the Baptists and Pentecostals.' He did not realise that... every prejudice excludes the one holding it from any possibility of right thinking. Many will not accept Jesus because he was Jewish... The Pharisees could not admit that a prophet could come from Galilee, John 7:52. Others took offence at his belonging to the lower class. They asked him in mocking tone, 'Is not this the carpenter's son?' Matthew 13:55... Flee any racial, national or denominational prejudice. Judge every person on his or her own merits. *Pastor Richard Wurmbrand*

Faith depends not on intellectual but on moral decisions.
Monsignor R Hugh Benson

'STIGMITIS'

July 2

So you should not pass judgment on anyone before the right time comes. Final judgment must wait until the Lord comes; he will bring to light the dark secrets and expose the hidden secrets of people's minds. *1 Corinthians 4:5 GNB*

When the popular theme is to blame a certain race or class for everything, people fall easy victims to the disease of 'Stigmitis' – the branding of many with the infamy of the few.
Wing Commander Edward Howell

If the wrong which people do fills you with such indignation and unbearable pain that you want to take vengeance on them, above all resist that feeling. At once go and seek suffering for yourself, as one guilty of the wrong done. Accept that suffering, endure it to the end, and your heart will be strengthened. You will understand how you are guilty yourself: you might have let your light shine on those who did wrong, and you did not do so. If your light had shone, it would have illumined the path for others, and they might perhaps have been saved from sinning.   *Feodor Dostoevsky*

Blaming someone else, or the other group, reveals the motive in us. Parents want the difficult child or difficult relative to change. Their motive is often a desire to have a quieter life in the family and home or that the neighbours will think more highly of them... We want the other crowd to change so that things will be easier for us and our crowd.

Paul Campbell and Peter Howard

THAT YE BE NOT JUDGED   July 3

Why, then, do you criticise your brother's actions, why do you try to make him look small? We shall all be judged one day, not by each other's standards, nor even by our own, but by the judgment of God.   *Romans 14:10-11*

For you will be judged by the way you criticise others and the measure you give will be the measure you receive. *Matthew 7:2*

This statement is not a haphazard guess, it is an eternal law of God... If you have been shrewd in finding out the defects in others, remember that will be the measure given to you. Life serves back in the coin you pay... The reason we see hypocrisy and fraud and unreality in others is because they are all in our hearts.   *Oswald Chambers*

We do exactly the reverse of what the Gospel bids us do. The Gospel bids us judge ourselves severely while it forbids us to judge our brethren... Who are we that we should judge our brethren, the servants of one another? To their own Master they stand or fall.   *St Francis de Sales*

How rarely we weigh our neighbour in the same balance in which we weigh ourselves.   *Thomas à Kempis*

THE STRANGE PHENOMENON OF PROJECTION July 4

Prepared as you are to instruct others, do you ever teach yourself anything? You preach against stealing, for example, but are you sure of your own honesty? You denounce the practice of adultery, but are you sure of your own purity?

Romans 2:21-22

Ever since Adam blamed Eve for giving him that apple, men – and women – have blamed others for what goes wrong. That achieves nothing. The radical revolutionary starts at the other end. He accepts for himself the changes he would like to see in others. Where people have done this, they have often become so different that they startled their friends and changed their enemies. And changed the trend of their age. Paul of Tarsus was a brilliant intellectual who led the violence against the early Christians. He became one of the toughest fighters for their idea – and turned the world upside down.

Sydney Cook and Garth Lean

Unless we are willing to help a person overcome his faults, there is little value in pointing them out. Robert J Hastings

Think of your own faults the first part of the night when you are awake and the faults of others the latter part of the night when you are asleep. Chinese Proverb

In any new country you visit, go on a basis, not of comparison but of appreciation. Dr Frank N D Buchman

UNSTINTING LOVE July 5

We see real love, not in the fact that we loved God, but that he loved us and sent his son to make personal atonement for our sins... If we love each other God does actually live within us, and his love grows in us towards perfection. 1 John 4:10 and 12

Take away love and our earth is a tomb. Robert Browning

Becoming a Christian so far as I could then (as a schoolboy) see, meant not to smoke or drink or muck around. The trouble was, I was still the centre of my own life. So for me, at that stage, it was a case of out of self, into Christ and back again! It didn't cost me very much. A challenge at Oxford to listen to God, meant taking seriously the next stage 'out to others'. That is really where the Cross came in, because I felt God was calling me to help others and lay my life down for them. *Brian Boobbyer*

You will find as you look back on your life that the moments that stand out, the moments when you have really lived, are the moments when you have done things in a spirit of love.

Professor Henry Drummond

HATING AND FORSAKING   July 6

These six things doth the Lord hate: yea, seven are an abomination unto him: A proud look, a lying tongue, and hands that shed innocent blood, an heart that deviseth wicked imaginations, feet that be swift in running to mischief, a false witness that speaketh lies, and he that soweth discord among brethren.

Proverbs 6:16-19

There are four stages in deliverance from sin: *Hate, Forsake, Confess, Restore.*

Hate: No one wants to forsake sin till he hates it. While we still love it, whether openly or in secret, we still cling to it inwardly, however much we may protest that we want to be free. When we really see it for what it is, the sight brings such loathing that we cannot be free fast enough.

Forsake: This means decision – not just for the present moment, but for ever. No provisional or temporary experimental forsaking will avail.

Confess: This is often the missing link, and the reason why so many constantly make resolutions and as constantly break them. The confession to someone who will not let you down or let you off, may be the way to bring you to the point of hating and forsaking. It is often not till we see our own sin through another person's eyes that we realise the heinousness of it.

Restore: This is the final stage which brings forgiveness and liberation. Restitution alone, according to the harm done, will enable Jesus to break the power of cancelled sin and set the prisoner free.   *Dorothy M Prescott*

THE VALLEY OF HUMILIATION July 7

The fear of the Lord is a training in wisdom and the way to honour is humility. *Proverbs 15:33 NEB*

Many who pray for humility would be extremely sorry if God were to grant it to them... They forget that to love, desire and ask for humility is loving, desiring and asking for humiliations.
Père Jean Nicolas Grou

I believe the first test of a truly great man is his humility.
John Ruskin

If I could give you information of my life, it would be to show how a woman of very ordinary ability has been led by God in strange and unaccustomed paths to do in his service what he has done in her. And if I could tell you all, you would see how God has done all, and I nothing. I have worked hard, very hard – that is all and I have never refused God anything.
Florence Nightingale

Knowledge of God gives love and knowledge of self gives humility. Humility is nothing but truth. What have we got that we have not received? asks St Paul. If I have received everything, what good have I of my own? If we are convinced of this we will never raise our head in pride... Self-knowledge puts us on our knees. *Mother Teresa*

AFTER A FALL July 8

Let the wicked leave their way of life and change their way of thinking. Let them turn to the Lord, our God; he is merciful and quick to forgive. *Isaiah 55:7 GNB*

I looked at my life in the light of absolute honesty. Floods of thoughts poured into my mind – the wrong things I'd done, the other women I'd messed around with, the way I'd used men, the stuff I'd knocked off from work, the money I'd fiddled in the shop stewards' committee. The rebellion and the pain I felt! That it should have to begin with yourself!... (Then he continues, having prayed fervently that God would help over the defeats in his life): When I came out of that church I felt so different I thought everyone was looking at me. I had talked about peace all my life, but I had never known what inner peace was until then.   *Les Dennison*

Who errs and mends, to God himself commends.
                                                  Miguel de Cervantes

After a fall it is a greater sin to withdraw from the fight, feeling sorry for yourself, than the original sin itself.   *Peter Howard*

UP AND DOING TO REBUILD   July 9

He is able to keep you from falling and to present you before his glory without fault and with unspeakable joy.   *Jude 24*

(Max Bladeck, a Ruhr miner who had been a Communist Party member for 26 years had responded to a greater revolution.) In the winter of 1951 Bladeck's ex-colleagues went after him. They knew he had a weakness for alcohol. They managed to get him drinking. They then sat him next to a particular woman on a bus on his way home and he publicly embraced her. Bladeck was so bitterly ashamed that he wrote to Buchman in America asking that none of Buchman's friends should call on him again. 'I have betrayed you,' he said. Buchman cabled back:

> 'Man-like it is to fall in sin;
> Fiend-like it is to dwell therein;
> Christ-like it is from sin to rise.

'"The blood of Jesus Christ, his son, cleanseth us from all sin." The biggest sinner can become the greatest saint. I have faith in the new Max.'
'I had expected anything else but not that,' Max told his friends later. 'I felt in the sentence he sent me the deepest message of Christianity and it came at the right time.'   *Garth Lean*

Jesus, meek and humble of heart, make my heart like yours.
                                                  St Thérèse of Lisieux

USING OUR MISTAKES

When I fall, I shall rise; when I sit in darkness the Lord shall be a light unto me.
Micah 7:8

A man who has committed a mistake and doesn't correct it is committing another mistake.
Confucius

Confession of every known sin is very important. Sometimes I ask myself a series of questions. Have I been trying to give the impression that I'm a better person than I really am? Am I being honest in all my words and actions?... Have I insisted on doing things about which my conscience is uneasy? Am I defeated in any part of my life?... If so, what am I doing about it? We need to allow God's Spirit to search our hearts.
Canon David Watson

When people read or hear it, the confession of my past sins arouses their hearts. No longer can they sleep in despair and say 'I can't'. They wake up to a love of your mercy and grace, and your grace, by making the weak aware of their weakness, makes them strong.
St Augustine

Help us, O Lord Christ, to stand for the hard right against the easy wrong. Help us not to lower our standards to win favours from others. Help us to do battle royally and to the end against all that thou dost condemn in us.
Rev John Hunter

IT MATTERS TO HIM

Who would dare to accuse us, whom God has chosen? God himself has declared us free from sin. Who is in a position to condemn? Only Christ Jesus, and Christ died for us, Christ also rose for us, Christ reigns in power for us, Christ prays for us!
Romans 8:33-34

God loves you as though you were the only person.
St Augustine

Every Christian has the potential to be a first-class disciple. This is because of the personal interest which our Master takes in each of his students... Prior to conversion my identity was vague and nebulous, for I had never discovered who I really was; but when I surrendered to Christ and became one of his disciples, the identity crisis was over.

Rev Selwyn Hughes © *CWR*

To Jesus every human being was a person. Matthew wasn't just a tax-gatherer; he was Matthew. Mary Magdalene was not just a sinner; she was Mary. Simon was not just a Pharisee; he was Simon. *Dr William Barclay*

We are called to a fully satisfying life once we have accepted that God, who cares, has chosen us for a particular work for him. *H P E*

THE ANSWER TO MATERIALISM July 12

Tell those who are rich in this present world not to be contemptuous of others, and not to rest the weight of their confidence on the transitory power of wealth but on the living God, who generously gives us everything for our enjoyment. Tell them to do good, to be rich in kindly actions, to be ready to give to others and to sympathise with those in distress. *1 Timothy 6:17-18*

For the fulfilment of his purpose God needs more than priests, bishops, pastors and missionaries. He needs mechanics and chemists, gardeners and street sweepers, dressmakers and cooks, tradesmen, physicians, philosophers, judges and shorthand typists... I do not serve God only in the brief moments I am taking part in a religious service, or reading the Bible, or saying my prayers, or talking about him in some book I am writing, or discussing the meaning of life with a patient or friend. I serve him quite as much when I am giving a patient an injection, or lancing an abscess, or writing a prescription, or giving a piece of good advice... I serve him by taking an interest in everything because he has created everything and has put me in his creation so that I may participate in it fully.

Dr Paul Tournier

Full life – 'life more abundant' involves living at war with materialism. It is the root of what is destroying our society and our country. Show me, Good Lord, how to fight this evil, starting in myself. *H P E*

WHERE TO START

The Lord is a refuge for the oppressed, a place of safety in times of trouble. Those who know you, Lord, will trust you; you do not abandon anyone who comes to you.   *Psalms 9:9-10 GNB*

Come close to God and he will come close to you. You are sinners; get your hands clean again. Your loyalty is divided; get your hearts made true once more.   *James 4:7 and 8*

For all of us, two roads stretch ahead. There is the road of self, the road of this world, with the trophies which it sometimes brings, and there is the royal road of the Cross, with its pain and its joy and its promise of 'an inheritance incorruptible and undefiled and that fadeth not away' not merely for ourselves but for a world which is so starved of the selfless endless love that it bequeaths... So, where to begin? The first step is to take time in quiet to listen to the deepest thing in your heart: what some call conscience, others the Holy Spirit... Then let God (or your conscience) show you how your life does not match up to absolute moral standards. However much of a mess your life may be in, God has the knack... of finding the end in the wool which helps the whole tangled ball to get straightened out.

Authors of The Secret

Say to yourself, 'I am loved by God more than I can either conceive or understand.' Let this fill all your soul and all your prayers. You will soon see that this is the way to find God.

Henri de Tourvillle

CHANGING HUMAN NATURE

What then... does the Lord your God ask of you? Only to fear the Lord your God, to conform to all his ways, to love him and to serve him with all your heart and soul.

Deuteronomy 10:12 NEB

Here below to live is to change, and to be perfect is to change often.   *Cardinal J H Newman*

Alec Smith is the son of the former Prime Minister of Rhodesia, Ian Smith. Alec was hooked on drugs like LSD and, for years, was a pusher himself. It was at this point that God, as he puts it, started to interfere in his life. He saw the musicals *Jesus Christ Superstar* and *Godspell* and, driving home alone one evening, a voice which seemed to be coming from the back of the car said: 'Go home and read the New Testament.' Alec eventually became a Christian and then, through meeting a group of people working with Moral Re-Armament, faced the question of how he could relate his personal change to the crisis in his nation, at that time divided by bitter civil war. 'I discovered', he said, 'that there is a difference between giving my life to God so that he can sort out my problems and giving my life to God to work towards establishing his authority in the power structure of my country.'   *Authors of* The Secret

THE HOME   July 15

Here we have no permanent home, but we are seekers after the city which is to come.   *Hebrews 13:14 NEB*

The strength of a nation is derived from the integrity of its homes.   *Confucius*

Happiness is to be found only in the home where God is honoured, where each one loves and helps and cares for the others.
                                         Blessed Théophane Vénard

> Our birth is but a sleep and a forgetting;
> The Soul that rises with us, our life's Star,
> Hath had elsewhere its setting,
> And cometh from afar;
> Not in entire forgetfulness,
> And not in utter nakedness,
> But trailing clouds of glory do we come
> From God, who is our home.   *William Wordsworth*

Where there is true piety in the home, purity of morals reigns supreme.   *Jean-Baptiste Vianney*

The most influential of all educational factors is the conversation in a child's home.   *Archbishop William Temple*

141

WHERE WARS BEGIN   July 16

What causes conflicts and quarrels among you? Do they not spring from the aggressiveness of your bodily desires? You want something which you cannot have, and so you are bent on murder; you are envious and cannot attain your ambition, and so you quarrel and fight. You do not get what you want, because you do not pray for it.   *James 4:1-2 NEB*

Peace demands a mentality and a spirit which, before turning to others, must first permeate the one who wishes to bring peace. Peace is first and foremost personal, before it is social. And it is precisely this spirit of peace which it is the duty of every true follower of Christ to cultivate.   *Pope Paul VI*

My religion is based on truth and non-violence. Truth is my God and non-violence is the means to reach him.

Mahatma Gandhi

Mankind must put an end to war, or war will put an end to mankind.   *John F Kennedy, 35th President of the USA*

A wave of absolute unselfishness throughout the nations would be the end of war.   *Dr Frank N D Buchman*

The king draws our wills to his will, and his will is our peace.

Dante Alighieri

WAR AND PEACE   July 17

Thou dost keep in peace men of constant mind, in peace because they trust in thee. Trust in the Lord for ever; for the Lord himself is an everlasting rock.   *Isaiah 26:3-4 NEB*

As far as your responsibility goes, live at peace with everyone.

Romans 12:18

In modern warfare there are no victors; there are only survivors.   *Lyndon B Johnson, 36th President of the USA*

> Waste of Muscle, waste of Brain,
> Waste of Patience, waste of Pain,
> Waste of Manhood, waste of Health,
> Waste of Beauty, waste of Wealth,

Waste of Blood and waste of Tears,
Waste of Youth's most precious years,
Waste of ways the Saints have trod,
Waste of Glory, waste of God – War!

G A Studdert-Kennedy

Only love – whereby came humility – can cast out the fear which is the root of all war.   *Thomas Merton*

Peace is not the absence of war. It is people becoming different. Most of us want to make peace by repenting of the other fellow's sins.   *Dr Frank N D Buchman*

THE COMMON FOE   July 18

We want to prove ourselves genuine ministers of God whatever we have to go through – patient endurance of troubles, hardship, desperate situations... Our sole defence, our only weapon, is a life of integrity.   *2 Corinthians 6:4 and 7*

Gentlemen, I must ask the forbearance of the men here tonight who are in intellectual difficulties if I speak to the men who are in moral degradation. It has come to my knowledge through the week from a bundle of letters from men now sitting in this room, that there are a large number with their backs to the wall. They are dead beat and I shall consider their cases first.

Professor Henry Drummond

Were one asked to select Drummond's finest achievement, one might safely mention the cleansing of student life at Edinburgh university. When he was an arts student, life in all the faculties, but especially the medical, was reckless, coarse, boisterous, and no one was doing anything to raise the tone. Twenty years afterwards 600 men, largely medics, met every Sunday evening for worship and conference under Drummond's presidency.

Dr John Watson, biographer of Professor Henry Drummond

As I am, so is my nation... Are you part of the disease or part of the cure?   *Dr Frank N D Buchman*

HOW IS PEACE MADE July 19

Those who live on the level of the spirit have the spiritual out-look, and that is life and peace. *Romans 8:6 NEB*

May the Lord of peace personally give you peace at all times and in all ways. The Lord be with you all. *2 Thessalonians 3:16*

Peace is never to be obtained but by the rooting out of sin.
Francis Hall

Pastor Richard Wurmbrand relates how an ex-communist captain, 'one of the worst torturers of Christians', found himself sharing a cell with Christians he had once arrested and beaten. He goes on: 'A boy of 12 entered, holding in his hand a flower for the captain's wife. The boy told him, "Captain, you are the one who put my father and mother in prison. Today is my mother's birthday. I always buy her a flower on this day. Because of you I have no mother to gladden today, but she was a Christian and taught me to love my enemies and reward evil with good. So I thought I would bring a flower to the mother of your children. Please take it to your wife and tell her about my love and about the love of Christ."'

Peace can be found nowhere except in simple obedience.
Archbishop François Fénelon

CAN ENEMIES BECOME FRIENDS? July 20

If, while we were his enemies, Christ reconciled us to God by dying for us, surely now that we are reconciled we may be perfectly certain of our salvation through his living in us.
Romans 5:10

If thine enemy be hungry, give him bread to eat; and if he be thirsty, give him water to drink. *Proverbs 25:21*

Could we read the secret history of our enemies, we should find in each person's life sorrow and suffering enough to disarm all hostility. *Henry W Longfellow*

I shall pass through this world but once. Any good thing therefore, that I can do, or any kindness that I can show to any human being, let me do it now. Let me not defer it or neglect it, for I shall not pass this way again.

Stephen Grellet, American Quaker

Does it never come into your mind to fear lest he should demand of you why you had not exercised toward your brother a little of that mercy which he, who is your master, so abundantly bestows on you? *Archbishop François Fénelon*

Where there is no love, pour love in, and you will draw out love. *St John of the Cross*

You see your enemy standing against you with his angry passion, his biting words, his provoking insults, his unrelenting hate... You need think only that he is a *man*. You love in him not what he is but what you would have him be, and thus when you love your enemy you love a brother... When Christ said, 'Father forgive them for they know not what they do', his will to forgive them was a will to transform them. *St Augustine*

THE PRICE OF PEACE   July 21

Thou dost keep him in perfect peace, whose mind is stayed on thee, because he trusts in thee. *Isaiah 26:3 RSV*

Peace is such a tremendous jewel that I would give anything for it – except truth. *Matthew Henry*

What Satan put into the heads of our remote ancestors was the idea that they could 'be like gods' – could set up on their own as if they had created themselves – be their own masters – invent some sort of happiness for themselves outside God, apart from God. And out of that hopeless attempt has come nearly all that we call human history – money, poverty, ambitions, war, prostitution, classes, empires, slavery – the long terrible story of man trying to find something other than God which will make him happy. *C S Lewis*

The time of business does not differ from the time of prayer; and in the noise and clutter of my kitchen, while several persons are at the same time calling for different things, I possess God in as great tranquillity as if I were upon my knees at the blessed sacrament. *Brother Lawrence*

AGAINST THE TIDE

For God has not given us a spirit of cowardice, but a spirit of power and love and a sound mind. *2 Timothy 1:7*

I have learned to be content whatever the circumstances may be. I know now how to live when things are difficult and I know how to live when things are prosperous... I am ready for anything through the strength of the one who lives within me.
Philippians 4:11-13

'Once to every man and nation comes the moment to decide.' That moment is here now: to persuade our own nation and the world to take a super-national view of their responsibilities and to accept a super-national sovereignty based on the will of God.
Peter Howard

We've tried living and thinking as we want. Now try living and thinking as God wants. Try living as we want the other fellow to live. Then our nation will be the spearhead of a new world order. *Dr Frank N D Buchman*

> For while the tired waves, vainly breaking,
> Seem here no painful inch to gain,
> Far back, through creeks and inlets making,
> Comes silent, flooding in, the main. *Arthur Hugh Clough*

A MORAL BACKBONE

We have set our faces against all shameful secret practices; We... speak the plain truth and so commend ourselves to every man's conscience in the sight of God. *2 Corinthians 4:2*

The crisis inherent in the political and economic situation today is a moral one... The day will surely come when a new Britain will be built. Those who do it will not pander; they will command the ancient values. *The Times, Feb 1963*

We hear much about the decay of moral standards and indeed we see that decay all around us, but we do not hear much about the way out from moral weakening and defeat, through the power of Christ. When I was an undergraduate in this university I sat up and took notice when I saw the lives of some of my friends becoming radically different. When I made investigation, I discovered that it was that they were being brought face to face with a virile all-answering Christian faith.

Bishop Cuthbert Bardsley

God never fails to provide occasions when either we challenge something that is wrong or lack the moral backbone to speak up. 'Then it is the brave man chooses, while the coward stands aside.'

P M and H P E

If your light had shone forth, it would have made clear the path for others, and the person who sinned would perchance be saved by your light.

Feodor Dostoevsky

ENDURING HARDNESS   July 24

We are hard-pressed on all sides, but we are never frustrated; we are puzzled, but never in despair. We are persecuted, but are never deserted; we may be knocked down but we are never knocked out!

2 Corinthians 4:8-9

During the First World War, a village behind the lines in the Somme valley had been shelled and there were many civilian casualties. The church too had been damaged, but it was the largest building available for a dressing station in the sudden emergency. The altar was turned into an improvised operating table. One of the casualties brought in was a young soldier who belonged to the village, and was at home on a few days leave. He was badly wounded and his leg would have to come off at once. 'You'll have to be brave,' said the doctor. 'This is going to be rather painful. We've got no anaesthetic – it was all destroyed when the hospital was hit.' The young man looked at the altar, and pointed with his hand towards the crucifix over it. 'I shall be all right,' he said. 'So long as I can look at him, I'll manage.'

F H Drinkwater

Suffering is the very best gift he has to give us. He gives it only to his chosen friends.

St Thérèse of Lisieux

Calvary is God's great proof that suffering in the will of God always leads to glory.

Warren Wiersbe

PERSECUTION

Persecution is inevitable for those who are determined to live
really Christian lives.   *2 Timothy 3:12*

William Tyndale (d1536) was a scholar who shared Wycliffe's
ideal of bringing the Bible to ordinary people in their own language. He went back to the original Hebrew Old Testament and
Greek New Testament to make his translation. Even the church
was still bitterly opposed to an English Bible and England grew
too hot for Tyndale and his unpopular views. He fled to the
Continent to finish translating... New Testaments were arriving
thick and fast in England but were not always falling into the
hands of sympathetic readers. Whenever a copy came to the
notice of church leaders they burned it, and there were public
bonfires outside St Paul's Cathedral for that very purpose... After months of torture in prison, he was condemned to death and
strangled, then burnt at the stake. But in spite of seeming failure, his dying prayer was answered. 'Lord, open the king of
England's eyes,' Tyndale prayed and when the first complete
Bible was printed in England, it had the king's blessing.

Mary Batchelor

The martyrs were bound, imprisoned, scourged, racked,
burned, rent and butchered – and they multiplied. *St Augustine*

Such is the law which God has annexed to the promulgation of
the Truth; its preachers suffer, but its cause prevails.

Cardinal J H Newman

WILLINGNESS TO BE MISUNDERSTOOD

He was oppressed, and he was afflicted, yet he opened not his
mouth... And he made his grave with the wicked, and with the
rich in his death; because he had done no violence, neither was
any deceit in his mouth.   *Isaiah 53:7 and 9*

One doctor said to another doctor: 'About the termination of a
pregnancy, I want your opinion. The father was a syphilitic.
The mother was tuberculous. Of the four children born, the first
was blind, the second died, the third was deaf and dumb, the
fourth also tuberculous. What would you have done?' 'I would

have ended the pregnancy.' 'Then you would have murdered Beethoven.'   *Maurice Baring*

> If you can keep your head when all about you
> Are losing theirs and blaming it on you...
> If you can wait and not be tired of waiting,
> Or being lied about, don't deal in lies,
> Or being hated, don't give way to hating
> And yet don't look too good nor talk too wise, . .
> Yours is the Earth and everything that's in it,
> And – which is more – you'll be a man my son!
>   *Rudyard Kipling*

If Jesus Christ be God and died for me, then no sacrifice can be too great for me to make for him.   *C T Studd*

BITTER SWEET   July 27

We know sorrow, yet our joy is inextinguishable. We have nothing to 'bless ourselves with' yet we bless many others with true riches. We are penniless, and yet we possess everything.
                                                2 Corinthians 6:10

No one stood by me the first time I defended myself; all deserted me... But the Lord stayed with me and gave me strength.
                                                2 Timothy 4:16-17 GNB

Nijule Sadunaite, a young Christian lady, said before the court in Lithuania, when she was sentenced for her faith: 'This is the happiest day of my life. I am tried for the cause of truth and love toward men... I have an enviable fate, a glorious destiny. My condemnation will be my triumph. I regret only to have done so little for people... but we must learn to love the person, even the one in error.' This you can only learn at the school of Jesus Christ.   *Pastor Richard Wurmbrand*

Don't search for God in far lands – he is not there. He is close to you. He is with you. Just keep the lamp burning and you will always see him. Watch and pray. Keep kindling the lamp and you will see how sweet is the Lord you love.   *Mother Teresa*

No strength of our own or goodness we claim;
Yet, since we have known the Saviour's great name,
In this our strong power for safety we hide –
The Lord is our power, the Lord will provide.

John Newton

SOMEBODY'S GOT TO BEGIN   July 28

On his journey, as he neared Damascus, a light from the sky
suddenly blazed around him, and he fell to the ground. Then
he heard a voice speaking to him, 'Saul, Saul, why are you persecuting me?' 'Who are you, Lord?' he asked. 'I am Jesus whom
you are persecuting,' was the reply. 'But now stand up and go
into the city and there you will be told what you must do.'

Acts 9:3-6

Frank Buchman looked at me and said, 'Young man, what the
country needs is not just one more good doctor. It needs an answer to selfish materialism, for without it, we may win the war
but we will certainly lose the peace.'...

I had to be back at work on Monday morning... Buchman
asked, 'Have you had guidance from God to go?'

I replied I didn't need God to tell me what to do – I had obli-
gations to meet. He suggested we listen to God together.

After a few moments he enquired, 'What thoughts did you
get?'

So I restated my position, 'My thought is to go.'

'That's strange,' he said, 'mine was "stay, stay, stay." Let's
listen some more... Should we pray together?'

So we did. As we were quiet, deep down I knew I was experiencing an undeniable sense of calling to join Buchman in his
work.' ...That decision was the toughest I ever had to make. I
stayed.   *Dr Paul Campbell*

You and I and each one of us can either add our weight behind
the push towards decadence, and so help to carry all of us into
the abyss: or we can, in the name of God, work to save the
world. Even now we can change the course of history.

Père Alphonse Gratry

STRENGTH IN WEAKNESS July 29

'My grace is sufficient for you; for where there is weakness, my power is shown the more completely.' Therefore I have cheerfully made up my mind to be proud of my weaknesses, because they mean a deeper experience of the power of Christ.

2 Corinthians 12:9

I myself was sick in prison with lung, spinal and intestinal tuberculosis and recurring jaundice. The 'medicines' I received were beatings, neglect and lack of food. Doctors in Oslo who later examined me and took X-rays could not believe at first that I had survived the Roumanian prison conditions with four vertebrae infected with tuberculosis, lungs like sieves, and without food and drugs. The healing virtue of Christ had proved to be the same as in the times of the gospel.

Pastor Richard Wurmbrand

It is a sign of strength, not of weakness, to admit that you don't know all the answers. John P Loughrane

God only asks from you what he gives you power to do.

Bishop W Walsham How

When God asks me to do something difficult, I have so often struggled to do it in my own strength, when I could trust him to provide all I need. H P E

THE GOOD FIGHT July 30

Fight the worthwhile battle of the faith, keep your grip on that life eternal to which you have been called, and to which you boldly professed your loyalty before many witnesses.

2 Timothy 6:12

This faith of ours is the only way in which the world can be conquered. 1 John 5:5

To fight for a new society is really a fight to change men and women, starting with ourselves. It's the most interesting way to live and can redirect the course of history. It is part of the struggle between good and evil which goes on in every single person. Why not get into the battle now? A fresh start takes only as long as it takes to make a decision. Then you can start enlisting others.   *Sydney Cook and Garth Lean*

Hatred does not come by hatred. Easily seen are the faults of others, but one's own faults are hard to see... Conquer the angry man by love; conquer the miser with generosity; conquer the liar with truth.   *The Buddha*

Give peace in our time O Lord; because there is none that fighteth for us, but only thou, O God.   *Book of Common Prayer*

REVOLUTION BY CONSENT   July 31

Take your stand then with truth as your belt, integrity your breastplate, the gospel of peace firmly on your feet, salvation as your helmet and in your hand the sword of the spirit, the word of God. Above all be sure to take faith as your shield, for it can quench every burning missile the enemy hurls at you.
Ephesians 6:14-16

The true revolutionary is passionate for what needs to be done and is not deterred by what people say cannot be done. He is not run by fear or flattery and is trusted because he tells the truth. He sees others as they could be and helps them to be their best; hates wrong but not wrong-doers. He is for absolute standards that will cut like a laser beam through the rottenness in our civilisation. He has put right everything in his life that he can and is out to put right what is wrong in the world.
Sydney Cook and Garth Lean

The greatest revolution of all time, whereby the cross of Christ will transform the world, is enlisting men today.
Dr Frank N D Buchman

He calls us to revolt and fight
With him for what is just and right,
To sing and live magnificat
In crowded street and council flat.   *Fred Kaan*

DEMOCRACY ON THE OFFENSIVE   August 1

The ultimate aim of the Christian ministry... is to produce the love which springs from a pure heart, a good conscience and a genuine faith.   *1 Timothy 1:5*

Every Christian prays, 'thy will be done, on earth, as it is in heaven.' It is nonsense to pray like that without seriously desiring what we are praying for. If I really want it then I must stand up for it, in my own life and in the lives of others, in the life of the nation and of the whole world, with all that I am and have, led by God, in community with others who feel the same obligation.   *Cardinal Cushing*

Addressing a Christian audience, *Peter Howard* said: 'Christianity is essential to democracy, if democracy is to work. Democracy without Christianity is a cart without a wheel, a seed without soil, a book without print.... The Christian spirit, which impresses on a man's heart and into his mind and thinking, be he rich or poor, employer or employed, the needs of the community before his own selfish interests, is the ingredient essential to reinvigorate Christianity.'

People must choose to be governed by God or they condemn themselves to be ruled by tyrants.   *William Penn*

A NEW PUBLIC OPINION   August 2

Everything that belongs to the world – what the sinful self desires, what people see and want, and everything in this world that people are so proud of – none of this comes from the Father; it all comes from the world. The world and everything in it that people desire is passing away; but those who do the will of God live for ever.   *1 John 2:16-17 GNB*

A new spirit can grasp the mind and muscle of every worker for a revolutionary conception of teamwork and maximum production. Friction between people causes more trouble than friction in machines. My mate and I learnt this at the bench. But when we got honest and said 'sorry' we had a team. Teamwork will not come by chance but by change. Labour has got to learn to work together with management and labour have got to learn to work together. *Duncan Corcoran*

We recognise the supreme importance of teamwork in an army and in an industry. And when the good people of the world are willing to be part of a great selfless team in the moral and spiritual field we shall change the world. *Edward T Perry*

The most effective way to ensure the value of the future is to confront the present courageously and constructively.

Rollo May

We in the media are unelected. We must turn the same eagle eye that we apply to other sectors of society onto what we ourselves do. *Martyn Lewis*

MAKING HISTORY   August 3

The people that do know their God shall be strong, and do exploits. *Daniel 11:32*

God purposed long ago in his sovereign will that all human history should be consummated in Christ, that everything that exists in heaven or earth should find its perfection and fulfilment in him. *Ephesians 1:10*

In the workings of history there must be felt the movement of a living God... I do not see why Christians should be shy of trusting in Providence, leaning upon it and making alliance with it, regarding it as a living and active agency, both in ourselves and in its movement over the length and breadth of history.

Professor Herbert Butterfield

The first law of history is not to dare to utter falsehood; the second is not to fear to speak the truth. *Pope Leo XIII*

The belief in that truth which was revealed through Christ – whether man is passionately opposed to it, or whether he makes every effort to realise it as his own destiny – has been the driving force of history ever since. *Erich Frank*

QUALITIES OF THE NEW TYPE OF PERSON

You must do your utmost from your side and see that your faith carries with it real goodness of life. Your goodness must be accompanied by knowledge, your knowledge by self-control, your self-control by the ability to endure. Your endurance too must always be accompanied by devotion to God; that in turn must have in it the quality of brotherliness, and your brotherliness must lead on to Christian love. *2 Peter 1:5-7*

I knew that here was a man of understanding sympathy, one who wouldn't be shocked, one who could help. Another thing I knew – that there was no professionalism about him, that he wouldn't think of me as 'a case', that he was a genuine man, genuinely interested in another man. I remember, too, I had the feeling that in this man there was plenty of time. Nothing suggested commercial bustle. He seemed to me to be living in a wonderful spiritual leisure.
Harold Begbie, speaking of his early meeting with Dr Frank Buchman

There is a simple idea which shocked me when I was a small child and which remains with me till now: the idea that we are, apparently, created in God's image. I can still hardly grasp the breadth of this idea. And every time I think about this, I feel that we should not behave the way we do.
Irina Ratushinskaya

WORLD RENAISSANCE

August 5

For God loved the world so much that he gave his only son, so that everyone who believes in him should not be lost, but should have eternal life. God has not sent his son into the world to pass sentence on it, but to save it. *John 3:16-17*

We cannot live for ever from one crisis to another, from one war to the next. We seek a hate-free, fear-free, greed-free world, where every nation can enrich the common life of all, where every man has his work to do. This, not recurring crisis and destruction, is the God-given destiny of mankind. Amid the failure of human wisdom, there is still one supreme source from whom all can draw new power, new hope, new illumination. God speaks directly to the heart of every man and woman who is prepared to listen and obey... 'All thy children shall be taught of the Lord, and great shall be the peace of thy children.'

The Earl of Athlone, in a BBC broadcast in 1939

No man is truly awake today who has not developed a supranational horizon to his thinking. No church is anything more than a pathetic, pietistic backwater unless it is first and fundamentally and all the time a world missionary church.

James S Stewart

May the God of hope fill you with all joy and peace, with such faith that by the dynamic of the Holy Spirit you overflow with hope.   *Romans 15:13*

REBUILDING THE WORLD   August 6

This faith of ours is the only way in which the world can be conquered.   *1 John 5:4*

Let God remake you so that your whole attitude of mind is changed.   *Romans 12:2*

The lifestyle of most western Christians and churches has no prophetic challenge at all to the affluent society all round. In fact it is scarcely distinguishable from it. We have, quite unconsciously, adopted the values and standards of the world... If we were willing to learn the meaning of real discipleship and actually to become disciples, the church in the west could be transformed and the resultant impact on society would be staggering.   *Canon David Watson*

'Set me aside Barnabas and Saul for the task to which I have called them,' said the Holy Spirit to the central team of committed Christians in the great city of Antioch around the year AD44. What was 'the task to which I have called them'? Nothing less, we now realise, than the capture of the Roman Empire. It took 300 years, but this was the start of the crucial opening phase which laid the lines for the future.   *K D Belden*

ABOVE MOODS   August 7

Fear thou not; for I am with thee; be not dismayed, for I am thy God. I will strengthen thee; yea, I will help thee.   *Isaiah 41:10*

If you believe in goodness and if you value the approval of God, fix your minds on whatever is true and honourable and just and pure and lovely and admirable.   *Philippians 4:8*

People often say to me in counselling sessions, 'I feel anxious, but I don't really know what I feel anxious about.' Anxiety arises out of our basic assumptions about life which we learned during our formative and developmental years. If we were brought up in a house with quarrelling parents, or where love was noticeably absent, then this can bring about a great degree of insecurity in us... The best object to pin anxiety to is the Lord Jesus Christ, for he alone has met everything we meet, and more.   *Rev Selwyn Hughes © CWR*

To the quiet mind all things are possible. What is the quiet mind? A quiet mind is one which nothing weighs on, nothing worries, which is free from ties and all self-seeking, is wholly merged into the will of God and dead to its own.

Meister Eckhart

ACHIEVING THE IMPOSSIBLE   August 8

Can you fathom the mystery of God, can you fathom the perfection of the Almighty?   *Job 11:7 NEB*

Jesus replied, 'What is humanly impossible is possible for God.'
Luke 18:27 GNB

George Müller, in the course of his life, distributed two million copies of the scriptures, equipped several hundred missionaries, built five large orphanages in which he educated 121,000 orphans. He received and administered a million and a half pounds sterling, and left at the age of 86 an estate worth £160. Muller never ran up bills and never bought supplies for which he could not pay on the spot. God provided, but only just what was needed.   *Garth Lean*

One reason why some people won't accept miracles today is that they believe they break scientific laws. But what is a scientific law? It's a generalisation of what normally happens. A Christian would go further and say that a scientific law is simply the way in which God normally acts, but there's no law which says that God must act in that way always. 'Our God is in heaven; he does whatever pleases him.' (*Psalm 115:3*)

Canon David Watson

God raises the level of the impossible. *Corrie ten Boom*

GREATNESS   August 9

Ascribe ye greatness unto our God. He is the rock, his work is perfect... a God of truth and without iniquity, just and right is he. *Deuteronomy 32:3-4*

One of the marks of true greatness is the ability to develop greatness in others. *J C Macauley*

I solemnly pledge myself before God and in the presence of this assembly: To pass my life in purity and to practise my profession faithfully. I will abstain from whatever is deleterious and mischievous... I will do all in my power to elevate the standard of my profession... With loyalty will I endeavour to aid the physician in his work and devote myself to the welfare of those committed to my care. *Florence Nightingale*

I long to accomplish a great and noble task, but it is my chief duty to accomplish small tasks as if they were great and noble. Green, the historian, tells us that the world is moved along, not only by the mighty shoves of the heroes, but also by the aggregate of the tiny pushes of each honest worker. *Helen Keller*

It is marvellous how our Lord sets his seal upon all that we do, if we will but attend to his working, and not think too highly upon what we do ourselves. *Monsignor R Hugh Benson*

My temptation is often to live small and safe within the limits of what I can do. Living under Christ's direction involves taking risks and letting his greatness carry me forward. *H P E*

CHARACTER   August 10

Set your minds, then, on endorsing by your conduct the fact that God has called and chosen you... If you live this sort of life a rich welcome awaits you as you enter the eternal kingdom of our Lord and Saviour, Jesus Christ.   *2 Peter 1:10-11*

Character is not in the mind. It is in the will.
Archbishop Fulton J Sheen

All the problems we face are rooted, not in capitalism, socialism, colour or class, but in one thing: character. New people with new motives will build a new world. No concept short of this tackles the root of the modern malaise.
Paul Campbell and Peter Howard

Character is what a person is in the dark.   *Dwight L Moody*

Anyone who stands against the shallowness and falseness of the prevailing trend is likely, at least at first, to feel isolated and alone, and may even experience a kind of terror, for he is likely to encounter powerful opposition. But if he persists, he comes to find himself carried into the full stream which is the true trend of history. Here he will be borne up and carried forward by God himself, supported by a mighty army of those who have remained faithful to God's destiny for them.   *Fred Ladenius*

BEYOND ARGUMENT   August 11

In this confidence let us build on to the hope that we profess without the slightest hesitation – for he is utterly dependable – and let us think of one another and how we can encourage each other to love and do good deeds.   *Hebrews 10:23-24*

Jesus said: You are eye witnesses of these things.   *Luke 24:48*

The Holy Spirit is no sceptic and the things he has written in our hearts are not doubts or opinions but assertions – sure and more certain than life itself.   *Dr Martin Luther*

The proof which comes home to my own mind that God is good is his dealings with myself. This proof any man may have – for it is a personal proof. Nothing can get rid of it, and it grows the more it is cultivated.   *Cardinal J H Newman*

The grace of God will do very little for us if we resolve to do nothing for ourselves. God calls us to co-operate with him in the perfecting of character.   *Dr Graham Scroggie*

DISCOVERY   August 12

How can any man learn what is God's plan? How can he apprehend what the Lord's will is?   *Wisdom 9:13 NEB*

For God has allowed us to know the secret of his plan, and it is this: he purposed long ago in his sovereign will that all human history should be consummated in Christ, that everything that exists in heaven or earth should find its perfection and fulfilment in him.   *Ephesians 1:9*

I said, 'God can change you and whenever you like.'

'But I don't believe in God,' he answered, as though that settled the matter.

'That doesn't alter God's position in the least. He doesn't depend on whether you believe in him. He is either there or he isn't, and you can easily find out.'

I added that you did not have to believe in electricity to find out if it was there; all you had to do was to turn on the light switch...

'There's a very simple way of discovering whether God is there or not', I told him.

'What's that?'

'If you ask him to come into your life and change it, he will either come or not. If he does, you'll know.'   *Garth Lean*

> Come my soul, thy suit prepare;
> Jesus loves to answer prayer.
> For his grace and power are such
> None can ever ask too much.   *John Newton*

ENDURE OR CURE   August 13

Jesus asked a man who had been ill for 38 years: 'Do you want to get well again?'   *Luke 5:5*

The whole problem is that you endure a thing rather than cure it. You would rather pay than pray. You would rather go on with your confusion, your grumbling, your complaints than change and have an answer. *Dr Frank N D Buchman*

Why not give Christianity a trial? The question seems a hopeless one after 2,000 years of resolute adherence to the old cry of 'Not this man, but Barabbas' – 'This man' has not been a failure yet, for nobody has ever been sane enough to try his way.

George Bernard Shaw

Thy way, not mine, O Lord,
However dark it be!
Lead me by thine own hand;
Choose out the path for me. *Horatius Bonar*

STEADFASTNESS   August 14

Be sober, be vigilant; because your adversary the devil, as a roaring lion, walketh about, seeking whom he may devour; whom resist steadfast in the faith, knowing that the same afflictions are accomplished in your brethren that are in the world. *1 Peter 5:8-9 AV*

The root of all steadfastness is in consecration to God.

Alex MacLaren

Spirituality really means 'Holy Spirit at work', a profound action of the Holy Spirit in his church, renewing that church from the inside. *Cardinal Leon Joseph Suenens*

In our age which stridently proclaims to the world that 'God is dead' and faith a sign of man's weakness and powerlessness, the news that God is not a God of inadequacy but a God of abundance, 'of complete satisfaction, able to do exceeding abundantly', heralds a new age of creative discovery.

Professor Theophil Spoerri

Even the woodpecker owes his success to the fact that he uses his head and keeps pecking away until he finishes the job he starts. *Coleman Cox*

Christians should have... such abundant life that in poverty they are rich, in sickness they are in spiritual health, in contempt they are full of strength, and in death full of glory.

Charles H Spurgeon

WITHOUT CAREFULNESS   August 15

I should like you to be free from worldly anxieties.

1 Corinthians 7:32

Don't worry about anything whatever; whenever you pray, tell God every detail of your needs in thankful prayer.

Philippians 4:6-7

There remain times when one can only endure. One lives on, one doesn't die and the only thing one can do is to fill one's mind and time as far as possible with the concerns of other people.   *Arthur C Benson*

If you find yourself loving any pleasure better than your prayers, any book better than the Bible... any person better than Christ, any indulgence better than the hope of heaven – take alarm!   *Thomas Guthrie*

> Faint not, nor fear, his arms are near,
> He changeth not, and thou art dear;
> Only believe, and thou shalt see
> That Christ is all in all to thee.   *J S B Monsell*

> Thou art the Way.
> Hadst thou been nothing but the goal
> I cannot say
> If thou hadst ever met my soul.

> I'll not reproach
> The road that winds, my feet that err.
> Access, Approach
> Art though, Time, Way, and Wayfarer.   *Alice Meynell*

THE WILL – WEAK OR STRONG   August 16

My own behaviour baffles me. For I find myself doing what I really loathe but not doing what I really want to do... But it cannot be said that 'I' am doing them at all – it must be sin that has made its home in my nature.   *Romans 7:15 and 17*

The enemy held my will and of it he made a chain and bound me. Because my will was perverse, it was changed to lust and lust yielded to become habit, and habit not resisted became necessity. My two wills, one old one new, one carnal one spiritual, were in conflict and in their conflict wasted my soul.
                                        St Augustine

Your life is without foundation if, in any matter, you choose on your own behalf.   *Dag Hammarskjöld*

Make this simple rule the guide of your life: to have no will but God's.   *Archbishop François Fénelon*

When we pray, 'Come, Holy Ghost, our souls inspire', we had better know what we are about. We cannot call upon the Creator Spirit in order to use omnipotence for the supply of our futile pleasures or the success of our futile plans. If we invoke him, we must be ready for the glorious pain of being caught by his power out of our petty orbit into the eternal purposes of the Almighty, in whose onward sweep our lives are as a speck of dust. The soul that is filled with the Spirit must have become purged of all pride or love of ease, all self-complacence or self-reliance; but that soul has found the only real dignity, the only lasting joy.

Come then, Great Spirit, come. Convict the world; and convict my timid soul.   *Archbishop William Temple*

SERENITY   August 17

It means bitter pain and agony for every human soul who works on the side of evil... But there is glory and honour and peace for every worker on the side of good.   *Romans 2:9-10*

We need the peace of God in our heart just as really for the doing well of the little things of our secular life as for the doing of the greatest duties of Christ's kingdom... We want heart-peace before we begin any day's duties, and we should wait at Christ's feet ere we go forth.   *J R Miller*

I think there is a place... for a sort of contemplation of the good, not just by dedicated experts but by ordinary people; an attention which is not just the planning of particular good actions but an attempt to look right away from self towards a distant transcendent perfection, a source of uncontaminated energy, a source of new and quite undreamt of virtue.   *Iris Murdoch*

Give us, O God, the vision that can see thy love in the world in spite of human failure. Give us the faith, the trust, the goodness in spite of our ignorance and weakness. Give us the knowledge that we may continue to pray with understanding hearts, and show us what each of us can do to set forth the coming of the day of universal peace.
Frank Bormann, Apollo 8, Christmas Eve 1968

INSIGHT   August 18

But it is the spirit of Almighty God that comes to human beings and gives them wisdom.   *Job 32:8 GNB*

Jesus did not need anyone to tell him what people were like; he understood human nature.   *John 2:25*

God has given you all a certain amount of spiritual insight.
1 John 2:20-21

Understanding is the reward of faith. Therefore do not seek to understand that you may believe, but believe that you may understand.   *St Augustine*

Such insights eventually brought me to realise how deeply sin resides not just in the many things that I do wrong but in the fact that I myself am wrong; that my nature, by itself, is so warped and marred that it is beyond my power to put it right... That is why we need a Saviour; to save us from ourselves, not just our actions.   *K D Belden*

God is always with us; why should we not always be with God?   *Archbishop William Ullathorne*

THE PURPOSE OF LIVING   August 19

This is the plan prepared for the whole earth, this the hand stretched out over all the nations. For the Lord of hosts has prepared his plan. Who shall frustrate it?   *Isaiah 14:26-27 NEB*

All who are ignorant of the purpose for which they live are fools and mad.   *John Calvin*

Jesus said that there were really two main principles of living on which all true morality and wisdom might be said to depend. The first was to love God with the whole personality, and the second to love everyone else as much and in the same way as you naturally loved yourself. If these two principles were obeyed, Christ said that you would be in harmony with the purpose of life, which transcends time.   *Canon J B Phillips*

God has a purpose and a plan – not only for the world but for every individual in it and for the smallest details in the life of the individual.   *Canon B H Streeter*

Almighty God, to whom great matters are never too great, and the smallest details never too small.   *Pope Gregory I*

The end of life is not to deny self, nor to be true, nor to keep the Ten Commandments – it is simply to do God's will.
Professor Henry Drummond

THE PURPOSE OF LIVING II   August 20

This is good and pleases God our Saviour who wants everyone to be saved and to come to know the truth. For there is one God and there is one who brings God and human beings together, the man Christ Jesus.   *1 Timothy 2:4-5 GNB*

An American doctor asked a militant young nationalist in Kenya (c1965), 'If you were speaking to American leaders, what would you ask for your country?' He said, 'I would ask them for teachers, doctors, engineers and all the people we need to help raise our standard of living.' He paused, then added with passion, 'But above all, we need young men and women who by godly discipline and purpose in their own lives can give our youth a new direction.'   *P M*

Free people are those who, as responsible children of the living God, fear no one, and aim towards total freedom from hate and fear and lust and arrogance.   *H P E*

It is a contradiction in terms to say that God exists but has no plan. And to say that his plan can only contemplate the big outline and not the minor details is to reduce his intelligence to the scale of ours.   *Canon B H Streeter*

THE ONLY THING THAT MATTERS   August 21

I look upon everything as loss compared with the overwhelming gain of knowing Christ Jesus my Lord... For now my place is in him and I am not dependent upon any of the self-achieved righteousness of the law.   *Philippians 3:8*

If there is anything in your life more demanding than longing after God, then you will never be a Spirit-filled Christian.
                                                                    A W Tozer

The chief characteristic of the devil, we have been told, is that he is a liar. In no sphere does this quality appear more vividly than in the whispers to the mind when instinct has very little control. 'Everyone does it', 'After all it's natural'... For the mind that is clear, these ancient slogans of compromise will be labelled for what they are and the mind will be on guard against the sophistry that tries to make right what it knows to be wrong.   *Kenaston Twitchell*

If you want to be of use get rightly related to Jesus Christ and he will make you of use.   *Oswald Chambers*

Consider the postage stamp; its usefulness consists in the ability to stick to one thing till it gets there.   *Josh Billings*

THIS ONE THING   August 22

I do concentrate on this: I forget all that lies behind me and with hands outstretched to whatever lies ahead I go straight for the

goal – my reward the honour of my high calling by God in
Christ Jesus.   *Philippians 3:13-14*

St Augustine, after his acceptance of the Christian faith at the
age of 32, wrote: Then we went in to my mother and told her, to
her great joy. We related how it had come about; she was filled
with triumphant exultation, and praised you who are mighty
beyond what we ask or conceive; for she saw that you had
given her more than, with all her pitiful weeping, she had ever
asked.   *St Monica had prayed for her son for 32 years*

I do not say I am without sin. I do say I live for one thing only,
to make Jesus Christ regnant in the life of everyone I meet.
                              Dr Frank N D Buchman

'This one thing I do' – to seek and obey God's will and to live
for others to find him – simplifies all the complexities of life and
is the secret of effective living.   *H P E*

THE PRACTICE OF THE PRESENCE   August 23

And he said, Go forth, and stand upon the mount before the
Lord. And behold, the Lord passed by, and a great and strong
wind rent the mountains, and brake in pieces the rocks before
the Lord; but the Lord was not in the wind; and after the wind
an earthquake; but the Lord was not in the earthquake: and after the earthquake a fire; but the Lord was not in the fire: and
after the fire a still small voice.   *1 Kings 19:11-12*

How can you expect God to speak in that gentle and inward
voice which melts the soul, when you are making so much
noise with your rapid reflections? Be silent and God will speak
again.   *Archbishop François Fénelon*

Our aim, remember, is to put our lives under God's control, and
find out whether he can speak clearly enough in our hearts for
us to know the steps he wants us to take. In all probability there
are things in our lives which will have to be cleared up before
God can really take control; and the first word God says to us
will be about these. At any rate let us begin by sitting quietly
for a few minutes thinking of our life in the light of what we
already know of God's will. The summary of Christ's teaching

under the headings of absolute honesty, absolute purity, absolute unselfishness and absolute love will help us.   *Rev Cecil Rose*

POWER TO FINISH   August 24

The Christ you have to deal with is not a weak person outside you but a tremendous power inside you. He was 'weak' enough to be crucified, yes, but he now lives by the power of God.

2 Corinthians 13:3-4

When Stanley went out to Africa in 1871 and found Livingstone, he spent months in his company, but Livingstone never spoke to Stanley about spiritual things. Throughout those months Stanley watched the old man. Livingstone's habits were beyond his comprehension and so was his patience. He could not understand Livingstone's sympathy for the Africans. For the sake of Christ and his gospel, the missionary doctor was patient, untiring, eager, spending himself and being spent for his master. Stanley wrote: 'When I saw that unwearied patience, that unflagging zeal, those enlightened sons of Africa, I became a Christian at his side, though he never spoke to me about it.'

Remember Jesus *for us* is all our righteousness before a holy God, and Jesus *in us* is all our strength in an ungodly world.

Robert Murray McCheyne

RESOLUTE TRUST   August 25

I will bless those who put their trust in me. They are like trees growing near a stream and sending out roots to the water.

Jeremiah 17:7-8 GNB

Jesus said: you must not let yourselves be distressed – you must hold on to your faith in me.   *John 14:1*

Many men and women believe that God is all-mighty and *may* do all; and that he is all-wisdom and *can* do all; but that he is all-love and *will* do all – there they stop short.

Mother Julian of Norwich

In all your affairs, rely wholly on God's Providence... Imitate little children, who with one hand hold fast to their father and with the other gather strawberries or blackberries along the hedges. So too, as you gather and handle the goods of this world with one hand, you must with the other always hold fast the hand of your heavenly Father, turning yourself to him from time to time to see if your actions or occupations be pleasing to him. *St Francis de Sales*

What is more elevating and transporting than the generosity of heart which risks everything on God's word?

Cardinal J H Newman

> He either fears his fate too much,
> Or his deserts are small,
> That dares not put it to the touch,
> To gain or lose it all. *Marquess of Montrose*

NOT IN OUR OWN STRENGTH   August 26

Apart from me you can do nothing at all... If you live your life in me, and my words live in your hearts, you can ask for whatever you like and it will come true for you. *John 15:5-7*

Some people are always telegraphing to heaven for God to send a cargo of blessings to them; but they are not at the wharfside to unload the cargo when it comes. *Rev F B Meyer*

One day his hostess went in to inspect Frank Buchman's room, not knowing that Frank was hidden in the part of the room formed by the 'L'. She heard Frank speaking. 'Lord,' he was saying, 'Lord, I can't do it.' She was deeply moved, learning as she could have learned in no other way what it cost Frank to make that Indian trip. But Frank's master had said, 'Go.' And he obeyed. It was indeed an undertaking of great heroism for a man who was unable to lift himself out of a chair or to walk unaided. But Frank uttered no complaint to anyone.

H W 'Bunny' Austin

Hold to Christ and for the rest be totally uncommitted.

Professor Herbert Butterfield

NONE OTHER THAT FIGHTETH FOR US

I will lift up mine eyes unto the hills, from whence cometh my help. My help cometh from the Lord, which made heaven and earth.   *Psalms 121:1-2*

God has said:
 'I will in no wise fail thee,
 Neither will I in any wise forsake thee.'
 We, therefore, can confidently say:
 'The Lord is my helper; I will not fear.'   *Hebrews 13:5-6*

The very vastness of the work raises one's thoughts to God, as the only one by whom it can be done. That is the solid comfort – he knows.   *Florence Nightingale*

I should as soon attempt to raise flowers if there were no atmosphere, or produce fruits if there were neither light nor heat as to regenerate people if I did not believe there was a Holy Spirit.
Henry Ward Beecher

Christ is the most unique person in history. No one can write a history of the human race without giving first and foremost place to the penniless teacher from Nazareth.   *H G Wells*

The whole future of the human race depends on bringing the individual soul more completely and perfectly under the sway of the Holy Spirit.   *Isaac T Hecker*

NOWHERE ELSE TO GO

God has given us eternal life, and this life has its source in his son. Whoever has the son has this life.   *1 John 5:11-12 GNB*

Philip said to him, 'Lord, show us the Father; that is all we need.'   *John 14:8 GNB*

I have been driven many times to my knees by the overwhelming conviction that I had nowhere else to go; my own wisdom and that of all around me seemed insufficient for that day.
President Abraham Lincoln

When we know what grace means, more than one precious thing emerges clearly. We know that our relationship to God depends not on our merits but on his love. We know that he loves us not for what we are, but because of what he himself is. We know that we are no longer left to face and fight life ourselves; but that there is open to us all the power and the strength of God. In grace there is release from the tension of unavailing effort, and the coming of power.   *Dr William Barclay*

God's promises of guidance are not given to save us the bother of thinking.   *Rev John R W Stott*

Always, when the situation seems impossible, God's guidance, when sought in the spirit of having nowhere else to go, becomes clear.   *P M and H P E*

OUR LIFE, NOT OUR HELPER   August 29

Then the word of the Lord came unto me saying... I ordained thee a prophet unto the nations. Then said I, Ah, Lord God! behold I cannot speak; for I am a child. But the Lord said unto me, Say not, I am a child; for thou shalt go to all that I shall send thee, and whatsoever I shall command thee that thou shalt speak. Be not afraid of their faces; for I am with thee to deliver thee, saith the Lord.   *Jeremiah 1:4-8*

I am come that they might have life and that they might have it more abundantly.   *John 10:10 AV*

Life is filled with meaning as soon as Jesus Christ enters into it.
Neil C Strait

Jesus Christ does not want to be our helper; he wants to be our life. He does not want us to work for him; he wants us to let him do his work through us, using us as we use a pencil to write with... The immediate, continual inspiration of God, as actually our only power of goodness, is our birthright, and must be our experience, if we are to live out God's will.
Andrew Murray

Life is designed to show us that God is enough for us.
Salvationist Catherine Booth at age of 100

171

GOD-GIVEN, NOT SELF-SOUGHT   August 30

I do assure you... that the gospel I preached to you is no human invention. No man gave it to me, no man taught it to me; it came to me as a direct revelation from Jesus Christ.

Galatians 1:11-12

No prophetic message ever came just from human will, but people were under the control of the Holy Spirit as they spoke the message that came from God.   *2 Peter 1:21 GNB*

Christ stimulates us, as no other great person stimulates us, but we find a power coming from him into our lives that enables us to respond. That is the experience that proves him to be the universal Spirit.   *Archbishop William Temple*

When God wants to move a mountain he does not take a bar of iron but he takes a little worm. The fact is that we have too much strength. We are not weak enough. It is not our strength we want. One drop of God's strength is worth more than all the world.   *Dwight L Moody*

What a man has, not from himself, but from God, he ought to regard not so much his own but God's. For no one has from himself the truth which he teaches or a righteous will but from God.   *St Anselm*

You will never need more than God can supply.   *J I Packer*

OUR KNOW-HOW OR GOD'S WISDOM   August 31

But if any of you lack wisdom, you should pray to God, who will give it to you; because God gives generously and graciously to all. But when you pray you must believe and not doubt at all.   *James 1:5-6 GNB*

Surely the essence of wisdom is that before we begin to act at all or attempt to please God, we should discover what it is that God has to say about the matter.   *Dr Martyn Lloyd-Jones*

Let your old age be childlike and your childhood like old age; that is, so that neither may your wisdom be with pride, nor your humility without wisdom.   *St Augustine*

It is a fact that those whose lives are daily being conformed to the word and purposes of God, will be given the ability to see issues more plainly.   *Malcolm Watts*

God grant me the serenity to accept things I cannot change, courage to change the things I can, and wisdom to know the difference.   *Reinhold Niebuhr*

HE IS COUNTING ON US

Jesus said: The prophets wrote, 'Everyone will be taught by God.' Anyone who hears the Father and learns from him comes to me.   *John 6:45*

To do the will of God – and only the will of God? It covers a wide field, from the factory floor, the office desk, the kitchen stove to career, money, the marriage bed, responsibility for the community and much else besides. It means not what I want but what Christ wants in every area of life. It means honesty, purity, unselfishness and love in every relationship, inside and outside the family. It means daily experience of the Cross.

K D Belden

The greatest gift which God of his bounty made at the creation, the gift most akin to his generosity, the gift which he values most highly, was the will's freedom, with which intelligent creatures, each and all, are endowed.   *Dante Alighieri*

When I respond to God's call, the call is God's and the response is mine; and yet the response is God's too; for not only does he call me in his grace, but also by his grace brings the response to birth within my soul.   *Professor John Baillie*

HE WILL FINISH WHAT
HE HAS BEGUN

Jude, a servant of Jesus Christ... to those who have obeyed the call, who are loved by God the Father and kept in the faith by Jesus Christ – may you ever experience more and more of mercy, peace and love!   *Jude 1*

Discipleship is not a slavish obedience to a set of principles, but a living dynamic contact with the person of Christ, who comes to indwell his disciples and live out his dynamic life within their beings. Every Christian is expected to be a first-class disciple, for there are no second-class citizens in the kingdom of God. The goal of discipleship is not simply to make us but to make us like Christ. For from the very beginning God decided that we should become like his son (*Romans 8:29*). At Pentecost the Holy Spirit came to make Christ available to each one of us, and places him not at our sides to be an instructor, but right at the core of our beings to be the driving force of our personalities.   *Rev Selwyn Hughes © CWR*

It is not finished, Lord.
There is not one thing done.
There is no battle of my life
That I have really won.
And now I come to tell thee
How I fought to fail,
My human, all too human, tale
Of weakness and futility.
And yet there is a faith in me,
That thou wilt find in it
One word that thou canst take
And make
The centre of a sentence
In thy book of poetry.   *G A Studdert-Kennedy*

After you have suffered a little while, the God of all grace, who has called you to his eternal glory in Christ, will himself restore, establish and strengthen you.   *1 Peter 5:10 RSV*

TRUST HIM   September 3

Trust in the Lord with all thine heart; and lean not unto thine own understanding. In all thy ways acknowledge him, and he shall direct thy paths.   *Proverbs 3:5-6*

He who trusts in himself is lost. He who trusts in God can do all things.   *St Alphonsus Liguori*

God expects us to trust him. Jesus was always grieved when the disciples failed in trust – when they woke him in panic during a storm or worried about lack of food. Trust is an act of will, which does not demand the security of certainty before it is made. It is an act of faith that God is love, and will do all in his good time and way.   *Dorothy M Prescott*

Cast off indecision, and doubt not in the least, when asking anything from God... Those who are divided in purpose waver before the Lord and altogether fail to obtain any of their requests. But those who are wholly perfect in the faith ask everything with reliance on the Lord and they receive.

Hermas in The Shepherd

God is full of compassion, and never fails those who are afflicted and despised, if they trust in him alone.

St Teresa of Avila

KNOCKING AT THE DOOR 1 September 4

'Ask, and you will receive; seek, and you will find; knock, and the door will be opened to you. For everyone who seeks will find, and the door will be opened to those who knock.

Matthew 7:7-8

The Light of the World is the title of a famous picture by Holman Hunt, painted in 1854. It portrays Christ, thorn-crowned, and carrying a lantern, knocking at a closed door. When the artist showed the completed picture to some friends, one pointed out what seemed to be an omission. 'You have put no handle on the door,' he said to Holman Hunt. The artist replied, 'We must open to the Light – the handle is on the inside.'

Anthony P Castle

Jesus told us 'to knock', 'to seek' and 'to ask', by which I understand him to mean that although the resources of God are always available, it is up to us to make use of them. I think too, that he may well have meant us to make spiritual experiments to try out, as it were, the divine resources.   *Canon J B Phillips*

Shame on us for being paupers when we were meant to be princes.   *Dr Martyn Lloyd-Jones*

KNOCKING AT THE DOOR 2 September 5

For all those who ask will receive, and those who seek will find, and the door will be opened to anyone who knocks.

Luke 11:10 GNB

We can accept what Christ has done without knowing how it works; indeed we certainly won't know how it works until we've accepted it.   *C S Lewis*

We have not to be discouraged because the answer does not come immediately... The world looks on to see how we shall behave ourselves under special trials and difficulties, what we shall do. If they find us waiting without fretting, without complaining, and especially without murmuring, then they may perceive that we are looking after the things of God and this may lead to blessing too.   *George Müller*

The daughter of Karl Marx once confessed to a friend that she had never been brought up in any religion and had never been religious. 'But', she said, 'the other day I came across a beautiful little prayer which I very much wish could be true.' 'And what was the prayer?' she was asked. Slowly the daughter of Karl Marx began repeating in German, 'Our Father, which art in heaven...'   *Robert Latham*

If you would have God hear you when you pray, you must hear him when he speaks.   *Thomas Brooks*

MY PEACE I GIVE UNTO YOU   September 6

Whenever you pray tell God every detail of your needs in thankful prayer, and the peace of God, which surpasses human understanding, will keep constant guard over your hearts and minds as they rest in Christ Jesus.   *Philippians 4:7*

How blest are the peacemakers. God shall call them his sons.
                                          Matthew 5:9

Peace flows from purity.   *Thomas Watson*

The peace of the soul consists in an absolute resignation to the will of God.   *Archbishop François Fénelon*

The springs of human conflict cannot be eradicated through institutions, but only through the reform of the human being.
                              General Douglas MacArthur

Peace is not an absence of war, it is a virtue, a state of mind, a disposition for benevolence, confidence, justice.

Baruch de Spinoza

Drop thy still dews of quietness,
Till all our strivings cease;
Take from our souls the strain and stress
And let our ordered lives confess
The beauty of thy peace.   *John Greenleaf Whittier*

GOD'S OVER-RULING PROVIDENCE   September 7

Look at the birds in the sky. They never sow nor reap nor store away in barns, and yet your heavenly Father feeds them. Aren't you much more valuable to him than they are?   *Matthew 6:26*

God's providence is not in baskets lowered from the sky, but through the hands and hearts of those who love him. The lad without food and without shoes made the proper answer to the cruel-minded woman who asked, 'But if God loved you, wouldn't he send you food and shoes?' The boy replied, 'God told someone, but he forgot.'   *George Butterick*

The acts of our maker ought always to be reverenced without examining, for they can never be unjust.   *Pope St Gregory I*

Lord, be thy word my rule,
In it may I rejoice,
Thy glory be my aim,
Thy promises my hope,
Thy holy will my choice,
Thy providence my guard,
Thine arm my strong support,
Thyself my great reward.

Bishop Christopher Wordsworth

GOD AT THE WHEEL   September 8

More than once I have heard God say that power belongs to him and that his love is constant. You yourself, O Lord, reward everyone according to his deeds.   *Psalms 62:11-12 GNB*

178

Christ was 'weak' enough to be crucified, yes, but he lives now by the power of God. We are weak as he was weak, but we are strong enough to deal with you for we share his life by the power of God.   *2 Corinthians 13:4*

It remains true that all things are possible with God; the intrinsic impossibilities are not things but non-entities.   *C S Lewis*

> No strength of our own or goodness we claim;
> Yet, since we have known the Saviour's great name,
> In this our strong tower for safety we hide, –
> The Lord is our power, the Lord will provide.
>
> *John Newton*

I am gradually learning to accept my age and to trust God and the Holy Spirit, rather than my own activism.   *Garth Lean*

> He wakes desires you never may forget,
> He shows you stars you never saw before,
> He makes you share the world's divine regret.
> How wise you were to open not – and yet
> How poor if you should turn him from the door.
>
> *Sydney Lynsight*

GOD IN NATURE   September 9

God saw all that he had made and it was very good.*Genesis 1:31*

Everything God made is good, and is meant to be gratefully used, not despised.   *1 Timothy 4:4*

When I love my God what is it that I love? I asked the earth and it answered, 'I am not he,' and everything that is in it said the same.

I asked the sea, the depths and the living creeping things, and they replied, 'We are not your God, seek above us.'

So I said to all these things that stand round the doors of my senses, 'Tell me about my God, since you are not he; tell me something of him.'

With a loud voice they cried out, 'He made us.'

My questioning them was my mind's desire, and their beauty was their answer.   *St Augustine*

Every flower of the field, every fibre of a plant, every particle of an insect, carries with it the impress of its maker, and can – if duly considered – read us lectures of ethics or divinity.

Thomas P Blount

What are the heavens, the earth, the sea, but a sheet of royal paper, written all over with the wisdom and power of God?

Thomas Brooks

ART IN THE SERVICE OF GOD   September 10

The heavens declare the glory of God; and the firmament showeth his handiwork.   *Psalms 19:1*

I believe the artist needs to be certain of and dependent on the existence of a creator, who not only made us but from whom we can receive strength and wisdom with which to continue our life on earth.   *W Heaton Cooper – Lakeland artist*

Some years ago I stood in a cathedral in Copenhagen, admiring as thousands before me, the beautiful statue known as Thorwaldsen's Christ. As I lingered there, deep in thought and admiration, a friend whispered: 'If you want to see the face, you must kneel before the feet.'   *Rev Selwyn Hughes © CWR*

We must create an art which is dangerous to evil.

Professor Lennart Segerstråle

All great art is the expression of man's delight in God's work, not his own.   *John Ruskin*

St Philip Neri lived in an age when literature and the arts were receiving their fullest development. He was anxious not to destroy or supersede, but to sanctify poetry and history and painting and music.   *Cardinal J H Newman*

HARMONY   September 11

Moreover we know that to those who love God, who are called according to his plan, everything that happens fits into a pattern for good.   *Romans 8:28*

Contentment with the divine will is the best remedy we can apply to misfortune... In the days of his earthly ministry, only those could speak to him who came where he was... But his ascension means that he is perfectly united with God; we are with him wherever we are present to God and this is everywhere and always.   *Archbishop William Temple*

What else can I do, a lame old man, but sing hymns to God? If I were a nightingale, I would do the nightingale's part; if I were a swan, I would do as a swan. But now I am a rational creature, and I ought to praise God; this is my work; I do it, nor will I desert my post, so long as I am allowed to keep it. And I exhort you to join me in this same song.   *Epictetus*

The glorious company of the Apostles praise thee. The goodly fellowship of the Prophets praise thee. The noble army of Martyrs praise thee... We therefore pray thee, help thy servants: whom thou hast redeemed with thy precious blood.

Book of Common Prayer

TREASURING THE MOMENT   September 12

Those who think they know something really don't know as they ought to know. But the person who loves God is known by him.   *1 Corinthians 8:2 GNB*

For it is in him, and in him alone, that all the treasures of wisdom and knowledge lie hidden.   *Colossians 2:3*

Every moment brings us more treasures than we can gather. The great value of the Now, spiritually viewed, is that it carries a message God has directed personally to us.

Bishop Fulton Sheen

Every person born into this world represents something new, something that has never existed before, something original and unique... and is called upon to fulfil his particular role in the world.   *Martin Buber*

There are two basic ways to learn... The first could be described as external listening, scholastic, catechistic and cultural. It means learning what the Lord has said. There is another way of learning, to listen to our inmost self. This gives a predominant place to the relationship between God and individuals.

Pope Paul VI

God's order, his good pleasure, his will, work and grace – as long as we live, all this is one and the same thing, God operating to make the soul like himself. Perfection is no more and no less than the soul's faithful co-operation in this work of God. Secretly and without our knowledge this purpose is realised in our souls, growing and increasing and being fulfilled.

J P de Caussade

MAN'S DEEPEST NEEDS September 13

My God will supply all that you need from his glorious riches in Christ Jesus. And may glory be to God and our Father for ever and ever. *Philippians 4:19-20*

The greatest need of mankind today – socially and individually – is a true sense of direction. Our world is like an Atlantic liner deprived of rudder, compass, sextant, charts and wireless tackle, yet compelled to go full steam ahead. There is magnificence, comfort, pulsating power... Is there available for man, if he so will, guidance in his dark and dangerous course from some wisdom higher than his own? *Canon B H Streeter*

It is very obvious that what is needed is not an effort, however well meant, to re-mould the Christian faith to suit the tastes of a crumbling civilisation, but resolute directing of the world's attention to the true content and promise of that faith. That way lies the hope of God's answer solving the basic problem – human nature – and sees our part fulfilled so long as we are living no longer by the dictates of our sinful nature, but in obedience to the prompting of the Holy Spirit. *J M Morrison*

Behold my needs, which I know not myself; see and do according to thy tender mercy. *Archbishop François Fénelon*

A HEAVENLY BANKING ACCOUNT   September 14

If you love money, you will never be satisfied; if you long to be rich, you will never get all you want. It is useless.

Ecclesiastes 5:10 GNB

You cannot serve God and the power of money at the same time.   *Luke 16:13*

There is none, in this whole city, who can say that I ever asked them for a penny; there is none, in the whole of England, who can say that I ever asked them for a penny; there is none under heaven, in the whole wide world, who can say that I ever asked them for a penny. To God, and to God alone, I went; and I did this because I knew ever since my conversion that one of the greatest necessities for the Church of God at large was an increase of faith. Therefore I determined to dedicate my whole life to this one great lesson, for the Church of God to learn and the world at large to learn: real, true, lasting dependence on God...

Greater and more manifest nearness of the Lord's presence I have never had than when after breakfast there were no means for dinner for more than 100 persons; or when after dinner there were no means for the tea, and yet the Lord provided the tea; and all this without one single human having been informed of our need.   *George Müller*

Nothing that is God's is obtainable by money.   *Tertullian*

> Boundless is thy love for me,
> Boundless then my trust shall be.   *Robert Bridges*

WHAT IS TRUE WEALTH?   September 15

Jesus looked steadily at him, and his heart warmed towards him. Then he said, 'There is one thing you still need. Go and sell everything you have and give the money away to the poor – you will have riches in heaven. And then come back and follow me.' At these words his face fell and he went away in deep distress, for he was very rich.   *Matthew 10:21-22*

The real measure of our wealth is how much we'd be worth if we lost all our money.   *John Henry Jowett*

It is preoccupation with possession, more than anything else, that prevents people from living freely and nobly.

Bertrand Russell

God is generous, but he also has the needs of the world and the advance of the kingdom in mind. Discipline over the use of resources applies as much to people with incomes, small or substantial, as it does to people who have lived without salary for many years. Large or small, what we have is meant to be at God's disposal once our commitment is made.   *K D Belden*

He is rich enough who is poor in Christ.   *St Jerome*

We have 'nothing to bless ourselves with' yet we bless many others with true riches. We are penniless, and yet in reality we have everything worth having.   *2 Corinithians 6:10*

'NOT YOURS, BUT YOU'   September 16

Not that I claim to have achieved (this knowledge of Christ), nor to have reached perfection already. But I keep going on, trying to grasp that purpose for which Christ Jesus grasped me.

Philippians 3:12

Suppose a man should make a ring for his fiancée, and she should love the ring more than the man who made it for her... Certainly let her love his gift, but what would we think of her if she should say, 'The ring is enough; I do not want to see his face again'? The man gave her the pledge just that he might himself be loved. God then has given you all these things. Love him who made them.   *St Augustine*

Frank Buchman, asked why he was so free from the preoccupation with minor matters and the anxieties besetting most people, and so unusually sensitive to the needs and welfare of others, replied: 'I once made the decision never to think of myself again.' To live out such a decision requires a determined switching of thought every time the demands for security, sex and success tempt us to self-centredness.   *Paul Campbell*

> Make me a captive, Lord,
> And then I shall be free;

184

Force me to render up my sword,
And I shall conqueror be.
I sink in life's alarms
When by myself I stand;
Imprison me within thine arms,
And strong shall be my hand.   *George Matheson*

STEWARDSHIP   September 17

But the Lord continued, 'Well, who will be the faithful, sensible
steward whom his master will put in charge of his household to
give them their supplies at the proper time? Happy is the servant if his master finds him so doing when he returns.
                                                    Luke 12:42-43

Another came saying, 'Lord behold here is thy pound which I
have kept laid up in a napkin; for I feared thee. And he saith
unto him, 'Thou wicked servant.'   *Luke 19:20-22*

It may be hard for a rich man to enter the kingdom of heaven,
but we have it on the same authority that admission is not to be
bought with a talent buried in a napkin.   *Geoffrey Faber*

Stewardship is the acceptance from God of personal responsibility for all of life and life's affairs.   *Roswell C Long*

Trusteeship brings the idea of accountability in this world before humans and before God in the life hereafter. We shall have
to develop social accounting... These concepts have important
economic consequences.
            *Prince Mohammad Al-Faisal Al-Saoud, Chairman of the
            International Association of Islamic Banks*

GOD'S PROVISION   September 18

Now to him who by his power within us is able to do infinitely
more than we ever dare to ask or imagine – to him be glory.
                                                    Ephesians 3:20-21

'Open thy mouth wide, and I will fill it;' this is, 'Ask great blessings from me, very great blessings, and I am ready to bestow them.' O what a precious, glorious promise for poor weak ones, as we are. 'Open thy mouth wide, and I will fill it.' The great point is to apply this to our various particular positions, and to the circumstances in which we are placed. *George Müller*

He did not say 'You will be spared storms, toil and suffering.' He did say, 'You will not be overcome.' God wants us to take these words seriously, so that in certain truth we may be strong, in good times and in bad. *Mother Julian of Norwich*

Wants are the fountains of felicity. *Thomas Traherne*

ENLIGHTENED SELF-INTEREST: IS IT ENOUGH? September 19

The wisdom that comes from above is first pure, then peace-loving, gentle, approachable, full of merciful thoughts and kindly actions, straightforward with no hint of hypocrisy.
James 3:17

I used to think enlightened self-interest was a good enough motive for anyone. Now I see that nobody can trust you on that basis. People are afraid that you will be their friend as long as you think it is in your interest, but that they will be discarded when it suits you. Behind my motive of self-interest was really a determination to be right and successful.
A Wall Street banker

Our strongest instinct is to self-preservation; grace's highest call is to self-sacrifice. *Paul Frost*

If employers change their motivation, is it possible to put people before money? The answer is 'yes'. It has happened in my family and industry in the last 45 years. Three times when it seemed economically impossible, my company has created employment to keep men working – in 1933, in the fifties and three years ago. When we have had difficult trading conditions I have taken a cut in salary in order to keep people working.
John Vickers

ENOUGH FOR EVERYONE'S NEED   September 20

If there be among you a poor man of one of thy brethren within any of the gates in thy land... thou shalt not harden thine heart, nor shut thine hand from thy poor brother. But thou shalt open thine hand wide unto him, and thou shalt surely lend him sufficient for his need.   *Deuteronomy 15:7-8*

Do you remember the generosity of Jesus Christ, the Lord of us all? He was rich, yet he became poor for your sakes so that his poverty might make you rich.   *2 Corinthians 8:9*

The king will say: I was an hungered, and ye gave me meat; I was thirsty and ye gave me drink; I was a stranger and ye took me in; naked and ye clothed me, I was sick and ye visited me; I was in prison and ye came unto me... Inasmuch as ye have done it unto one of the least of my brethren ye have done it unto me.
Matthew 25: 35-36,40 AV

When we come before our heavenly Father and he says, 'Did you feed them, did you give them to drink, did you clothe them, did you shelter them?' and we say, 'Sorry Lord, but we did give them 0.3 percent of our gross national product,' I don't think it will be enough.   *Barbara Ward*

The rich may have to live more simply, that the poor may simply live.   *Club of Rome*

THE ECONOMICS OF   September 21
UNSELFISHNESS

Jesus sat opposite the Temple alms box and watched the people putting their money into it. A great many rich people put in large sums. Then a poor widow came and dropped in two little coins... Jesus said to his disciples: 'This poor widow has put in more than all the others. For they have all put in what they can easily afford, but she in her poverty who needs so much, has given away her whole living.'   *Mark 12:41-43*

In this interdependent economic world, the doctrine of 'every nation for itself' is as dangerous a philosophy as the doctrine of 'every man for himself.'   *Prime Minister Harold Wilson*

The cause of this world's state is not economic; the cause is moral. It is there where the evil lies. It is the want of religion which we ought to possess. If I may use a phrase which is common in a great movement in this country and elsewhere, what you want are God-guided personalities which make God-guided nationalities, to make a new world. All other ideas of economic adjustment are too small really to touch the centre of the evil.   *The Marquess of Salisbury,*
                        Speaking in the House of Lords, 1936

The man who lives by himself for himself is apt to be corrupted by the company he keeps.   *Charles H Parkhurst*

LIFE'S HARVEST   September 22

Do not deceive yourselves; no one makes a fool of God! People will reap exactly what they sow. If they sow in the field of their natural desires, from it they will gather the harvest of death; if they sow in the field of the Spirit they will gather the harvest of eternal life.   *Galatians 6:7-8 GNB*

Five years ago I came to believe in Christ's teaching and my life suddenly changed. I ceased to desire what I had previously desired, and began to desire what I formerly did not want. What had previously seemed to me good seemed evil. It happened to me as it happens to a man who goes out on some business and on the way suddenly decides that the business is unnecessary and returns home.   *Count Leo Tolstoy*

If we have been defeated let us not be discouraged; there is forgiveness. But do not let us think lightly of defeat, as though it did not matter. It cost God Calvary to forgive my 'smallest' sin.   *Amy Carmichael*

Let us endeavour so to live that when we come to die even the undertaker will be sorry.   *Mark Twain*

MONEY – SERVANT OR TYRANT?   September 23

For the love of money is the source of all kinds of evil. Some have been so eager to have it that they have wandered away from the faith and have broken their hearts with many sorrows.

1 Timothy 6:10 GNB

It is no regret to me that I was not the son of a rich man. My father indeed had riches but of the mind, not of the pocket. The least valuable thing a parent can endow a strong healthy son with is money. Counsel, correction and example should count for more in equipping him for the battle of life.   *Lord Nuffield*

Money can buy the husk of many things, but not the kernel. It buys you food but not appetite; medicine but not health; acquaintances but not friends; servants but not faithfulness; days of joy but not peace and happiness.   *Henrik Ibsen*

Money, needless to say, is one of the places where we are most reluctant to yield control. 'Capital is sacred', even from God... True commitment means that all our resources – income, capital, possessions, prospects – are given to God to use as he directs.   *K D Belden*

Money certainly provides the basic necessities of life and for some it is the main purpose of living. But money never made anyone rich in peace of mind or real purpose.   *P M*

SACRIFICE, NOT SURPLUS   September 24

I will not offer to the Lord my God whole offerings that have cost me nothing.   *2 Samuel 24:24 NEB*

The principle of sacrifice is that we choose to do or to suffer what, apart from our love, we should not choose to do or to suffer.   *Archbishop William Temple*

When Kim Beazley entered the Australian Parliament at the age of 28, he was tipped as Prime Minister of a future Labour Government. In 1953, however, he reached a profound turning point in his personal life and public career. 'I have made a decision,' he said, 'to concern myself daily with the challenge of how to live out God's will; to turn the searchlight of absolute honesty on to my motives; to try to see the world with the clarity of absolute purity; to take as radar through the fog of international affairs absolute love.'... Wrote Alan Reid, at that time doyen of Australia's political journalists, 'Powerful, office-hungry individuals fear that his idealism and his current determination to pursue the truth, whatever the price, could cost the Labour Party the next election. The story they are assiduously peddling is, "Beazley has lost his balance." So the word has gone out, "Destroy him!"' They neither destroyed Beazley nor deflected him from his purpose. He was ultimately elected to the second highest office in the party and became Minister for Education.   *Authors of* The Secret

A WORLD BUILT FOR HEROISM   September 25

One day a longing came over David, and he exclaimed, 'If only I could have a drink of water from the well by the gate of Bethlehem!' At this the heroic three made their way through the Philistine lines and drew water from the well by the gate of Bethlehem and brought it to David. But David refused to drink it; he poured it out to the Lord and said, 'God forbid that I should do such a thing! Can I drink the blood of these men who risked their lives for it?'   *2 Samuel 23:15-17 NEB*

Martyred for his faith in AD 145, Polycarp, Bishop of Smyrna, in answer to the request, 'Have some respect for your age. Swear by the divinity of Caesar. If you take the oath I will let you go,' replied: '86 years have I served him and he has done me no wrong. How then can I blaspheme my Saviour and King?'

Nothing less than a living sacrifice is demanded. Not a loan, but a gift; not a compromise, but a sacrifice; not our poorest, but our best; not a dead but a living offering. Each drop of our blood, each ounce of our energy, each throb of our heart we must offer to God.   *Joseph Pearce*

A saint is not faultless: he does not always think or behave wisely: one who has occasion to oppose him is not always wrong or foolish... He, or she, is canonised because his personal daily life was lived, not merely well, but at an heroic level of Christian faithfulness and integrity.   *Donald Attwater*

190

ONE INCREASING PURPOSE   September 26

I alone know my purpose for you, says the Lord... If you invoke
me and pray to me, I will listen to you. If you search with all
your heart, I will let you find me, says the Lord.

Jeremiah 29:11-13 NEB

This is good and it pleases God our Saviour, who wants everyone to be saved and to come to know the truth.

1 Timothy 2:4 GNB

A little one shall become a thousand, and a small one a strong
nation: I the Lord will hasten it in his time.   *Isaiah 60:22*

To put the world in order we must first put the nation in order;
to put the nation in order we must first put the family in order;
to put the family in order, we must cultivate our personal life,
we must first set our hearts right.   *Confucius*

Every life should have a purpose to which it can give the energies of its mind and the enthusiasms of its heart. That life without a purpose, will be a prey to the perverted ways waiting for
the uncommitted life.   *Neil C Strait*

> I have life before me still
> And thy purpose to fulfil;
> Yea, a debt to pay thee yet;
> Help me, sir, and so I will.   *Gerard Manley Hopkins*

GROWING   September 27

We are not meant to remain as children at the mercy of every
chance wind of teaching and the jockeying of men who are expert in the crafty presentation of lies. But we are meant to hold
firmly to the truth in love, and to grow up in every way into
Christ, the head.   *Ephesians 4:14,15*

Growth is the only evidence of life.   *Cardinal J H Newman*

There was a Chinese diplomat at this party... I went up and in-
troduced myself. We started talking... He said (about the Christians in China): 'They were intensely interested in people's
souls. And they were very interested in filling their churches.
But we (Communists) were interested in the nation. We had a

191

plan for the nation. That's why we won China.'   *Peter Howard*

Happy is he who makes daily progress and who considers not what he did yesterday but what advance he can make today.
St Jerome

I am the sort of man who writes because he has made progress, and makes progress – by writing.   *St Augustine*

NOT CHANGE OF CONDUCT   September 28
BUT CHANGE OF CHARACTER

He that walketh uprightly walketh surely.   *Proverbs 10:9*

Anyone who is joined to Christ is a new being; the old is gone, the new has come.   *2 Corinthians 5:17 GNB*

Those who are simply living in the world and growing characters, however finely they may be developing their character, cannot understand too plainly that they are not fulfilling God's will. They are really outside a great part of God's will altogether... they miss the private part, the secret whispering of God to the ear, the constant message from earth to heaven, 'Lord what wilt thou have me to do.'
Professor Henry Drummond

It was said of Bishop Logan Roots of China: 'His concern was to develop people of character and have them placed at the service of the nation.'

WILL CHANGE OF   September 29
CIRCUMSTANCES DO IT?

I have learned to be content whatever the circumstances may be. I know now how to live when things are difficult and I know how to live when things are prosperous.
Philippians 4:11-12

I have suffered from ill-health during the last few years. To a large extent this was my own fault, for I accepted hundreds of demands on my time which were out of all proportion to my real strength... I have read a great deal during the last few years, but I have never discovered anything that even remotely helps those who have to endure such times of depression unless it be found in, or derived from, the teachings of Jesus Christ.

Canon J B Phillips

Difficulties are the voice of God speaking to us. God speaks to us through events, through circumstances. And when these are hard to bear he is trying to make us less reliant upon ourselves, teaching us to have more confidence in him... Difficulties are not obstacles between God and ourselves – they are the way to him... This carrying of the cross is totally compatible with peace, security, happiness.   *Cardinal Basil Hume*

Difficulties prove people.   *Johannes von Goethe*

WILLINGNESS TO CHANGE   September 30

All of us who are Christians have no veils on our faces but reflect like mirrors the glory of the Lord. We are transformed in ever increasing splendour into his own image, and this is the work of the Lord who is the Spirit.   *1 Corinthians 3:18*

How do you change? By listening to God; because as the sun is always shining, so God is constantly speaking. How do you listen to God? The best time is in the morning before all distractions and activities intervene. How can I listen to God, you ask me. This is the answer: you write.   *Père Alphonse Gratry*

There are no galley slaves in the royal vessel of divine love – every person works his oar voluntarily.

Bishop Jean Pierre Camus

The Cross is something that can be taken up or left, just as we choose. It is not illness (that comes to all) or bereavement (that also is the common lot of us all). It is something voluntarily suffered for the sake of the Lord Jesus, some denial of self, that would not be if we were not following him.   *Amy Carmichael*

SELF-DISCIPLINE   October 1

Everyone has to be consecrated by the fire of the discipline.
Mark 9:49 Moffatt

Leonore is a young Australian. After graduating from university, she spent eight unhappy and disillusioning months on the
dole, and became very bitter and full of self-pity. 'It destroys a
lot in you if you don't know why you're alive,' she said... 'How
dare God put me through such misery?' Soon there was nothing
left but prayer. A 'clear quiet voice' seemed to say to her: 'You
get your relationship with me straight and everything else will
fall into place.'.. 'Slowly, as I began to put God first in every
area of my life,' she said, 'my bitterness was healed, I escaped
from the prison of self-pity and discovered not only a reason for
existing but also a true sense of direction and purpose.'
Authors of The Secret

What we must look for here (in education) is firstly, religious
and moral principles; secondly, gentlemanly conduct; thirdly,
intellectual ability. *Thomas Arnold, Headmaster of Rugby 1828–42*

You give but little when you give of your possessions. It is
when you give of yourself that you truly give.   *Khalil Gibran*

A MIRACLE OF THE SPIRIT   October 2

If our lives are centred in the Spirit, let us be guided by the
Spirit... The Spirit produces in human life fruits such as these:
love, joy, peace, patience, kindness, generosity, fidelity, tolerance and self-control.   *Galatians 5:25,22–23*

The world needs a miracle. Miracles of science have been the
wonder of the age. But they have not brought peace and happiness to the nations. A miracle of the Spirit is what we need.
Dr Frank N D Buchman

The divine art of miracle is not an art of suspending the pattern
to which events conform but of feeding new events into the pattern.   *C S Lewis*

The Incarnation is the most stupendous event which can ever
take place on earth, and after it and henceforth I do not see how

we can scruple at any miracle on the ground of it being unlikely
to happen. *Cardinal J H Newman*

God made us and we wonder at it. *Spanish Proverb*

The whole future of the human race depends on bringing the
individual soul completely and perfectly under the sway of the
Holy Spirit. *Isaac T Hecker*

SIMPLICITY October 3

Thy testimonies are wonderful; therefore doth my soul keep
them. The entrance of thy words giveth light; it giveth understanding unto the simple. *Psalms 119:129–130*

Love's secret is always to be doing things for God and not to
mind because they are such very little ones. *Frederick W Faber*

A holy Christian life is made up of a number of small things:
Little words, not eloquent sermons;
Little deeds, not miracles of battle
Or one great, heroic deed of martyrdom;
The little constant sunbeam, not the lightning.
Andrew Bonar

Should not the little things of our daily life be as relatively perfect as the lesser creatures of God (a butterfly's wing) are absolutely perfect? Ought we not to glorify God in the formation of
each letter that we write, and as Christians to write a more legi-
ble hand? Ought we not to be more thorough in our service, not
simply doing well that which will be seen and noticed, but as
our Father makes many a flower to bloom unseen in the lonely
desert, so to do all we can do, as under his eyes, though no
other eye ever take note of it. *Dr Hudson Taylor*

MATURITY October 4

So we preach Christ to everyone. With all possible wisdom we
warn and teach them in order to bring each one into God's
presence as a mature individual in union with Christ. To get

this done I toil and struggle, using the mighty strength which Christ supplies and which is at work in me.

Colossians 1:28-29 GNB

As God's picked representatives, purified and beloved, put on that nature which is merciful in action, kindly in heart and humble in mind. Accept life and be most patient and tolerant with one another, always ready to forgive if you have a difference with anyone.   *Colossians 3:12-13*

Maturity begins to grow when you can sense your concern for others outweighing your concern for yourself.

John MacNaughton

The law of Christian maturity demands that we lose ourselves in concern for others. One must not wait until all problems at home are solved before beginning to address oneself to those of the neighbour. In fact awareness of the immensity of the tasks and problems of progress which face humanity as a whole can stir individuals to work more seriously for progress in their own society.   *Pope Paul VI*

God will not look you over for medals, degrees or diplomas but for scars.   *Elbert Hubbard*

Spiritual maturity comes not by erudition but by compliance with the known will of God.   *D V Lambert*

MENTAL FIGHT   October 5

I will pray with my spirit but I will pray also with my mind. I will sing with my spirit, but I will sing also with my mind.

1 Corinthians 14:14-15 GNB

Occupy your minds with good thoughts or the enemy will fill them with bad ones; unoccupied they cannot be.

Sir Thomas More

What the world expects of Christians is that they should speak out, loud and clear, and that they should voice their condemnation in such a way that never a doubt, never the slightest doubt could arise in the heart of the simplest person.   *Albert Camus*

This is the very point at which so many draw back – I would have done so myself if I could – and proceed no further with Christianity. An impersonal God – well and good. A subjective God of beauty, truth and goodness, inside our own heads – better still. A formless life-force surging through us, a vast power which we can tap – best of all. But God himself, alive, pulling at the other end of the cord, perhaps approaching at an infinite speed, the hunter, king, husband – that is quite another matter.

C S Lewis

It is thoughts of God's thinking which we need to set us right and, remember, they are not as our thoughts.   *W M Macgregor*

THEY LIVE   October 6

For he is destined to reign until God has put all enemies under his feet; and the last enemy to be abolished is death.

1 Corinthians 15:25-26

I have come to bring them life in its fullness.   *John 10:10*

The conquest of death is the final achievement of religion. No religion is worth its name unless it can prove itself more than a match for death.   *L P Jacks*

Death, the only immortal who treats us all alike, whose pity and whose peace and whose refuge are for all – the soiled and the pure, the sick and the poor, the loved and the unloved.

Mark Twain

In the blest fellowship of saints
Is wisdom, safety and delight;
And when my heart declines and faints,
It's raised by their heat and light.   *Richard Baxter*

Take care of your life and the Lord will take care of your death.

George Whitefield

If you were arrested for being a Christian, would there be enough evidence to convict you?   *David Otis Fuller*

LIFE IS A GIFT October 7

All of us should eat and drink and enjoy what we have worked
for. It is God's gift. *Ecclesiastes 3:13 GNB*

Sin pays its servants; the wage is death. But God gives to those
who serve him; his free gift is eternal life through Jesus Christ
our Lord. *Romans 6:23*

God wants us to approach life full of expectancy that God is
going to be at work in every situation as we realise our faith in
him. *Colin Urquhart*

I have a very vehement, violent, over-impressionable nature,
which gets ridiculously over-roused, jarred, confused. Hence I
have a big job to drop, drop, drop all this feverishness, and to
listen as docilely as I can, to think, will and pray... The minute I
at all attain to these dispositions, fruitfulness succeeds.

Baron F von Hügel

> God give me work
> Till my life shall end;
> And life
> Till my work is done. *Winifred Holtby*

THE GOAL IN SIGHT October 8

The time for my departure has arrived. The glorious fight that
God gave me I have fought, the course that I was set I have
finished, and I have kept the faith. The future for me holds the
crown of righteousness which the Lord, the true judge, will give
me in that day – and not, of course, only to me but to all those
who have loved what they have seen of him.

2 Timothy 4:6-8

None of these things move me, neither count I my life dear to
myself so that I might finish my course with joy!
Acts 20:24 – St Paul, on his way to Jerusalem facing death

And I saw there was an Ocean of Darkness and Death; but an
infinite Ocean of Light and Love flowed over the Ocean of
Darkness; and in that I saw the infinite love of God. *George Fox*

We must aim to have a Christianity which, like the sap of a tree, runs through twig and leaf of our character and sanctifies all.

Bishop J C Ryle

Each of us has something to do which is not easy. God takes care it shall be so. If things were easy where would be the fight? How should we be trained for heavenly service? But there is no need ever to be overcome. God makes provision for victory, never for defeat.

Amy Carmichael

SELF-FORGETFULNESS October 9

Don't forget what I teach you, my son. Always remember what I tell you to do.

Proverbs 3:1 GNB

We should not forget to do good and to share our good things with others, for these are the sort of sacrifices God will accept.

Hebrews 13:16

We are most ourselves when we most lose sight of ourselves.

Cardinal J H Newman

An humble knowledge of thyself is a surer way to God than a deep search after learning... Christ will come unto thee, and show thee his own consolation, if thou prepare for him a worthy mansion within thee.

Thomas à Kempis

There was a day when I died to George Müller, his opinions and preferences, taste and will; died to the world, its approval or censure; died to the approval or blame even of my brethren or friends; and since then I have striven only to show myself approved unto God.

George Müller

The centre of God's will is our only safety.

Corrie ten Boom

NO NESTLING October 10

Live in such a way as to cause no trouble either to Jews or Gentiles or to the church of God. Just do as I do; try to please everyone in all that I do, not thinking of my own good, but of the good of all so that they might be saved.

1 Corinthians 10:32-33 GNB

The world, and the things that are in it, will one day be folded up like an Arab's tent; you are not to live exclusively for this life. *Archbishop Fulton Sheen*

There was a period in my life when my interest in a girl pushed most other considerations into the periphery. Being in love is one of life's great gifts, but I had let it come before my calling. When I put my commitment to God first I discovered that she was not the right girl for me. It was painful but it also set her free to find the road she was meant to take. At the same time it was a step towards finding my wife. *Jens-J Wilhelmsen*

> Not for ever in green pastures
> Do we ask our way to be:
> But the steep and rugged pathway
> May we tread rejoicingly. *L M Willis*

I am persuaded that nothing is thriving in my soul unless it is growing. *Robert M McCheyne*

THE MORAL TEST   October 11

Let your heart therefore be perfect with the Lord our God, to walk in his statutes and to keep his commandments.

1 Kings 8:61

Build up your strength in union with the Lord and by means of his mighty power. Put on all the armour that God gives you, so that you will be able to stand up against the devil's evil tricks.

Ephesians 6:10-11 GNB

We get nowhere with people till we make the moral test... (Jesus sees) that behind our intellectual difficulties is deep moral need – an attempt to find satisfaction in what can never satisfy... Christ meets you at the point of your deepest need.

Dorothy M Prescott

Christian life means a walking; it goes by steps. There is a straight fence run for us between right and wrong. There is no sitting on that fence. No; only walking, one side or the other.

Robert W Barbour

Strive we then to think aright; that is the first principle of moral life. *Blaise Pascal*

O God, forasmuch as without thee we are not able to please thee; mercifully grant, that thy Holy Spirit may in all things direct and rule our hearts. *Book of Common Prayer*

KEEP ON KEEPING ON   October 12

Thine ears shall hear a word behind thee, saying, This is the way, walk ye in it, when ye turn to the right hand and when ye turn to the left. *Isaiah 30:21*

Let God remake you so that your whole attitude of mind is changed. Thus you will prove in practice that the will of God is good, acceptable to him and perfect. *Romans 12:2*

God will hold us responsible as to how well we fulfil our responsibilities to this age and take advantage of our opportunities. *Dr Billy Graham*

Pure motives will make a clear flame. Impure motives are the smoke that clogs the flame. *Sydney Cook*

God Almighty has set before me two great objects, the suppression of the slave trade and the reformation of manners.

William Wilberforce, written in his early morning journal, shortly after asking God to direct his life

God has plenty of time. It is our ambitious time-scale that makes us impatient... A woman, said Jesus, put yeast into a half a hundredweight of dough (laughter from the women in the crowd). Nothing much happened – not for hours. A man planted a seed in the earth. Nothing happened – for months. 'Be patient, you lot,' he tells us, 'you want everything to happen in your lifetime so you can claim credit for it.' *Donald Simpson*

WHAT ARE YOU GUIDED BY? October 13

The Lord says, 'I will teach you the way you should go; I will instruct you and advise you.' *Psalms 32: GNB*

What we see happening to men and women in the Acts of the Apostles is what happens when God is really allowed to take over and run our lives himself. Our fundamental need is for him to be in charge. Our fundamental sin is that we have not allowed him to be. We may have referred some of our difficulties and questions to him. We may have accepted portions of his programme for us – selected according to taste – but we have not given him complete command. The self-run life has been our trouble. *Rev Cecil Rose*

What I believe to be absolutely necessary for a guide of souls is a faith unfeigned, the love of God and our neighbour, a burning zeal for the advancement of Christ's kingdom, with a heart and life wholly devoted to God. *John Wesley*

No man can give at the same time the impression that he himself is clever and that Jesus Christ is mighty to save. *James Denny*

NOTHING IN MY HAND October 14

I will bless those who put their trust in me. They are like trees growing near a stream and sending out roots to the water. They are not afraid when hot weather comes, because their leaves stay green; they have no worries when there is no rain; they keep on bearing fruit. *Jeremiah 17:7-8 GNB*

He who trusts in himself is lost. He who trusts in God can do all things. *St Alphonsus Liguori*

As in a game of cards, so in the game of life, we must play with what is dealt out to us and the glory consists not so much in winning as in playing a poor hand well. *Josh Billings*

If we would avoid a senseless natural philosophy we must always start with this principle: that everything in nature depends on the will of God. *John Calvin*

Nothing in my hand I bring,
Simply to thy cross I cling.
Naked, come to thee for dress;
Helpless, loók to thee for grace;
Foul I to the fountain fly;
Wash me, Saviour, or I die.   *A M Toplady*

OBEDIENCE LIBERATES   October 15

The world of creation cannot as yet see reality, not because it
chooses to be blind, but because in God's purpose it has been so
limited – yet it has been given hope. And the hope is that in the
end the whole of created life will be rescued from the tyranny
of change and decay, and have its share in that magnificent liberty which can only belong to the children of God.

                                        Romans 8:21-22

Obedience is the key and prompt action. This will free you
with the right thing to say when you are feeling dumb.   *H P E*

Our most devouring need is liberty – liberty to stop sinning; to
leave the prison of our passions and shake off the fetters of the
past... It is a cleaner world we want; a purer air or any air at all,
for our higher selves.   *Professor Henry Drummond*

My gracious Lord, I own thy right
To every service I can pay;
And call it my supreme delight
To hear thy dictates and obey.   *Philip Doddridge*

THE WAY OF OBEDIENCE   October 16

For he, who had always been God by nature, did not cling to
his privileges as God's equal, but stripped himself of every advantage by consenting to be a slave by nature and being born a
man. And, plainly seen as a human being, he humbled himself
by living a life of utter obedience.   *Philippians 2:6-7*

Man has become an intellectual giant but stays a moral dwarf.
His brain has swollen. His hands grow strong. His heart is

shrunken... There are men who worship mind... They say man is a thinking beast. They do not believe in God. But they cannot consider that anything more wonderful than their own intelligence exists. They worship man's mind, especially their own, as others worship flesh.   *Peter Howard*

Members of a church were startled when they arrived one Sunday morning to find their church doors locked. Pinned to the wood was this notice: 'You have been coming here long enough. Now go and do it.' Jesus had something similar to say to some of his so-called disciples: 'Why do you call me Lord, Lord, and do not do what I say?' *(Luke 6:46)*.

Canon David Watson

The golden rule for understanding in spiritual matters is not intellect, but obedience.   *Oswald Chambers*

CULTIVATING CHARACTER OR DOING GOD'S WILL?   October 17

If you have to choose between a good reputation and great wealth, choose a good reputation. The rich and the poor have this is common; the Lord made them both.   *Proverbs 22:1 GNB*

So then, my brothers and sisters, try even harder to make God's call and his choice of you a permanent experience.

2 Peter 1:10 GNB

Stuart Sanderson owned a woollen mill in Galashiels in the Scottish borders and lived in a beautiful home overlooking the town. Sanderson was a good Presbyterian and devoted church elder, but he had a sharp temper and was accustomed to getting his own way... In the 1920s he... decided that his life should be run not for profit but on the basis of God's will. In the 1930s his mill, like a great many others in Gala, was hit by the depression. Friends advised him to sell up and get out, as some of his companions were doing. But, in a time of quiet, God told him that he must neither sell his mill nor sack a single one of his employees. Instead he was told to sell his home, his car and the family silver, put the proceeds into the business and move into a small cottage in the mill grounds. Sanderson obeyed. His mill stayed open during the depression years; not one of his workers lost their jobs. *Authors of* The Secret

Lord, what wilt thou have me to do? *Acts 9:6 AV*

PEACE AT THE HEART OF THE WHIRLWIND

If someone has done you wrong, do not repay him with a wrong. Try to do what everyone considers to be good. Do everything on your part to live in peace with everybody.
Romans 12:17-18 GNB

Peace demands a mentality and a spirit which, before turning to others, must first permeate him who wishes to bring peace. Peace is first and foremost personal, before it is social. And it is precisely this spirit of peace which it is the duty of every true follower of Christ to cultivate. *Pope Paul VI*

If we have not quiet in our minds, outward comfort will do no more for us than a golden slipper on a gouty foot. *John Bunyan*

> Breathe through the heats of our desire
> Thy coolness and thy balm;
> Let sense be dumb, let flesh retire;
> Speak through the earthquake, wind and fire,
> O still small voice of calm. *John Greenleaf Whittier*

REST

Thou wilt keep him in perfect peace, whose mind is stayed on thee; because he trusteth in thee. *Isaiah 26:3*

There are ten strong things. Iron is strong but fire melts it. Fire is strong, but water quenches it. Water is strong, but the clouds evaporate it. Clouds are strong, but wind drives them away. Man is strong, but fears cast him down. Fear is strong, but sleep overcomes it. Sleep is strong, yet death is stronger. But loving-kindness survives death. *The Talmud*

Dispose our soul for tranquillity, O God, that the loving know-ledge of contemplation may the more grow and the soul will feel it and relish it more than all other things whatever; because it brings with it peace and rest, sweetness and delight without trouble.   *St John of the Cross*

It is known to many that we need solitude to find ourselves. Perhaps it is not so well known that we need solitude to find our fellows. Even the Saviour is described as reaching mankind through the wilderness.   *Havelock Ellis*

PATTERN FOR A NEW WORLD   October 20

Fight to the death for truth, and the Lord God will fight on your side.   *Ecclesiasticus 4:28 NEB*

And looking around at those who were sitting in the circle about him, he said, 'Here are my mother and my brothers. Whoever does the will of God is my brother, my sister, my mother. '   *Mark 3:34-35 NEB*

It was dawn in a remote village in the Papua-New Guinea Highlands in the early 1930s. A reveillé blown on conch shells summoned the villagers to gather with the chief and elders of the tribe. They met in silence, half an hour of silence together. Then they pooled the thoughts which the Spirit of God had given them. Not long before, this was a head-hunting tribe, dominated by their witch doctors. On this day, as they do week by week now, they are listening together to the living God. And he is altering the whole pattern of their lives. Head-hunting is out. They have made peace, over splendid feasts, with neighbouring tribes.   *K D Belden*

As long as you refuse to change yourself, the world will not change either. The world can change if you change. If you become a new person, the new world will become possible.
                                        Père Alphonse Gratry

THE DESTINY OF US ALL   October 21

We know that in all things God works for good with those who
love him, those he has called according to his purpose. Those
whom God had already chosen he also set apart to become like
his Son.   *Romans 8:28–29*

Is our Christianity concerned not only with my personal
salvation and my family's, not only with my nation, but with
God's plan for the whole world and the whole of history? Each
person has a part and is responsible for the future of the world.
                              Bishop Rendtorff of Kiel University

We are not permitted to choose the frame of our destiny. But
what we put into it is ours.   *Dag Hammarskjöld*

Mr Stand-fast speaks at the end of his journey, 'I have formerly
lived by hearsay and faith but now I go where I shall live by
sight and shall be with him in whose company I delight myself.'
                                                    John Bunyan

God-guided people, to build God-guided nations, is the destiny
of our age.   *Dr Frank N D Buchman*

THE LOVE THAT CASTS OUT FEAR   October 22

The fear of the Lord is the beginning of wisdom.   *Proverbs 9:10*

There is no fear in love; perfect love drives out all fear. So then,
love has not been made perfect in anyone who is afraid,
because fear has to do with punishment.   *John 4:18 GNB*

I am astonished at the image of God that many Christians carry
around in their minds. In response to my question, 'How do
you see God?' I have heard them say things like, 'I see him as
distant, uncommunicative, indifferent, always angry with me,
unconcerned with my needs, punitive, harsh, demanding, at-
tending to the needs of others before me, etc etc'... If, however,
we see him as loving, forgiving, generous and considerate, then
by that secret law of the soul... our lives will take on those
positive qualities.   *Rev Selwyn Hughes © CWR*

If we try to look at the complex issues of the world with the eye of faith, what is revealed? We acknowledge first of all, God's love for us, from which flows a growing love for him. Springing from this grows a love for all his people in some area of the world, or some area of life, a multiplicity of callings which spring from the same motivation.   *John Lester and Pierre Spoerri*

Do not be afraid – I will save you. I have called you by name – you are mine. When you pass through the deep waters, I will be with you.   *Isaiah 43:1-2 GNB*

FEAR-FREE   October 23

The Lord is merciful and loving, slow to become angry and full of constant love... As a father is kind to his children, so the Lord is kind to those who honour him.   *Psalms 103:8 and 13 GNB*

The wise man in the storm prays God not for safety from danger but for deliverance from fear. It is the storm within which endangers him not the storm without.   *Ralph Waldo Emerson*

I had lost all faith and hope of discovering the truth. By this time my mother had come to me following me over sea and land with the courage of piety and relying upon you in all perils. For they were in danger in a storm, and she reassured even the sailors – who ordinarily reassure travellers newly ventured upon the deep – promising them safe arrival because thus you had promised her in a vision.   *St Augustine*

My blood ran cold at the idea of recounting my almost non-existent experience of a few hours to 80 to 100 people I had never met before. But I knew something had happened to me since the night before, that Jesus Christ had come into my agnostic heart. I knew that my life was already different deep down inside, even if my understanding of what all this meant was practically zero. So I went along and at the appropriate moment told them about it with unexpected ease for someone so pulverisingly shy and self-conscious as I was, and found it the beginning of the deepest friendships I had ever known... This was my introduction to the fact that the Christian life is designed to be lived in teamwork.   *K D Belden*

Fear nothing but sin.   *George Herbert*

THREE LEVELS OF LIFE   October 24

A man can live at one of three levels – instinct, conscience or grace. At the instinctive level, we do what we want; at the conscientious level we do (or try to do) what we ought; at the level of grace we do what God wants.   *Dorothy M Prescott*

INSTINCT
The Lord said: Cattle know who owns them, and donkeys know where their master feeds them. But that is more than my people know; they don't understand at all.   *Isaiah 1:3 GNB*

Even storks know when it is time to return; doves, swallows and thrushes know when it is time to migrate. But my people, you do not know the laws by which I rule you.
Jeremiah 8:7–8 GNB

CONSCIENCE
Then David's conscience began to trouble him, and he said to his men, 'May the Lord keep me from doing any harm to my master, whom the Lord chose as king. I must not harm him in the least, because he is the king chosen by the Lord!' So David convinced his men that they should not attack Saul.
1 Samuel 24:5-7 GNB

GRACE
But by God's grace I am what I am, and the grace that he gave me was not without effect. On the contrary, I have worked harder than all the other apostles, although it was not really my own doing, but God's grace working with me.
1 Corinthians 15:10 GNB

THOUGHTS ON PRAYER   October 25

Go to the Lord for help, and worship him continually.
1 Chronicles 16:11 GNB

This poor man cried, and the Lord heard him, and saved him out of all his troubles.   *Psalms 34:6*

We have courage in God's presence, because we are sure that he hears us if we ask him for anything that is according to his will. He hears us whenever we ask him.   *1 John 5:14–15 GNB*

Prayer is conversation with God.   *St Clement of Alexandria*

Pray as if everything depended on God and act as if everything depended on oneself.   *St Ignatius of Loyola*

Prayer is practised for its own sake. It is its own purpose. There has to grow within us a desire for prayer, a nostalgia for prayer, a taste for prayer... It is not because we are drawn to prayer that we first begin to pray more often. We have to begin prayer and then the desire and the taste for it comes.   *Cardinal Basil Hume*

Really to pray is to stand to attention in the presence of the king and to be prepared to take orders from him.

Archbishop Donald Coggan

FAITHFUL IN LITTLE THINGS   October 26

Think of a ship; big as it is and driven by such strong winds, it can be steered by a very small rudder, and it goes wherever the pilot wants it to go. So it is with the tongue; small as it is, it can boast about great things. Just think how large a forest can be set on fire by a tiny flame!   *James 3:4–5 GNB*

We are too fond of our own will. We want to be doing what we fancy mighty things; but the great point is to do small things, when called to them, in the right spirit.   *Richard Cecil*

Little things come daily, hourly, within our reach, and they are not less calculated to set forward our growth in holiness than are the greater occasions which occur but rarely. Moreover, fidelity in trifles and an earnest seeking to please God in little matters is a test of real devotion and love. Let our aim be to please our dear Lord perfectly in little things and to attain a spirit of childlike simplicity and dependence.   *Père Jean N Grou*

We can do little things for God; I turn the cake that is frying on the pan, for love of him; and that done, if there is nothing else to call me, I prostrate myself in worship before him who has given me grace to work; afterwards I rise happier than a king.

Brother Lawrence

THE POWER OF A CONSISTENT LIFE — October 27

In conclusion, my brothers and sisters, fill your minds with those things that are good and that deserve praise; things that are true, noble, right, pure, lovely and honourable. Put into practice what you have learnt and received from me, both from my words and from my actions. *Philippians 4:8–9 GNB*

Make sure that your endurance carries you all the way without failing, so that you may be perfect and complete, lacking nothing. *James 1:4 GNB*

It is right to be contented with what we have but never with what we are. *James Mackintosh*

The trouble with too many Christians is that they are more concerned about their own doctrine of holiness than they are about being clothed with the beauty of Christ's purity.
Monsignor R Hugh Benson

There is no single definition of holiness; there are dozens, hundreds. But there is one I am particularly fond of; being holy means getting up every time you fall, with humility and joy.
Dom Helder Camara

The silent power of a consistent life. *Florence Nightingale*

Out of self, into Christ, for others – make this a fresh decision at the start of every day. *Dr Frank N D Buchman*

ILLUMINATION — October 28

This is how the judgment works: the light has come into the world, but people love the darkness rather than the light, because their deeds are evil. All those who do evil hate the light and will not come to the light, because they do not want their evil deeds to be shown up. But those who do what is true come to the light in order that the light may show that what they did was in obedience to God. *John 3:19–21 GNB*

Just as the light releases oxygen from the plant, so Christ's light, acting on the cells of personality, releases great aims: the militancy of a great compassion, the strategy of a great commitment, the will to fight. To expose our lives to the light by listening to God's guidance excites moral and neuro-chemical action which affects the way we think, look, talk, eat, walk and work. Everything becomes new. *Dr Paul Campbell*

To the Church, Pentecost brought light, power, joy. There came to each illumination of mind, assurance of heart, intensity of love, fullness of power, exuberance of joy. No one needed to ask if they had received the Holy Ghost. Fire is self-evident, so is power! *Samuel Chadwick*

THE GREAT GAMBLE   October 29

Abraham, when hope was dead within him, went on hoping in faith, believing that he would become 'the father of many nations'. He relied on the word of God which definitely referred to 'thy seed'. *Romans 4:16 GNB*

Hope remains untaxable even in my country. So I declare to you today that I am full of hope. I have faith that the ordinary person will rise to the challenge of our times. *Peter Howard*

The will responds to total demands. It has peace only when there is singleness of purpose demanding total effort. Its basic need is to give everything for something great... to live for an objective relevant to the problems of the age.

Paul Campbell and Peter Howard

> He was a gambler too, my Christ,
> He took his life and threw
> It for a world redeemed.
> And ere his agony was done,
> Before the westering sun went down,
> Crowning that day with its crimson crown,
> He knew that he had won. *G A Studdert-Kennedy*

NO NEUTRALITY

I offer you the choice of life or death, blessing or curse. Choose life and then you and your descendants will live; love the Lord your God, obey him and hold fast to him. *Deuteronomy 30:19–20*

An honest man with an open Bible and a pad and pencil is sure to find out what is wrong with him very quickly.   *A W Tozer*

The crucial issue for all of us, surely, is to be so aware of the needs and issues of the world and so open to the Spirit of God, that we are always ready to take the next step in God's purposes and never rule out the possibility of being used to play a part beyond our dreams, however insignificant or remote we may feel from great affairs.   *K D Belden*

Every time a Christian cheats on his income tax, he perverts and obscures the Gospel.   *John Sanderson*

Let us pray for the whole state of Christ's Church militant here in earth.   *Book of Common Prayer*

> Soldiers of Christ arise,
> And put your armour on,
> Strong in the strength that God supplies...
> Wrestle and fight and pray,
> Tread all the powers of darkness down
> And win the well-fought day.   *Charles Wesley*

SPIRITUAL FITNESS

Keep yourself in constant training for a godly life. Physical training has some value but spiritual exercise is valuable in every way, because it promises life both for the present and for the future.   *1 Timothy 4:7 GNB*

So live that God can say 'hello' to you at any time of day or night.   *Dr Frank N D Buchman*

The first mark of a Christian is a deep reverence for persons as destined for eternity with God. The second is a kind of heavenly serenity which is able to draw the sting of suffering. And the third is the humility of a man or woman who has known authentically the presence of God. *Archbishop A M Ramsey*

Never be ashamed to own you had been in the wrong; 'tis but saying you are wiser today than you were yesterday.

Jonathan Swift

Jesus promised his disciples three things – that they would be completely fearless, that they would be serenely happy and in constant trouble. *F R Maltby*

Discipleship is more than getting to know what the teacher knows. It is getting to be what he is. *Juan Carlos Ortiz*

WHAT ARE SAINTS? November 1

Do ye not know that the saints shall judge the world?
1 Corinthians 6:2 AV

You will be able to thank the Father because you are privileged to share the lot of the saints who are living in the light. For he rescued us from the power of darkness, and re-established us in the kingdom of his beloved Son. *Colossians 1:12-13*

God creates out of nothing. Wonderful, you say. Yes to be sure, but he does what is still more wonderful. He makes saints out of sinners. *Søren Kierkegaard*

I expect you to be saints and very great saints! because sanctity is not a luxury but a mere duty according to Christ's teaching.
Maximilian Kolbe

What are saints? Are they exalted beings, commemorated in stained glass windows, who were somehow born with special spiritual gifts which made goodness come easier to them than to us ordinary mortals? Or are they, rather, people like those whom Jesus described in the beatitudes?... Each of us, the most unsaintly as well as the most spiritually minded, has a next step which will take him nearer to God; and all he asks of us is that we will take that step. *Dorothy M Prescott*

THEY SHALL INHERIT THE EARTH November 2

You are no longer a slave but a son or daughter. And since that is what you are, God will give you all that he has for his heirs.
Galatians 4:7 GNB

This faith of ours is the only way in which the world can be conquered. *1 John 5:4*

The saints are God's jewels, highly esteemed by and dear to him; they are a royal diadem in his hand. *Matthew Henry*

Joan of Arc was a being so uplifted from the ordinary run of mankind that she finds no equal in a thousand years... she embodied the natural goodness and valour of the human race in unexampled perfection. Unconquerable courage, infinite

215

compassion, the virtue of the simple, the wisdom of the just, shone forth in her. *Sir Winston Churchill*

> And Satan trembles when he sees
> The weakest saint upon his knees. *William Cowper*

The serene silent beauty of a holy life is the most powerful influence in the world, next to the might of the spirit of God.
Charles H Spurgeon

What saint has ever won his crown without first contending for it? *St Jerome*

How blest are they of a humble and gentle spirit. They will win the world. *Matthew 5:5*

LIVING OUR FAITH   November 3

Now faith means that we have full confidence in the things we hope for; it means being certain of the things we cannot see.
Hebrews 11:1

In an essay entitled 'Wanted – a New Pleasure' which was widely read in the thirties, Aldous Huxley wrote that the world needed a new drug: 'If we could sniff or swallow something that would abolish solitude, attune us to our fellows with a glowing exultation of affection and make life in all its respects not only worth living, but divinely beautiful and significant, and if this heavenly transfiguring drug were of such a kind that we could wake up next morning with a clear head and undamaged constitution – then it seems to me, all our problems would be wholly solved and earth would become a paradise.' I once discussed these matters with Huxley... and he agreed that some people had this thing and that its name was Faith. *Garth Lean*

For faith is the beginning and the end is love and God is the two of them brought into unity. After these comes whatever else makes up a Christian gentleman. *St Ignatius of Antioch*

If a man believes and knows God he can no longer ask, 'What is the meaning of my life?' But by believing he actually lives the meaning of his life. *Karl Barth*

216

ONE WORLD November 4

God who made the world and all that is in it, being Lord of both heaven and earth, does not live in man-made temples... From one ancestor he has created every race of men to live over the face of the whole earth. *Acts 17:24-26*

Skin colour does not matter to God, for he is looking upon the heart... When we are standing at the foot of the Cross there are no racial barriers. *Dr Billy Graham*

Hardened Mau Mau leaders generally refused to listen when white men spoke; but here was a force of all races and backgrounds united in a common battle for a new world. Peter Howard was one of those who spoke. He said: 'I was born white. I couldn't help it, could I?' He had their interest. He said, 'I am a proud man and I come from a proud race. Now I see that it was the pride of men like me which has created so much tragedy for the world. But I have made up my mind to change.' *Bremer Hofmeyr, South Africa*

The world and all that is in it belongs to the Lord; the earth and all who live in it are his. *Psalms 24:1-2 GNB*

All of creation waits with eager longing for God to reveal his children. *Romans 8:19 GNB*

SPIRITUAL POWER November 5

Even those who are young grow weak; young people can fall exhausted. But those who trust in the Lord for help will find their strength renewed. *Isaiah 40:30-31 GNB*

The Christ you have to deal with is not a weak person outside you, but a tremendous power inside you. He was 'weak' enough to be crucified, yes, but he now lives by the power of God. *2 Corinthians 13:3-4*

The absence of the cutting edge of Christ's standards is only too apparent as you look at the lives of some Christians, and of our own often enough. Yet the battle we are called to demands the steel of God's fullest claims upon us if we are going to capture the hearts and minds of men and women under the pressures

of today, or meet the chaotic confusion in so many people's
lives.   *K D Belden*

We see modern miracles in other people's lives when we pay
the price in the discipline and passion of our own... 'According
to your faith be it unto you.' 'Large petitions with you bring.
You are coming to a king.' Those who deal trenchantly with sin,
and expect miracles see the miracles come to pass.
                                                      Peter Howard

EMBRACING THE 'NOW'   November 6

To love is to obey the whole law. You must do this, because you
know that the time has come for you to wake up from your
sleep. For the moment when we will be saved is closer now
than when we first believed.   *Romans 13:10-11 GNB*

The moment passed is no longer; the future may never be; the
present is all of which man is the master.   *Jean-Jacques Rousseau*

The longer I live and the older I grow, the more convinced I am
that there are times when we must sit quietly at the feet of
Jesus, and only let God speak to our souls.   *D L Moody*

Live in the perfection of the present moment – God's gift – and
of the person you are with. Or do you spoil it by thinking of six
other things to do, or people to see, in future?   *Roland Wilson*

Throughout the whole New Testament there runs the conviction that the time looked forward to by the prophets has in fact
arrived in history with the advent of Jesus Christ... The time of
Jesus is 'kairos' – a time of opportunity. To embrace the opportunity means salvation, to neglect it disaster. There is no third
course.   *John Marsh*

Do not walk through time without leaving worthy evidence of
your passage.   *Pope John XXIII*

THE PURPOSE OF DISCIPLINE November 7

Happy is the person whom God corrects! Do not resent it when he rebukes you. *Job 5:17 GNB*

The Lord corrects those he loves, as parents correct a child of whom they are proud. Happy is anyone who becomes wise – who gains understanding. There is more profit in it than in silver. *Proverbs 3:12-14 GNB*

Life must be based on positive and permanent values. The value of love will always be stronger than the value of hate; since any nation which employs hatred is eventually torn to pieces by hatred within itself. The value of truth and sincerity is always stronger than the value of lies and cynicism. No process has been invented which can permanently separate people from their own hearts and consciences or prevent them from seeing the results of their own false ideas. *President F D Roosevelt*

God never strikes except for motives of love and never takes away but in order to give. *Archbishop François Fénelon*

Think not of undisturbed repose until the flesh is dropped. There is a ceaseless cycle of sorrow and temptation here. But despise not the scourge. It has a teaching voice. It is held by a loving Father's hand. *Henry Law*

In the last resort both love and life resolve themselves into spiritual staying power. And there is no spiritual staying power without lifelong unrelenting discipline. *Elisabeth Herman*

DISCIPLINE OF TONGUE November 8

The human tongue is physically small, but what tremendous effects it can boast of! A whole forest can be set ablaze by a tiny spark of fire and the tongue is a fire, a whole world of evil... Blessing and curses come out of the same mouth – surely, my brothers, this never ought to happen! Have you ever known a spring to give sweet and bitter water at the same time?
James 3:5-6 and 10

On the wall of his refectory, for all to see, was a verse which said: 'If anyone likes to tell stories against people behind their backs, let him know that this table is no place for him.' When fellow-bishops protested that surely this was not to be taken too seriously, Augustine replied that if they took that verse off the wall he would go and eat his meal by himself.

Possidius, biographer of St Augustine

Nature has given a man one tongue, but two ears, that we may hear from others as much as we speak. *Epictetus*

It is unworthy of a Muslim to injure another's reputation, to curse anyone, to abuse anyone or to talk vainly.

The Sayings of Mohammed

Many a saint, for want of keeping a tight rein, and that constantly, over some corruption which they have thought they have got the mastery of, has been thrown out of the saddle... The humble Christian is the wary Christian. *William Gurnall*

Be careful how you think; your life is shaped by your thoughts.

Proverbs 4:23 GNB

PLAN FOR VICTORY   November 9

It is sin which gives death its sting, and it is the law which gives sin its power. All thanks to God, then, who gives us the victory over these things through our Lord Jesus Christ.

1 Corinthians 15:57

A Moravian missionary named George Smith went to Africa. He had been there only a short time and had only one convert, a poor woman, when he was driven from the country. He died shortly afterwards, on his knees, praying for Africa. He was considered a failure. But a company of men stumbled on the place where he had prayed and found a copy of the scriptures he had left. As a result they met the one poor woman who was his convert... 100 years later his mission counted more than 13,000 living converts who had sprung from the ministry of George Smith. *A J Gordon*

If Christ is with us, who is against us? You can fight with confidence where you are sure of victory. With Christ and for Christ, victory is certain. *St Bernard of Clairvaux*

There can be no victory where there is no combat.

Richard Sibbes

I die the king's good servant, but God's first.

Sir Thomas More, before his execution

THE DANGEROUS VOYAGE OF LIFE   November 10

Do not love the world or anything that belongs to the world. If you love the world, you do not love the Father. Everything that belongs to the world – what the sinful self desires, what people see and want, and everything in this world that people are so proud of – none of this comes from the Father; it all comes from the world. The world and everything in it that people desire is passing away; but those who do the will of God live for ever.

1 John 2:15-17 GNB

When Moses threw the wand into the Red Sea, the sea quite contrary to the expected miracle, did not divide itself to leave a dry passage for the Jews. Not until the first man had jumped into the sea did the waves recede.   *Jewish legend*

Gladys, the new maid sat on the edge of the bed and surveyed her small store of belongings: a Bible, a book of devotional readings, and about three and a half old pence. It seemed impossible to think of getting to China, yet she was absolutely sure that God had called her to go and tell the people there about him. She hadn't been accepted by a missionary society, but still she knew she must go. She put her few possessions together, laid her hand on them and prayed: 'O God. Here's me. Here's my Bible. Here's my money. Use us, God.'

Mary Batchelor. The story of Gladys Aylward, missionary in China,
was told in the film The Inn of the Sixth Happiness.

Cardinal Wolsey: Cromwell, I charge thee, fling away ambition:
    By that sin, fell the angels; how can man, then,
    The image of his Maker, hope to win by't?...
    Had I but served my God with half the zeal
    I served my king, he would not in mine age
    Have left me naked to mine enemies.

Shakespeare – Henry VIII

FAITH November 11

If you have faith no bigger even than a grain of mustard seed, you will say to this mountain, 'Move from here to there!' and it will move; nothing will prove impossible for you.

Matthew 17:20 NEB

So with faith; if it does not lead to action, it is in itself a lifeless thing. *James 2:17 NEB*

Belief is a truth held in the mind. Faith is a fire in the heart.

Joseph Newton

Ultimately, faith is the only key to the universe. The final meaning of human existence, and the answers to the questions on which all our happiness depends cannot be found in any other way. *Thomas Merton*

Faith without knowledge leads to the conceit of ignorance, and knowledge without faith begets a stony heart. Therefore only as these two are well blended do they become the basis of good deeds. *Buddhist scripture*

All I have seen teaches me to trust the creator for what I have not seen. *Ralph Waldo Emerson*

'I do believe,' the boy's father burst out. 'Help me to believe more.' *Mark 9:24*

THE FRUIT OF OBEDIENCE November 12

Just as the mass of people were made sinners as a result of the disobedience of one man, in the same way the mass of people will all be put right with God as the result of the obedience of one man. *Romans 5:19 GNB*

The surest evidence of our love to Christ is obedience to the laws of Christ. Love is the root, obedience the fruit.

Matthew Henry

One of the things in this world which we do well to remember is that every situation is an opportunity. One of the great

222

missionary stories is the story of Mary Reed. In India she was haunted and oppressed by the fate of the lepers, for in those days nothing was done for them. She herself took ill with an illness which no one could diagnose. A visit to a hill station made no difference. She was sent home, and still no one could place her trouble. She had a numbness in one of her fingers and a stubbornly unhealable spot on her face. At last a doctor realised what was the matter with her. She had contracted leprosy herself. She was told the news. What was her reaction? Her reaction was to go down on her knees and to thank God that he had made her a leper, for now she could spend her life with the lepers for whom her heart was sore.   *Dr William Barclay*

Every revelation of God is a demand and the way to knowledge of God is by obedience.   *Archbishop William Temple*

ACCEPTANCE   November 13

Let the words of my mouth, and the meditation of my heart, be acceptable in thy sight, O Lord, my strength and my redeemer.
Psalms 19:14

May God, the source of patience and encouragement, enable you to have the same point of view among yourselves by following the example of Christ Jesus... Accept one another, then, for the glory of God as Christ has accepted you.
Romans 15:5 and 7 GNB

We need only obey. There is guidance for each of us and by lowly listening we shall hear the right word.
Ralph Waldo Emerson

For Bede, the holy man of Northumbria and the first English historian, the perfection of Christian life lay not in renunciation but in acceptance.   *Gervase Mathew*

You are not accepted by God because you deserve to be or because you have worked hard for him but because Jesus died for you.   *Colin Urquhart*

ACCEPTING ONESELF November 14

For what seems to be God's 'foolishness' is wiser than human wisdom, and what seems to be God's 'weakness' is stronger than human strength. Now remember what you were, my brothers and sisters, when God called you. From the human point of view few of you were wise or powerful or of high social standing. God purposely chose what the world considers nonsense to shame the wise, and he chose what the world considers weak to shame the powerful.   *1 Corinthians 1:25-27 GNB*

If we stand in the openings of the present moment, with all the length and breadth of our faculties unselfishly adjusted to what it reveals, we are in the best condition to receive what God is always ready to communicate.   *T C Upham*

Relying on God has to begin all over again, every day, as if nothing had yet been done.   *C S Lewis*

'God can't make anything out of such poor material as I am,' we say in effect. But once we do accept ourselves as we are, and 'love ourselves' because God made us and loves us, then he can begin to work miracles in us, and it seems as if all the riches of personality in us begin to be liberated – often even our health and appearance are transformed.   *Dorothy M Prescott*

I am inclined to think that to forgive ourself is sometimes the hardest kind of forgiveness. Self is the inmost entrenchment at which the unforgiving spirit makes its last stand... The prodigal would have never come home had he been unable to forgive himself... And this unwillingness to forgive oneself is the last refuge of the selfish spirit.   *Thomas Martin Lindsay*

DETACHMENT November 15

I had rather be a doorkeeper in the house of my God, than to dwell in the tents of wickedness. For the Lord God is a sun and shield; the Lord will give grace and glory; no good thing will he withhold from them that walk uprightly.   *Psalms 84:10-11*

'Your problems are mixed up with the things you love most and which count most to you,' said Archbishop Temple. Self-love shows itself in the love of praise and popularity and social success... We develop what we are pleased to call sensitiveness, but what we can better call touchiness. Then self-pity creeps in. We feel inferior, we positively hug failure and point to previous defeats as evidence of our limitations... Then self-importance often gives rise to jealousy and makes us run on our position and reputation, though inwardly defeated.   *Loudon Hamilton*

You have an ego – a consciousness of being an individual. But that doesn't mean that you are to worship yourself, to think constantly of yourself, and to live entirely for self.

Dr Billy Graham

I find that living under God's direction, for others, requires an essential detachment from love of praise, popularity or success.

H P E

DEATH TO SELF   November 16

Jesus said: If anyone wants to come with me, he must forget self, carry his cross and follow me. For whoever wants to save his life will lose it; but whoever loses his life for my sake will find it.   *Matthew 16:24-25*

The cross that Jesus tell us to carry is the one that we least willingly take up ourselves – the cross of self-denial in order that we might live for the glory of the Father.   *Colin Urquhart*

The foolish man is full of selfishness; he toils day and night, greedy for wealth, as if he will never grow old or die.

Jainist saying

Self-admiration is the death of the soul. To admire ourselves as we are is to have no wish to change. And with those who don't want to change, the soul is dead.   *Dr William Barclay*

There is no other way to live the Christian life than by a continual death to self.   *Archbishop François Fénelon*

IN THE CRUCIBLE

And throughout the land two-thirds of the people will die. And I will test the third that survives and will purify them as silver is purified by fire. I will test them as gold is tested. Then they will pray to me, and I will answer them. I will tell them that they are my people, and they will confess that I am their God.

Zechariah 13:8-9 GNB

Britain declared a state of emergency in Kenya in 1953 because of the Mau Mau terrorist movement. About to arrive in East Africa, I heard to my horror that of the 22,000 Christians in Kenya less than 1,000 remained. One of these, Andrew Kaguru, continued to preach in his church, despite a threat to his life. One morning before daybreak terrorists came to his house and ordered him to take the Mau Mau oath. This he refused to do. He was battered to death. The Kikuyu Christians asked their fellow believers: 'Do not pray that we may be kept safe. Pray that we may be kept faithful.' *P M*

Adversity is the trial of principle. Without it a man hardly knows whether he is honest or not. *Henry Fielding*

We must become so pure in heart – and it needs much practice – that we shall see God. That explains life – why God puts man and woman in the crucible and makes them pure by fire.

Professor Henry Drummond

USES OF ADVERSITY

You imitated us and the Lord, and even though you suffered much, you received the message with the joy that comes from the Holy Spirit. So you became an example to all believers in Macedonia and Achaia. *1 Thessalonians 1:6-7*

Adversity is not necessarily an evil. Beethoven composed his deepest music after becoming totally deaf. Pascal set down his most searching observations about God and man, life and death, in brief intervals of release from a prostrating illness.

Robert McCracken

A Christian is someone who shares the sufferings of God in the world. *Dietrich Bonhoeffer*

During this century we have lived through a chapter of history in which one climax has followed another... At the beginning of the First World War many assumed that it was the war to end all wars. Communists believed that Communism would transform the world... We have witnessed... great tides of history... Great aims may not always be attainable, but they produce greatness; small aims produce mediocrity.

John Lester and Pierre Spoerri

Suddenly my guest rounded on me with passion and said, 'How can you believe in God when you see the undeserved suffering in the world? How can God allow it? Are you not bitter about what happened to your wife?' It dawned on me that I had been given the answer to the 'problem of suffering'. I could only say that I honestly was not bitter because, although I had no philosophic answer in theory, in my personal experience Bridget had demonstrated that suffering, though painful, could be turned to gold – in fact gold that had been freely given to other people. *H P E*

IN TIME OF TROUBLE   November 19

Leave your troubles with the Lord, and he will defend you; he never let honest people be defeated.   *Psalms 55:22 GNB*

Don't worry over anything whatever; whenever you pray tell God every detail of your needs in thankful prayer, and the peace of God, which surpasses human understanding, will keep constant guard over your hearts and minds as they rest in Christ Jesus.   *Philippians 4:6-7*

The Lord gets his best soldiers out of the highlands of adversity.
Charles H Spurgeon

Whilst I continue on this side of eternity, I never expect to be free from trials, only to change them. For it is necessary to heal the pride of my heart that such trials should come.
George Whitefield

Disappointments come not by our own folly, they are the trials or corrections of heaven; and it is our own fault if they prove not to our advantage... No pain, no palm; no thorn, no throne; no gall, no glory; no cross, no crown.   *William Penn*

DELIVERANCE   November 20

How lovely on the mountains are the feet of the herald who comes to proclaim prosperity and bring good news, the news of deliverance.   *Isaiah 52:7 NEB*

Jesus told Nicodemus... that he must be born again through the spirit. Nicodemus was someone who lived a decent sort of life by human standards. But it was a legalistic life because God's law and spirit were not within him. Once Bishop Taylor Smith, when preaching on the need for new birth, said: 'You could even be an archdeacon and not be born again.' Afterwards the archdeacon of that church wrote to him saying: 'Mine has been a hard legal service. I did not know what the matter was until you spoke to me in the service yesterday.' Later that archdeacon experienced the new birth and his life was transformed.
Canon David Watson

There does exist a great liberating power that can transform us and perhaps situations around us, from inside... Those of us who are Christians will call this liberating force God, or the redeeming power of Jesus Christ.   *Pierre Spoerri*

> From all that terror teaches,
> From lies of tongue and pen,
> From all the easy speeches
> That comfort cruel men,
> From sale and profanation
> Of honour, and the sword,
> From sleep and from damnation,
> Deliver us, Good Lord.   *G K Chesterton*

THANKSGIVING   November 21

Offer to God the sacrifice of thanksgiving and pay your vows to the most high.   *Psalms 50:14 NEB*

Never stop praying. Be thankful whatever the circumstances may be. For this is the will of God for you in Christ Jesus.

1 Thessalonians 5:17-18

We should spend as much time in thanking God for his benefits as we do in asking him for them.   *St Vincent de Paul*

A true Christian is someone who never for a moment forgets what God has done for him in Christ, and whose whole comportment and whole activity have their root in the sentiment of gratitude.   *Professor John Baillie*

I own that I am disposed to say grace upon 20 other occasions in the course of the day besides my dinner. I want a form for setting out upon a pleasant walk, for a moonlight ramble, for a friendly meeting or a solved problem. Why have we none for books, those spiritual repasts?   *Charles Lamb*

God is he who created the heavens and the earth and sent down water from the clouds, then brought with it the fruits as a sustenance for you... And he has made subservient to you the night and the day. And he gives you of all that you ask him and if you count God's favours you will not be able to number them; surely man is very ungrateful.   *The Koran*

Bless the Lord, O my soul: And all that is within me,
    bless his holy name.
Bless the Lord, O my soul, and forget not all his benefits.

Psalms 103:1-2

AUTHORITY   November 22

He taught with a ring of authority.   *Mark 1:22*

I am convinced that people are open to the Christian message if it is reasoned with authority and proclaimed as God's word.

Dr Billy Graham

My parents had brought me up with clear standards of right and wrong and to know and experience God's guidance. I am grateful that they did. It certainly gave my childhood a richness, stability and happiness that many of my friends envy. But never once did they put pressure on me to commit myself to their way of life – and every initiative towards it was left to me. The adventure of their way of life and its relevance to what was going on in the world was a powerful magnet. I took each step in learning how to live because I saw that it worked for them and for other people I met. *Geoffrey Lean*

Stir up that inner fire which God gave you at your ordination through my hands. For God has not given us a spirit of fear, but a spirit of power and love and a sound mind. *2 Timothy 1:6-7*

A NEW TYPE OF PERSON November 23

Anyone who is joined to Christ is a new being; the old has gone, the new has come. All this is done by God, who through Christ changed us from enemies into his friends and gave us the task of making others his friends also. *2 Corinthians 5:17-18 GNB*

The great issue of our times is whether God and spirit or people and matter are masters of the globe. Most people through history have found it more reasonable to believe in a God who made them and the world we live in, who gave each of us liberty of choice, moment by moment, and a knowledge in our hearts of evil and good; who sees in this world a chance for those whom he made to grow in character and develop in the liberty of his children. *Dr Frank N D Buchman*

As I have read about the saints like Francis of Assisi, Clare and Thérèse of Lisieux, what has been revealed is not a duty, nor a task but a love affair with Christ: men and women who so submit to Christ's presence that they become lost in him, and begin to reflect Christ himself.

Countless actions over the centuries have ensured that 'divine' love is known in the world. Perhaps this is the basic struggle in the world. Will our negative human qualities – ambition, lust, bitterness, greed – dominate and become the engine of society, or will love be allowed to become the driving force?

Dr John Lester

THE CREATIVE MINORITY November 24

Go in by the narrow gate. For the wide gate has a broad road which leads to disaster and there are many people going that way. The narrow gate and the hard road lead out into life and only a few are finding it. *Matthew 7:13-14*

Convictions are the main springs of action, the driving powers of life. What we live are our convictions. *Francis C Kelly*

If we expect disaster we will get disaster. If we expect and fight for success, we will get success. We need a determination to create a new society. There are those who say that our problems are too complex for simple solutions. But the basic moral decisions we have to make are often very simple, though the implementation may be complex and demand all the faculties of thought, science, energy and imagination of which we are capable. *Neville Cooper*

If five per cent of any body of people are wholly convinced about anything, they can swing the rest. The final decision as to what the future of a society shall be depends not on how near the organisation is to perfection but on the degree of worthiness of its individual members. *J C Smuts*

The kingdom of Heaven is like a tiny grain of mustard-seed which a man took and sowed in his field. As a seed it is the smallest of them all, but it grows to be the biggest of all plants. It becomes a tree, big enough for birds to come and nest in its branches. *Matthew 13:31-32*

THE ORDINARY PERSON November 25

Then the Lord ordered him, 'Go, with all your great strength and rescue Israel from the Midianites. I myself am sending you.' Gideon replied, 'But Lord, how can I rescue Israel? My clan is the weakest in the tribe of Manasseh and I am the least important member of my family.' *Judges 6:14-15 GNB*

The ordinary person who wills to have a mind freed from the shackles of impure imagery, an eye that looks at things squarely and brooks deception neither of self nor of others, a hand that will not spare itself in work, and a heart that will express without reserve its honest convictions and genuine affections, will often outstrip the brilliant genius, who is shackled and ultimately overthrown by impurity, dishonesty, selfishness or atrophy of heart.   *Henry B Wright*

There was I, a college student, cold, selfish, cynical, sneering at the poor boys from the factories and slums... sinful, and I felt it as never in my life before, as soon as Moody began to speak... I felt shrivelled in selfishness. There was this man who had never entered a college or high school, using bad grammar but shaking half a continent in America and upsetting the colleges and cities of Great Britain. Before he had finished a great thirst had sprung up in my heart... That night marked the turning point in my life.   *Rev Sherwood Eddy*

The ordinary person can do the extraordinary thing if he is in touch with God.   *Dr Frank N D Buchman*

A NEW SOCIAL ORDER   November 26

Righteousness makes a nation great; sin is a disgrace to any nation.   *Proverbs 14:34*

The truth is that we neither live nor die as self-contained units. At every turn life links us to the Lord.   *Romans 14:6-7*

When people change, the structure of society changes. And when the structure of society changes, people change. Both go together and both are necessary.
Hans Böckler, President of the German
Trades Union Federation

We have gone a long way to change the evils that have affected the people of South Africa for the past 300 years.
President Nelson Mandela on the first
anniversary of democratic elections

The main object of religion is not to get man into heaven but to get heaven into him.   *Thomas Hardy*

Neither civilisation nor Christianity can be promoted alone. In fact they are inseparable.   *David Livingstone*

HOMEWARD BOUND

Whom have I in heaven but thee? And there is none upon earth that I desire beside thee. My flesh and my heart faileth; but God is the strength of my heart and my portion for ever.

Psalms 73:25-26

There are many rooms in my Father's house and I am going to prepare a place for you. *John 14:2 GNB*

If you insist on having your own way, you will get it. Hell is the enjoyment of your own way for ever. If you really want God's way with you, you will get it in heaven. *Dorothy L Sayers*

Any philosophy which deals only with the here and now is not adequate. *Dr Billy Graham*

We treat sensible and present things as realities, and future and eternal things as fables; whereas the reverse should be our habit. *Richard Cecil*

In sure and certain hope of the resurrection to eternal life through our Lord Jesus Christ; who shall change our vile body that it may be like unto his glorious body, according to the mighty working, whereby he is able to subdue all things to himself. *The Burial Service in the Book of Common Prayer*

We are warned again and again not to value this world as a permanency. Neither our security nor our true wealth is rooted in this passing life. *Canon J B Phillips*

Today many people fear death. Helping them involves sharing with them the joy of the vision of being homeward bound. *P M*

ASPIRATION

Not that I claim to have reached perfection already. But I keep going on, trying to grasp that purpose for which Christ Jesus grasped me. *Philippians 3:12*

I have immortal longings in me. *William Shakespeare*

I have a dream that one day this nation will rise up and live out the true meaning of this creed: 'We hold these truths to be self-evident that all men were created equal.' I have a dream that one day on the red hills of Georgia, the sons of former slaves and the sons of former slave-owners will be able to sit down together at the table of brotherhood... I have a dream that my four little children will one day live in a nation where they will not be judged according to the colour of their skin but by the content of their character. I have a dream that one day every valley shall be exalted, every hill and mountain shall be made low, the rough places will be made plain, and the crooked places will be made straight and the glory of the Lord shall be revealed and all flesh shall see it together.

Dr Martin Luther King

I asked for Peace –
My sins arose,
And bound me close,
I could not find release.
I asked for Truth –
My doubts came in
And with their din
They wearied all my youth.
I asked for thee –
And thou didst come
To take me home
Within thy heart to be.

D M Dolben

If you aim at nothing you hit it.

Dorothy M Prescott

A GOOD LISTENER   November 29

You, Lord, give perfect peace to those who keep their purpose firm and put their trust in you.   *Isaiah 26:3 GNB*

Our minds are like crows. They pick up everything that glitters no matter how uncomfortable our nests get with all that metal in them.   *Thomas Merton*

Lift up your heart to him, sometimes even at your meals and when you are in company; the least little remembrance will

always be acceptable to him. You need not cry very loud. He is
nearer to us than we are aware of.   *Brother Lawrence*

Almighty God influences us and works in us through our
minds, not without them or in spite of them.

Cardinal J H Newman

The person who does most for others is a quiet person, unhurried, a good listener, who wastes no time thinking of themselves but is centred in God.   *H P E*

To thee, O Lord, we turn for peace... but grant us too the
blessed assurance that nothing shall deprive us of that peace,
neither ourselves nor our foolish earthly desires, nor my wild
longings nor the anxious cravings of my heart.

Søren Kierkegaard

GRACIOUS LIVING   November 30

Just as sin ruled by means of death, so also God's grace rules by
means of righteousness, leading us to eternal life through Christ
Jesus our Lord.   *Romans 5:21 GNB*

My colleagues often ask me: 'How is it you manage to talk so
intimately with people?' I think the answer is never to let ourselves become accomplices in any attempts at evasion, never to
let ourselves fly off at a tangent when the conversation shows
signs of turning down into the depths, to be ready ourselves at
all times to face any problem, any question, however indiscreet.

Dr Paul Tournier

I fancy that as we grow older, as we think longer and work
harder and learn to sympathise more intelligently, the one thing
we long to be able to pass on to people is a vast commanding
sense of the grace of the eternal. Compared with that, all else is
but small dust of the balance.   *Hugh R Mackintosh*

I sincerely wanted to do much for the people in my charge. But
what was lacking was the gracious living which would make it
easy for them to tell me their problems. I was too often in a
hurry and my driving was sometimes fearsome.

A former Colonial administrator

The best thing to give to your enemy is forgiveness;
  – to your opponent, tolerance;
  – to a friend, your ear;
  – to your child, good example;
  – to a father, reverence;
  – to your mother, conduct that will make her
    proud of you
  – to yourself, respect;
  – to all men, charity.   *Benjamin Franklin*

FREEDOM: GIFT AND DECISION December 1

Live as free people; do not, however, use your freedom to cover up any evil, but live as God's slaves. Respect everyone, love your fellow-believers, and honour God.   *1 Peter 2:16-17 GNB*

So Jesus said to the Jews who believed in him, 'If you are faithful to what I have said, you are truly disciples. And you will know the truth and the truth will set you free.'   *John 8:31-32*

Love produces freedom, above all freedom from self, which allows people to become single-minded and wholly given... The cost of experiencing that freedom is the abandonment of self in favour of God, submission to the imprisonment of God's will. The resulting experience of joy and love is one of liberation. A heart which loves is a heart which is free.   *Dr John Lester*

When we speak with God, our power of addressing him, of holding communion with him, and listening to his still small voice, depends upon our will being one and the same with him.
Florence Nightingale

Give me the liberty to know, to think, to believe and to utter freely, according to conscience, above all other liberties.
John Milton

Plant your feet firmly therefore within the freedom that Christ has won for us.   *Galatians 5:1*

SELF-WILL CROSSED OUT December 2

Do not be like your ancestors and your fellow-Israelites who were unfaithful to the Lord their God. As you can see he punished them severely. Do not be stubborn as they were but obey the Lord.   *2 Chronicles 30:7-8 GNB*

May your kingdom come, and your will be done on earth as it is in heaven.   *Matthew 6:10*

The will is the deciding factor in everything that we do. In every sphere of life it settles alternatives.   *Frederick Wood*

God, having placed good and evil in our power, has given us

full freedom of choice; he does not keep back the unwilling, but embraces the willing.   *St John Chrysostom*

> And I will place within them as a Guide
> My umpire Conscience, whom if they will hear,
> Light after light well used they shall attain,
> And to the end persisting, safe arrive.   *John Milton*

The whole duty of man is summed up in obedience to God's will.   *George Washington*

FREE WILL   December 3

When he made man in the beginning, he left him free to take his own decisions; if you choose you can keep the commandments; whether or not you keep faith is yours to decide.
                                              Ecclesiasticus 15:15 NEB

The will is not free... the affections love as they do and the will chooses as it does because of the state of the heart and... the heart is deceitful and desperately wicked.   *A W Pink*

The will can be made to conform by pressure. That is why relative standards are so popular and why absolute standards are so necessary. The relative moral standard yields before the demands of the will. The absolute standard cuts across the will and demands change... To surrender our own will is like giving up life itself. It is a dying to self. One great revolutionary said of his experience 'I die daily.' It has been called 'taking up the cross'.   *Paul Campbell and Peter Howard*

The centre of God's will is our only safety.
    The words of Betsie ten Boom to others when she and they were facing death by starvation and beatings in a Nazi concentration camp.

THE GREAT POSITIVE   December 4

But you belong to God, my children, and have defeated the false prophets, because the spirit who is in you is more powerful than the spirit in those who belong to the world.

1 John 4:4 GNB

In all things you yourself must be an example of good behaviour. Be sincere and serious in your teaching. Use sound words that cannot be criticised.

Titus 2:7-8 GNB

The highest recommendation of Bishop Aidan's teaching to all was that he and his followers lived as they taught. He never sought or cared for any worldly possessions, and loved to give away to the poor whatever he received from kings or wealthy folk.

The Venerable Bede

> Fill every part of me with praise...
> So shall each fear, each fret, each care
> Be turned into a song
> And every winding in the way
> The echo shall prolong.

Horatius Bonar

Grant to us thy humble servants that by thy holy inspiration we may think those things that be good, and by thy merciful guiding may perform the same.

Book of Common Prayer

THE HOLY SPIRIT   December 5

If you love me, you will obey my commandments. I will ask the Father and he will give you another helper, who will stay with you for ever. He is the spirit who will reveal the truth about God.

John 14:15-17 GNB

If you believe that you have within you a master who would teach you eternal wisdom, say to this master as resolutely and as plainly as you would say it to a man standing before you, 'Master, speak. I am listening.'

But when you have said, 'I am listening', it is necessary that you should indeed listen. This seems obvious, but it is altogether essential.

What am I to do in practice? Here is my answer; you are to *write*. Do not trust to memory. Memory is faithful and accurate only in the actual presence of the objects. Memory is a faculty that forgets. When the heavenly light of ideas shines upon it, memory thinks that this light will not be withdrawn. Do not believe it. When the light has gone, memory will grow dim.

Père Alphonse Gratry

> Come, Holy Spirit...
> Wash away the dirt,
> Water the dry places;
> Heal the wounds;
> Bend the rigid mind;
> Warm the cold heart;
> Direct the wayward will.
>
> *Thirteenth century prayer to the Holy Spirit*

BORN AGAIN   December 6

For through the living and eternal word of God you have been born again as the children of a parent who is immortal, not mortal.   *1 Peter 1:23 GNB*

Conviction, were it never so excellent, is worthless until it convert itself into conduct.   *Thomas Carlyle*

No man who, through the deliberate act of surrender of the human will to absolute standards of purity, honesty, unselfishness and love, has once felt the coursing of these immortal powers in his spirit can ever after find any experience of this new life tame or commonplace.   *Henry B Wright*

Mrs Penn-Lewis read book after book on the Holy Spirit. Finally she decided, 'I will go straight to God... I want the deliverance that Peter got at Pentecost.' Later, 'I knew in my spirit that he had come... Christ suddenly became to me a real person.'

Mark Guldseth

The Holy Spirit is always original and no negative ever comes from his inspiration.   *Dorothy M Prescott*

THOUGHTS ON HUMILITY December 7

Live a life that measures up to the standard God set when he called you. Be always humble, gentle and patient. Show your love by being tolerant with one another. *Ephesians 4:1-2 GNB*

Humility is the hall-mark of the child of God.
Dr Martyn Lloyd-Jones

A black South African leader told me he thought the only good white man was a dead one. He had decided to hold a major demonstration in Johannesburg. Violence might have ensued... Shortly before it was due to begin, a young Afrikaner student had come to his house in the African township. He said 'I have come to say sorry. I have blamed you but remained arrogant... I am sorry.' The black man was astonished. He told his people, 'We must delay our demonstration.' *Dr John Lester*

> Who sweeps a room as for thy laws,
> Makes that and th' action fine. *George Herbert*

OPEN TO NEW THINKING December 8

My thoughts are not your thoughts, neither are your ways my ways, saith the Lord. For as the heavens are higher than the earth, so are my ways higher than your ways, and my thoughts than your thoughts. For as the rain cometh down, and the snow from heaven, and returneth not thither, but watereth the earth, and maketh it bring forth and bud, that it may give seed to the sower and bread to the eater: So shall my word be that goeth forth out of my mouth; it shall not return unto me void, but it shall accomplish that which I please, and it shall prosper in the thing whereto I sent it. *Isaiah 55:8-11*

A new world philosophy is needed, a world philosophy capable of creating a new era of constructive relationships between individuals and nations. A new statesmanship and a new leadership will ensue from this heightened quality of thinking and living. This world philosophy will emerge as people begin to get their direction from the living God. It will be within the framework of a hate-free, fear-free, greed-free quality of living... People today are ready to believe that human wisdom has failed. A situation is growing up in which people will want God to speak to them.   *Dr Frank N D Buchman*

> There are more things in heaven and earth, Horatio,
> Than are dreamt of in your philosophy.
> *William Shakespeare*

'GREAT' AND 'SMALL'   December 9

Even your smallest and humblest family will become as great as a powerful nation. When the right time comes, I will make this happen quickly. I am the Lord!   *Isaiah 60:22 GNB*

If you are to judge the world do you consider yourselves incapable of settling such infinitely smaller matters?
1 Corinthians 6:2

There is nothing small in the service of God.   *St Francis de Sales*

The scriptures are a river, if I may put it in this way, in which a lamb may walk and an elephant may swim.   *Pope Gregory I*

Detailed care for people. I have never known anyone who knows so quickly and so surely what is going on inside another person as Frank Buchman. In a room full of people he has an unerring eye for the one who specially needs help, or encouragement, a stimulating challenge or maybe a drastic warning. He used to tell us, 'You've got to be so sensitive that if the other fellow has a hole in his shoe, your foot gets cold.'
Rev Alan Thornhill

Do little things as if they were great, because of the majesty of the Lord Jesus Christ who dwells in thee.   *Blaise Pascal*

NOW OR NEVER   December 10

For God's word is: At an acceptable time I hearkened to thee, and in a day of salvation did I succour thee. Now is the 'acceptable time', and this very day is the 'day of salvation'.

2 Corinthians 6:2

In darkness there is no choice. It is light that enables us to see the differences between things; and it is Christ who gives us light.

Augustus W Hare

Absolute moral standards are not just questions of individual conduct today. They are the conditions of national survival... Wherever people give human beings the place in their lives that God alone should have, slavery has begun. There is no neutrality in the battle between good and evil.

Dr Frank N D Buchman

The power of choosing good or evil is within the reach of us all.

Origen of Alexandria

There is a time when we must firmly choose the course we will follow, or the relentless drift of events will make the decision.

Herbert V Prochnow

Help each other to stand firm in the faith every day, while it is still called 'today'... These words are still being said for our ears to hear:

> Today if ye shall hear his voice
> Harden not your hearts.

Hebrews 3:13,15

THOUGHTS ON PURITY   December 11

Who may go up the mountain with the Lord? And who may stand in his holy place? He who has clean hands and a pure heart, and who has not set his mind on falsehood, and has not committed perjury.

Psalms 24:3-4 NEB

Every one of you should learn to control his body, keeping it pure and treating it with respect... The calling of God is not to impurity but to the most thorough purity, and anyone who makes light of the matter is not making light of a man's ruling but of God's command.

1 Thessalonians 4:4 and 7-8

The strength of a nation is measured by its fight for purity. When this moral bastion goes, infection creeps through the whole fabric of society. Then honesty depends only on the possibility of getting caught. Loyalty lasts only as long as it is expedient. Co-operation must pay an obvious cash dividend, or give way to 'each man for himself'. This civilisation – that means your children and grandchildren – will know suffering beyond any calculation unless we know these facts and start to fight.   *Kenaston Twitchell*

The impure then cannot love God; and those who are without love of God cannot really be pure. Purity prepares the soul for love, and love confirms the soul in purity.

Cardinal J H Newman

Holiness consists primarily, not in the absence of faults, but in the presence of spiritual force, of love creative, love triumphant.

Baron Friedrich von Hügel

THE THOUGHT LIFE   December 12

Be careful how you think; your life is shaped by your thoughts.

Proverbs 4:23 GNB

Fill your minds with those things that are good and deserve praise; things that are true, noble, right, pure, lovely and honourable.   *Philippians 4:8 GNB*

At every point right living begins with right thinking.

Bruce J Milne

Believe it, Christians, for a certain truth that, when you come to die, your thoughts will not be: what a figure have I made in the world; how pleasantly have I passed my days;... and what wealth will I leave behind me? No, no. But such as these following will be your reflections: how have I spent my life; how have I employed my time and my health; how have I improved the talents with which God entrusted me; what good have I done in the world; have I brought up my children in the fear of God; have I been true and just in my dealings; have I lived in the fear of God and worshipped him both in public and in private according to my ability?   *Bishop Thomas Wilson*

The most important thought I ever had was that of my individual responsibility to God.   *Daniel Webster*

Whatever I in this life may yet reflect,
that you will give me;
And whatever I shall not attain,
that, plainly, you have purposed for others.

Alexander Solzhenitsyn

ASKING   December 13

We receive from him whatever we ask, because we obey his commands, do what pleases him... Those who obey God's commands live in union with God and God lives in union with them. And because of the spirit that God has given us we know that God lives in union with us.   *1 John 3:22 and 24 GNB*

God insists that we ask, not because he needs to know our situation, but because we need the spiritual discipline of asking.

Catharine Marshall

There is a force that can outmatch all others and which, if we will, can shape the future. It is the mighty onslaught of a new spirit challenging people and nations to a change of heart. It is the cumulative effect of millions of people who listen to God and obey.   *Senator Bankhead*

All my discoveries have been made in answer to prayer.

Sir Isaac Newton

Lord we know not what we ought to ask of thee; thou only knowest what we need.   *Archbishop François Fénelon*

The Spirit also comes to help us, weak as we are. For we do not know how we ought to pray; the Spirit himself pleads with God for us in groans that words cannot express.   *Romans 8:26*

UNITY   December 14

Among the large number who had become believers there was complete agreement of heart and soul.   *Acts 4:32*

When anyone is united to Christ, there is a new world; the old order has gone, and a new order has already begun.

2 Corinthians 5:17

Some of us worked long enough in a shipbuilding district to know that welding is impossible except the materials to be joined are at white heat temperature.   *George F McLeod*

We are one hunk of ground, water, air, clouds, floating around in space. From here it really is one world.

Frank Bormann, speaking from the moon

In necessary things, unity; in doubtful things, liberty; in all things charity.   *Richard Baxter*

> Wherever in the world I am,
> In whatsoe'er estate,
> I have a fellowship of hearts
> To keep and cultivate.   *Anna Letitia Waring*

FACTS, NOT FEELINGS   December 15

As long as you obey his commands, you are safe and a wise person knows how and when to do it.   *Ecclesiastes 8:5 GNB*

It is a fact that our faith is not to be based on individual feelings – but it is equally true that our faith is suspect if it is not accompanied by the certain feeling of the peace that is beyond human understanding.   *P M*

When depressed or confused, the *fact* is that God is there. And if the *will* is there, he will surely guide. The Holy Spirit is the most intelligent source of information in the world today. Everywhere, when people let him, he is teaching them how to live.   *Dr Frank N D Buchman*

Our main business is not to see what lies dimly at a distance, but to do what lies clearly at hand.   *Thomas Carlyle*

When Christ comes in, the wonder is not that one has emotion, but the wonder is that one can be so restrained.

Rev E Stanley Jones

FIRE ON THE EARTH December 16

I came to set the earth on fire, and how I wish it were already kindled. *Luke 12:49 GNB*

The supreme need of the church is the same in the twentieth century as in the first; it is men on fire for Christ.

James S Stewart

I am never better than when I am on full stretch for God.

George Whitefield

Lord, we believe, we accept, we adore,
Less than the least though we be;
Fire of love, burn in us, burn evermore
Till we burn out for thee.

O for the pure prayer power that prevails,
That pours itself out for the lost,
Victorious prayer in the Conqueror's name:
The Lord of Pentecost. *Amy Carmichael*

O thou who camest from above,
The pure celestial fire to impart,
Kindle a flame of sacred love
On the mean altar of my heart.

There let it for thy glory burn
With inextinguishable blaze,
And trembling to its source return
In humble prayer, and fervent praise. *Charles Wesley*

FOR EVERYONE EVERYWHERE December 17

For as the scripture says, 'As surely as I am the living God, says the Lord, everyone will kneel before me, and everyone will confess that I am God.' *Romans 14:11 GNB*

Let us love one another because love comes from God. Whoever loves is a child of God and knows God. *1 John 4:7 GNB*

One of the urgent functions of the church today is to proclaim from the housetops that it is possible for a nation, as for an individual, to progress materially and to regress spiritually... to feed, clothe and educate our children yet so to neglect their spiritual welfare as to set their feet on the path to destruction; to be so with-it as to be 'without him'; to refuse the absolutes of God's law and to land in the sands of moral chaos.

Archbishop Donald Coggan

You are writing a gospel,
A chapter a day,
By the deeds that you do
And the words that you say,
Men read what you write,
If it's false or it's true;
Now what is the gospel
According to you?

Anon

Attempt great things for God; expect great things from God.

William Carey

THE NEW ERA   December 18

Let your eyes look straight before you, fix your gaze on what lies ahead.   *Proverbs 4:25 NEB*

Our hopes are set on new heavens and a new earth which God has promised us, in which justice will make its home.

2 Peter 3:13

Despair not for the future of the world. Out of its heart will yet come those who shall lift it up to a new level... God knows where to find them. And, when the times are darkest, they shall lead forth a host of pilgrim spirits.   *Rev F B Meyer*

The first feast that God prepares for us is the gospel feast. The menu is superlative – 'the peace which transcends all understanding' Philippians 4:7; 'inexpressible and glorious joy' 1 Peter 1:8; 'love that surpasses knowledge' Ephesians 3:19; 'total forgiveness' 1 John 1:9; 'life to the full' John 10:10; and 'glorious freedom' Romans 8:20, among other things. Ever since the death and resurrection of Jesus, this gospel feast has been ready and God has been saying 'Come'. *Canon David Watson*

The power of Christ's Cross and Resurrection is greater than any evil which man could or should fear. *Pope John Paul II*

THE MEANING OF CHRISTMAS December 19

They went into the house, and when they saw the child with his mother Mary, they knelt down and worshipped him. They brought out their gifts of gold, frankincense, and myrrh, and presented them to him. *Matthew 2:11 GNB*

Of the wise men come from the East: It was no summer progress. A cold coming they had of it at this time of the year, just the worst time of the year to take a journey, and specially a long journey in. The ways deep, the weather sharp, the days short, the sun farthest off, and the very dead of winter.
Bishop Lancelot Andrewes

God has humbled himself, and still we are proud! Great is the wretchedness of our pride; but greater still is the mercy of God's humility. *St Augustine*

The character of the Creator cannot be less than the highest he has created, and the highest is that babe born to Mary on that first Christmas morning. *A Ian Burnett*

> O Holy Child who came to birth
> To heal the hates of all the earth,
> Shatter our poor selective care
> With love for all men everywhere. *Bremer Hofmeyr*

DIVINE INTERVENTION December 20

Before the words were out of his mouth, a voice spoke from heaven: 'King Nebuchadnezzar, listen to what I say! Your royal power is now taken away from you. You will be driven away from human society.' *Daniel 4:31-32 GNB*

But an angel of the Lord said to Philip, 'Get up and go south down the road which runs from Jerusalem to Gaza, out in the desert.' ...The Spirit said to Philip, 'Approach this carriage, and keep close to it.' *Acts 8:26-27*

A S Candler Jnr of Coca Cola tells how he desperately tried to overcome the problem of drink. He dealt with the symptoms of his problem but failed to see that the root cause was his unsurrendered self. One night as he was being driven home, half-drunk, by his chauffeur, the Holy Spirit spoke to his heart in these words: 'You must renounce yourself; you must reject yourself; you must surrender yourself.' Notice the Spirit did not say, 'You must stop drinking,' but 'Surrender yourself.'

Rev Selwyn Hughes © CWR

God has created me to do him some definite service; he has committed some work to me which he has not committed to another. I have my mission – I never may know it in this life, but I shall be told it in the next. *Cardinal John Henry Newman*

> But O what sight appears
> Within that lowly door!
> A manger, stall and swaddling clothes?
> A child and mother poor.
> Our sinful pride to cure
> With that pure love of thine,
> O be Thou born within our hearts,
> Most holy child divine. *C Coffin*

GOD'S VALUES AND OURS   December 21

As the scripture says: 'What no one ever saw or heard, what no one ever thought could happen, is the very thing God prepared for those who love him.' But it was to us that God made known his secret by means of his Spirit. The Spirit searches everything, even the hidden depths of God's purposes.

1 Corinthians 2:9-10 GNB

Just as in the beginning, God said 'Let there be light' and there was light, so at the moment appointed for our new birth, he said 'Let there be life' and there was life. *J A Motyer*

It is good that somewhere in the world there are people who realise that Christ is born. There were only a few shepherds at the first Bethlehem, and it is the same now. The ox and the ass understood more of the first Christmas than the High Priests in Jerusalem. And it is the same today. *Thomas Merton*

Alexander, Caesar, Charlemagne and I have founded empires. But on what did we rest the creation of our genius? Upon force. Jesus Christ founded his empire on love; and at this hour millions of people would die for him. *Napoleon Bonaparte*

The coming of Christ by way of a Bethlehem manger seems strange and stunning. But when we take him out of the manger and invite him into our hearts, then the meaning unfolds and the strangeness vanishes. *Neil C Strait*

THE SIGN OF THE STRONGEST   December 22

The Lord gives strength to his people and blesses them with peace. *Psalms 29:11 GNB*

The Lord stood by me and gave me strength.
2 Timothy 4:17 NEB

When I was in the army I had to do all kinds of seemingly annoying and unnecessary things as part of my training in submission and obedience. This habit of obedience has to be so ingrained that in the heat of the battle one would do instantly and unquestioningly whatever one's commanding officer ordered. In a spiritual battle God can wonderfully use and bless those soldiers who obey instantly and unquestioningly.
Canon David Watson

The most difficult thing in the world is to become poor in spirit.
Dr Martyn Lloyd-Jones

God only asks from you what he gives you power to do.
Bishop W Walsham How

Humility is the surest sign of strength. *Thomas Merton*

> May the strength of God pilot us,
> May the power of God preserve us,

May the wisdom of God instruct us,
May the way of God direct us,
May the shield of God defend us,
May the host of God guard us against the snares of evil
and the temptations of the world.
May Christ be with us,
Christ before us,
Christ in us,
Christ over us.   *St Patrick*

ON EARTH PEACE   December 23

Now I will lie down in peace and sleep; for thou alone, O Lord,
makest me live unafraid.   *Psalms 4:8 NEB*

To be controlled by the Spirit results in life and peace.
                                              Romans 8:6 GNB

I have always loved the story of Bishop Quayle, the great
American bishop. For years he worried himself to death about
his church and his clergy and his work and about all the things
that had to be done. He used to sit up half the night worrying
about all kinds of things. Then one night, as he sat worrying, he
tells us that he heard God's voice as clearly as if it had been
someone sitting in the same room; and God was saying,
'Quayle, you go to bed. I'll sit up for the rest of the night!' And
thereafter there was in Quayle a wonderful serenity, for he had
learned to cast his burden on the Lord.   *Dr William Barclay*

Few things more adorn and beautify a Christian profession
than exercising and manifesting the spirit of peace.   *A W Pink*

Stayed upon Jehovah
Hearts are fully blessed,
Finding, as he promised,
Perfect peace and rest.   *Frances Ridley Havergal*

If there is something that our divided world without peace
needs then it is people who in the name of Christ will cross
boundaries to lessen their neighbour's need.   *Mother Teresa*

THE STAR December 24

The wise men listened to the king and then went on their way, to Bethlehem. And now, the star, which they had seen in the east, went in front of them until at last it shone immediately above the place where the little child lay. The sight of the star filled them with indescribable joy. So they went into the house and saw the little child with his mother Mary. And they fell on their knees and worshipped him. *Matthew 2:9-10*

> As with gladness men of old
> Did the guiding star behold,
> As with joy they hailed its light,
> Leading onward, beaming bright,
> So, most gracious Lord, may we
> Evermore be led to thee. *William Chatterton Dix*

Keep thy heart in a soft and tractable estate, lest thou lose the imprints of God's hands. *St Irenaeus*

> Love came down at Christmas.
> Love all lovely, Love Divine;
> Love was born at Christmas,
> Star and angels gave the sign. *Christina G Rossetti*

THE CHRIST CHILD December 25

Well then, the Lord himself will give you a sign; a young woman who is pregnant will have a son and will name him Immanuel. *Isaiah 7:14 GNB*

When the angels went away from them back to heaven, the shepherds said to one another, 'Let's go to Bethlehem and see this thing that has happened, which the Lord has told us.' So they hurried off and found Mary and Joseph and saw the babe lying in the manger. *Luke 2:15-16 GNB*

There is only one way of being faithful to the Incarnation and that is to become an embodied testimony to the living God. Perhaps the core of the apologetic task in every age is to be created in lives rather than in arguments. *Gabriel Marcel*

O little town of Bethlehem,
How still we see thee lie!
Above thy deep and dreamless sleep
The silent stars go by.
Yet in thy dark streets shineth
The everlasting light;
The hopes and fears of all the years
Are met in thee tonight.   *Phillips Brooks*

THE WISE MEN   December 26

Jesus was born in the town of Bethlehem in Judea, during the
time when Herod was king. Soon afterwards some men who
studied the stars came from the east to Jerusalem and asked,
'Where is the baby born to be king of the Jews? We saw his star
when it came up in the east and we have come to worship him.'
Matthew 2:1-2 GNB

If you long for wisdom, keep the commandments and the Lord
will give it you in plenty.   *Ecclesiasticus 1:26 NEB*

Wise men came from afar, guided by a star, at that first Christmas. May each one of us, illumined from afar, bring a gift to all
mankind that will be more acceptable than any earthly reward.
Dr Frank N D Buchman

Every thought, word, action, silence and self-expression in the
incarnate life of the Word of God is full of spiritual significance
and effectiveness.   *Monsignor R Hugh Benson*

The first visitors to a home after the birth of a child are usually
family and friends. It was different when Jesus was born. Local
people, about their ordinary business, were alerted by God's
angels, who told them precisely where that very day their Saviour had been born. Then came wise men from the east, already
forewarned of the birth and asking where the King of the Jews
could be found. These may well have been non-Jews, the first
Gentiles to pay homage to God's only son.   *P M*

CHRISTMAS LASTS FOR EVER — December 27

Love knows no limit to its endurance, no end to its trust, no fading of its hope; it can outlast anything. Love never fails. ...In this life we have three lasting qualities – faith, hope and love. But the greatest of them is love. *1 Corinthians 13:7-8 and 13*

> For O! eternity's too short
> To utter all thy praise. *Joseph Addison*

We must aim above all at a spiritual renewal, a liberation from the mere following of conventions, a new departure in our way of thinking. More than anything else we must lament our shortcomings before God and the community of our brethren.
Pope Paul VI

> Christmas has its special magic,
> Long may it last and vanish never.
> To lose it early would be tragic,
> For Christmas lasts for ever. *H P E*

AFTER THE STAR — December 28

He gives me new strength. He guides me in the right paths, as he has promised. Even if I go through the deepest darkness, I will not be afraid, Lord, for you are with me... I know that your goodness and love will be with me all my life, and your house will be my home as long as I live. *Psalms 23:3-4 and 6 GNB*

For yourselves keep faithful to what you heard at the beginning. If you do you will be living in fellowship with both the Father and the Son. And that means sharing his own life for ever as he has promised. *1 John 2:24-25*

Are you willing to believe that love is the strongest thing in the world and that the blessed life which began in Bethlehem 1,900 years ago is the image and brightness of eternal love? Then you can keep Christmas. And if you keep it for a day, why not always? *Henry van Dyke*

What God-given faculty is it that enables us to recognise the word of God as the word of God and not as a mere human opinion or doctrine? From my own experience, that is from my own knowledge of my own inner truth, I believe this recognition of God's word to be a valid part of human experience. And when I find, as I have done over the last 30 years, that this inner experience is shared by thousands in various parts of the world, I am convinced that here is an authentic part of human existence which is all too often ignored. *Canon J B Phillips*

Turn the harsh hearts to humbleness,
Sweeten the sour, inflame the cold,
So may we live your miracle,
Accept the new – and leave the old. *Peter Howard*

When Christ came into the world peace was sung; and when he went out of the world peace was bequeathed. *Francis Bacon*

BEST IS YET TO BE December 29

These are the people who have come safely through the terrible persecution. They have washed their robes and made them white with the blood of the Lamb... Never again will they hunger or thirst; neither sun nor any scorching heat will burn them, because the Lamb who is in the centre of the throne, will be their shepherd, and he will lead them to springs of living water. And God will wipe away every tear from their eyes.

Revelation 7:14-17 GNB

These two dimensions cannot be separated: on the one hand, the moral demands God makes of people; on the other, the demands of his saving love – the gift of his grace – to which God in a certain sense has bound himself. What else is the redemption accomplished in Christ, if not precisely this? God desires the salvation of us all, he desires that humanity find that fulfilment to which he himself has destined it, and Christ has the right to say that his yoke is easy and his burden, in the end, light. *Pope John Paul II*

Not with the cross of the Saviour behind you, but with your own cross behind the Saviour. *Cyprian Norwid*

Seek Christ and you will find him and with him everything else thrown in. *C S Lewis*

GOOD RESOLUTIONS AND THE GRACE OF GOD

Let us hold fast the confession of our faith without wavering, for he who promised is faithful.   *Hebrews 10:23*

Patrick listened – and thought about himself. He knew that there were areas of his own life that would need a thorough clean-up if he was to find a new direction. He was not without a faith. He had been brought up a Catholic, but in Australia he had certainly not kept to the straight and narrow. 'I got a new vision. That was the first thing and then I made certain decisions... I loved my father and respected him, but we could not communicate... By simply telling my Dad about the shames and hurts in my life, it broke down all the barriers.'   *Geoffrey Gain*

Would not the carrying out of one single commandment of Christ, 'Love one another', change the whole aspect of the world and sweep away prisons and strife and all the strongholds of the devil? Two thousand years have nearly passed and people have not yet understood that one single commandment of Christ, 'Love one another'.   *Friedrich Max Müller*

> Father let me dedicate
> All this year to thee,
> In whatever worldly state
> Thou wilt have me be;
> Not from sorrow, pain or care
> Freedom dare I claim;
> This alone shall be my prayer,
> 'Glorify thy name.'   *L Tuttiet*

SUPPOSE!

Be concerned with the heavenly things, not with the passing things of earth. For, as far as the world is concerned, you are already dead and your true life is a hidden one in God through Christ.   *Colossians 3:2-3*

There is a kind of love that is demanding, that asks for a return of love, or else shuts off its flow. Absolute love is undemanding. It continues to care, to work for the other's welfare, whether there is any response or not, and even when rebuffed. Write down the places where your love has been demanding. Where would you and I be if God turned off his love every time we spurn it or are ungrateful or indifferent?   *Edward T Perry*

'We know that all things work together for good to them that love God.' The idea is not that we do work for God, but that we are so loyal to him that he can do his work through us.

Oswald Chambers

If we knew how to listen to God, we should hear him speaking to us, for God does speak. He speaks in his gospel, he speaks also through life – that new gospel to which we ourselves add a page each day.   *Abbé Michel Quoist*

All things are possible to him that believes.   *Mark 9:23*

Ring out false pride in place and blood,
The civic slander and the spite;
Ring in the love of truth and right,
Ring in the common love of good.

Ring in the valiant man and free,
The larger heart, the kindlier hand;
Ring out the darkness of the land,
Ring in the Christ that is to be.

Alfred, Lord Tennyson

Index of Authors

BAXTER, Richard (1615-91)	Jun 22, Oct 6, Dec 14
BAZOZ, Dr A	Jan 4
BEA, Cardinal (1881-1968)	Apr 30
BEDE, The Venerable (673-735)	Mar 27, Dec 4
BEECHER, Henry Ward (1813-87)	May 9, Aug 27
BEETHOVEN, Ludwig van (1770-1827)	Mar 22
BEGBIE, Harold (1871-1929)	Aug 4
BEKR, Abu	Feb 26
BELDEN, Kenneth D	Jan 8,20, Feb 13, Apr 21,24, 27, May 1,17,28, Jun 1, Aug 6,18, Sept 15,23,29, Oct 20,23,30, Nov 5,
BENNETT, Arnold (1876-1931)	Feb 27,
BENSON, Arthur C (1862-1925)	Aug 13
BENSON, Monsignor R Hugh (1971-1914)	Jan 20, Jul 1, Aug 9, Oct 27, Dec 26
BERNARD, St of Clairvaux (1090-1153)	Nov 9
BILLINGS, Josh (1818-85)	Aug 21, Oct 14
BLAKE, William (1757-1827)	Jan 11
BLANCHARD, John	Mar 12, 17, Apr 8
BLOUNT, Sir Thomas (1649-97)	Sept 9
BÖCKLER, Hans	Nov 26
BODE, J E (1816-74)	Jan 21, May 11
BONAR, Andrew (d.1892)	Oct 3
BONAR, Dr Horatius (1808-89)	Jan 26, Aug 13, Dec 4
BONAVENTURA, St (1221-74)	May 15
BONHOEFFER, Dietrich (1906-45)	Apr 9, Nov 18
BOOBBYER, Brian	Feb 1,22, Mar 26, Jul 5
BOOM, Betsie ten	Dec 3
BOOM, Corrie ten	Apr 2, Jun 30, Aug 8, Oct 9,
BOOTH, Catherine Bramwell	Apr 28, Aug 29
BOOTH, General William (1829-1912)	May 31, Oct 20
BORMANN, Frank	Aug 17, Dec 14
BOSCO, St John (1815-1888)	Mar 10
BREADY, J W	Apr 19
BRIDGES, Robert (1844-1930)	Mar 24, Sept 14
BROOKS, Bishop Phillips (1833-97)	Mar 10, 21, Dec 25
BROOKS, Thomas (1608-80)	Apr 29, Sept 5, 9
BROWNING, Elizabeth Barrett (1806-61)	Jun 2
BROWNING, Robert (1812-89)	Mar 29, Jul 5,
BRUNNER, Emil (1889-1955)	Jan 6
BUBER, Martin (1878-1965)	Sept 12
BUCHMAN, Dr Frank N D (1878-1961)	Jan 25, 28, Feb 10,14, Mar 3,7,19, Apr 6,7,11, May 27, Jun 7,8,30, Jul 4,16,17,18,22, Aug 13,22, Sept 27, Oct 2, 21,27,31, Nov 23,25, Dec 8,10,15,26
BUDDHA, The (c BC 563-483)	July 30

BUNYAN, John (1628-88)   Oct 18, 21
BURKE, Edmund (1729-97)   Feb 11
BURNETT, A Ian   Dec 19
BUSHNELL, Horace (1802-76)   Apr 2, Jun 20
BUTTERFIELD, Sir Herbert (1900-1979)   Aug 3, 26
BUTTERICK, George   Sept 7
CALVIN, John (1509-64)   Jan 6, 11, Jun 16, 21, Aug 19,
                                                 Oct 14
CAMARA, Dom Helder   Oct 27
CAMPBELL, Dr Paul (1912-1995)   Jan 22, 31, Mar 20, 26, Apr 8,
                                                 May 17, 21, 23, 26, Jun 28,
                                                 Jul 28, Sept 16, Oct 28.
  With Peter Howard: Feb 2, Mar 21, May 15, Jun 4,
                                                 Jul 2, Aug 10, Oct 29, Dec 3
CAMUS, Albert (1913-1960)   Jan 3, Oct 5
CAMUS Bishop Jean-Pierre (1582-1652)   Jan 13, 28, Sept 30
CAREY, William (1761-1834)   Dec 17
CARLYLE, Thomas (1795-1881)   Jan 3, 12, Dec, 6, 15
CARMICHAEL, Amy (1867-1951)   Mar 6,8, Sept 22,30, Oct 8,
                                                 Dec 16
CARRETTO, Carlo   Jan 15, Apr 24, May 26
CARTER, Sydney   Mar 27
CASTLE, Anthony P   Sept 4
CECIL, Richard (1748-1810)   Oct 26, Nov 27
CERVANTES, Miguel de (1547-1616)   Jul 8
CHADWICK, Samuel (1832-1917)   Oct 28
CHAMBERS, Oswald   Jan 19, Feb 5,8,19,29, Mar
                                                 8,15, Apr 27, May 25, Jul 3,
                                                 Aug 21, Oct 16, Dec 31
CHEKHOV, Anton (1860-1904)   Jun 23
CHESTERTON, G K (1874-1936)   Nov 20
CHORLEY, H Fothergill   Jun 5
CHRYSOSTOM, St John (347-407)   May 19, Dec 2
CHURCHILL, Sir Winston (1874-1965)   Feb 25, Apr 13, Nov 2
CLEMENT of Alexandria, St (c.150-220)   Sept 9, Oct 25
CLOUGH, Arthur Hugh (1819-61)   Jul 21
COFFIN, C (1676-1749)   Dec 20
COGGAN, Archbishop Donald   Jan 3, Feb 13, May 1, Jun 16,
                                                 Oct 25, Dec 5,17.
COLE, W Owen   Jun 9
COLLIER, Jeremy (1650-1726)   May 24
COLWELL Brothers   Feb 29
CONFUCIUS (BC550-478)   Apr 4, Jul 10,15, Sept 26
CONKLIN, Edward (1863-1952)   Apr 10
COOK, Sydney   Oct 12
  With Garth Lean: Jul 4,30,31
COOPER, Heaton   Sept 10
COOPER, Neville   Nov 24
CORCORAN, Duncan   Aug 2

261

COWPER, William (1731-1800)	Jan 14,19, May 22, Nov 2
COX, Coleman	Aug 14
CRANMER, Archbishop Thomas (1489-1556)	Jan 12
CROMWELL, Oliver (1599-1658)	May 22
CRONIN, Dr A J (1896-1981)	May 30
CUSHING, Cardinal	Aug 1
DALAI Lama	Jun 11
DANTE ALIGHIERI (1265-1321)	Jul 16, Sept 1
DAVIDMAN, Joy	May 22
DAVIES, S J	Apr 3
de CHARDIN, P Teilhard (1881-1955)	Apr 11
de CAUSSADE, J P (1675-1751)	Feb 24, Apr 22
DECK, Northcote	Jun 22
DENK, Hans	Mar 3
DENNISON, Leslie	Jul 8
DENNY, James	Oct 13
DIX, William Chatterton (1837-98)	Dec 24
DODD, C H (1884-1973)	Jun 6
DODDRIDGE, Philip (1702-51)	Oct 15
DOLBEN, D M (1848-67)	Nov 28
DONNE, John (1573-1631)	Mar 2
DOSTOEVSKY, Feodor (1821-81)	Jul 2, 23, Sept 12
DRAKE, Sir Francis (1540-96)	May 7
DRINKWATER, F H	Jul 24
DRUMMOND, Prof Henry (1851-97)	Jan 12,17, Feb 1, Mar 12, May 12, Jul 5,18, Aug 19, Sept 28, Oct 15, Nov 17
DRYDEN, John (1631-1700)	Feb 25
DUNN, Ronald	Mar 12
DYKE, Henry van (1852-1933)	Dec 28
ECKHART, Meister (1260-1327)	Feb 26, Aug 7
EDDY, Sherwood	Nov 25
EDISON, Thomas A (1847-1931)	Jan 23
EDWARDS, Jonathan (1703-57)	Apr 22
EINSTEIN, Albert (1879-1955)	Jan 9, Apr 10
ELIOT, George (1819-80)	Jan 3
ELIOT, Thomas S (1888-1965)	Mar 2
ELIZABETH II Queen	Jun 9
ELLIOTT, Elisabeth (1836-97)	Jun 16
ELLIS, H Havelock (1859-1939)	Oct 19
EMERSON, Ralph Waldo (1803-82)	Feb 9, Mar 13, Apr 23, May 15, Oct 23, Nov 11,13
EPICTETUS (60-120)	Jan 24, Sept 11, Nov 8
FABER, Frederick W (1814-63)	Apr 13, May 2, Oct 3
FABER, Geoffrey	Sept 17
FÉNELON, Archbishop François (1651-1715)	Jan 18, May 4, Jun 18, 19, Jul 19, 20, Aug 16, 23, Sept 6, 13, Nov 7, 16, Dec 13

FIELDING, Henry (1707-54)	Nov 17
FOSTER, John	Apr 5
FOX, George (1624-91)	Feb 19, Oct 18
FRANCIS of Assisi, St (1181-1226)	Mar 28
FRANCIS, Brendon	Apr 17
FRANCIS de Sales, St (1567-1622)	Mar 7, Jul 3, Aug 25, Dec 9
FRANK, Erich	Aug 3
FRANKLIN, Benjamin (1706-90)	Feb 15, Nov 30
FROMM, Erich	Jun 9
FROST, Paul	Sept 19
FRY, Elizabeth (1780-1845)	Jan 7
FULLER, David Otis	Oct 6
GAIN, Geoffrey	Dec 30
GANDHI, Mahatma Mohandas (1869-1948)	Jan 18, Jul 16
GANDHI, Rajmohan	Feb 24, Jun 8
GAY, Frances	Apr 19
GIBBON, Dr Monk	Feb 9
GIBRAN Khalil (1833-1931)	Oct 1
GLUBB, Sir John Bagot (1897-1986)	May 8
GOETHE, Johann W von (1749-1832)	Sept 29
GORDON, A J	Nov 9
GRAHAM, Dr Billy	Apr 1, Oct 12, Nov 4, 15, 22, 27
GRATRY, Père Alphonse (1805-72)	Jan 11, Jul 28, Sept 30, Oct 20, Dec 5
GREGORY I, St Pope (c540-604)	Apr 25, Aug 19, Sept 7, Dec 9
GRELLET, Stephen	Jul 20
GRENFELL, Sir Wilfred (1865-1940)	Apr 26
GRIDER, Kenneth	Jun 17
GRIFFITH, Allan	Mar 28
GROU, Père Jean N (1731-1803)	Jul 7, Oct 26
GUINESS, Os	May 15
GULDSETH, Mark	Dec 6
GURNALL, William	Nov 8
GUTHRIE, Thomas (1803-1873)	Aug 15
HALL, Francis	Jul 20
HAMBRO, President C J	May 19
HAMILTON, Loudon	Mar 18, Nov 15
HAMMARSKJÖLD, Dag (1905-61)	Jan 27, May 5, Aug 16, Oct21
HANNON, Peter	Jan 23
HARDY, Thomas (1840-1928)	Nov 26
HARE, Augustus W (1792-1834)	Dec 10
HARRIS, J Rendel (1852-1941)	Jan 6
HASTINGS, Robert J	Jul 4
HAVERGAL, Frances Ridley (1836-79)	Apr 24, Dec 23

HAZLITT, William (1778-1830)	Jul 1
HEBER, Bishop R (1783-1826)	May 18
HECKER, Isaac T (1819-88)	Aug 27, Oct 2
HENRY, Matthew (1662-1714)	Mar 25, Jun 18,24, Jul 21, Nov 2,12
HENRY, William	Feb 3
HERBERT, George (1593-1633)	Oct 23, Dec 7
HERMAN, Elisabeth	Nov 7
HERMAS (2nd century)	Sept 3
HESSION, Roy	May 10
HICKS, Roger	Jan 10
HILL, Rev Roland	May 7
HOFMEYR, Bremer	Apr 16, Nov 4, Dec 19
HOLME, Reginald (1909-92)	Feb 15
HOLTBY, Winifred (1898-1935)	Oct 7
HOPKINS, Gerard Manley (1844-89)	Sept 26
HORE-RUTHVEN, James	Jun 2
HOW, Bishop W Walsham (1823-97)	Jul 29, Dec 22
HOWARD, Peter (1908-65)	Jan 5,26,27,31, Feb 13,21,28, Mar 2,4,14,15, Apr 23,29, May 16, Jun 7, Jul 8,22, Aug 1, Sept 27, Oct 16,29, Nov 5, Dec 28
With Dr Paul Campbell:	Feb 2, Mar 21, May 15, Jun 4, Jul 2, Aug 10, Oct 29, Dec 3
HOWELL, Wing Commander Edward	Jul 2
HUBBARD, Elbert (1859-1915)	Oct 4
HÜGEL, Baron Friedrich von (1852-1925)	Jan 28, Apr 22, Oct 7, Dec 11
HUGHES, Rev Selwyn © CWR	Jan 30, Feb 16,21, Mar 24, Apr 12, Jul 11, Aug 7, Sept 2,10, Oct 22, Dec 20
HUGO, Victor (1802-85)	Mar 20, Apr 3
HUME, Cardinal Basil	May 14, Sept 29, Oct 25
HUMMEL, Charles	Jan 29
HUNTE, Conrad	May 19
HUNTER, Rev John	Feb 12, Jul 10
IBISH, Professor Ibish	Mar 11, Jun 26
IBSEN, Henrik (1828-1906)	Sept 23
IGNATIUS, Loyola St (1491-1556)	Apr 21, May 30, Oct 25
IGNATIUS of Antioch, St (c35-c107)	Nov 3
INGE, Dean William R (1860-1954)	Jan 29, Feb 28, Jun 22
IRENAEUS, St (c125-202)	Jan 10, Dec 24
JACKS, L P (1860-1955)	Oct 6
JAMES, William (1842-1910)	Apr 14
JASPER, Hilys	Apr 29
JEROME, St (c340-420)	Apr 23, Sept 15,27, Nov 2
JEROME, Jerome K (1859-1927)	May 8

LEWIS, Martyn	Aug 2
LIGUORI, St Alphonsus (1696-1787)	Sep 3, Oct 14
LINCOLN, President Abraham (1809-65)	Aug 28
LINDSAY, Thomas Martin (1843-1914)	Nov 14
LIVINGSTONE, David (1813-73)	Feb 9, Apr 15, Aug 24, Nov 26
LLOYD-JONES, Dr Martyn	Jan 16,17, Feb 29, Jun 26, Aug 31, Sept 4, Dec 7, 22
LONG, Boswell C	Sept 17
LONGFELLOW, Henry W (1807-82)	Jul 20
LOUGHRANE, John P	Jul 29
LOWELL, J R (1819-91)	Apr 28
LUTHER, Dr Martin (1483-1546)	Feb 13, 25, Apr 15, Jun 19, Aug 11
LYNSIGHT, Sydney	Sept 8
LYTE Henry Francis (1793-1847)	Jan 16
MACARTHUR, General Douglas (1880-1864)	Sept 6
MACAULEY, J C	Mar 19, Aug 9
MACDONALD, George (1824-1905)	Mar 5
MACKINTOSH, Hugh R (1870-1936)	Nov 30
MACKINTOSH, Sir James (1765-1812)	Oct 27
MACGREGOR, W M	Oct 5
MACLAREN, Alexander (1826-1932)	Mar 31, Aug 14
MACNAUGHTEN, John	Oct 4
MANDELA, Nelson	Jun 11, Nov 26
MALTBY, F R	Oct 31
MANNING, Cardinal Henry E (1808-92)	Apr 22
MARCEL, Gabriel (1889-1973)	Feb 6, Dec 25
MARSH, John	Nov 6
MARSHALL, Catharine	Dec 13
MATHESON, George (1842-1906)	Sept 16
MATHEW, Rev Gervase O P (1905-76)	Nov 13
MAX MÜLLER, Friedrich (1823-1900)	Dec 30
MAY, Rollo	Aug 2
McCRACKEN, Robert	Nov 18
McCHEYNE, Robert Murray (1813-43)	Jun 17, Aug 24, Oct 10
McLEOD, George F, Lord (b1895)	Dec 14
MERTON, Thomas (1915-68)	Mar 23, Jul 17, Nov 11,29, Dec 21
MEWTON, Dr Margaret	Jan 15, Jun 23
MEYER, Rev F B (1847-1929)	Jan 21,26, Feb 15, Mar 9, 16,26, May 9, Jun 13, Aug 26,18
MEYNELL, Alice (1847-1922)	Aug 15
MILLER J R	Aug 17
MILNE, Bruce J	Dec 2
MILTON, John (1608-74)	Dec 1, 2
MOHAMMAD, Prince el Farad al Saoud	Sept 17

266

MOHAMMED, The Prophet (570-632)	Jun 28, Nov 8
MONSELL, J S B (1811-75)	Jan 16, Aug 15
MONTGOMERY of Alamein, Viscount (1887-1976))	Jun 19
MONTINI, Archbishop	Jan 2
MONTROSE, Marquess of (1612-50)	Aug 25
MOTYER, J A	Dec 21
MOODY, Dwight L (1837-99)	Feb 12, Apr 10,20, May 18, Jun 28, Aug 10, 30, Nov 6
MORE, Sir Thomas (1478-1535)	Oct 5, Nov 9
MORGAN, Dr Campbell	Jan 23
MORRISON, John M	May 29, Sept 13,
MUGGERIDGE, Malcolm (1903-90)	Jan 4, Apr 7,
MÜLLER, George (1805-98)	May 3, Sept 5,14,18, Oct 9
MURDOCH, Dame Iris	Aug 17
MURRAY, Andrew	Aug 28
NA, Tolon (1896-1986)	Apr 8
NAPOLEON, Bonaparte (1769-1821)	Dec 21
NEWMAN, Cardinal J H (1801-90)	Jan 6,16, Mar 31, Apr 5,11, May 13, Jun 2, Jul 14,25, Aug 11,25, Sept 10,27, Oct 2,9, Nov 29, Dec 12,20
NEWTON, Sir Isaac (1642-1727)	May 3, Dec 13
NEWTON, John (1725-1807)	Jan 13, Feb 1, 14, May 3, Jul 27, Aug 12, Sept 8
NEWTON, Joseph	Nov 11
NEWQUIST, David	Mar 13
NIEBUHR, Professor Reinhold (1892-1971)	Aug 31
NIGHTINGALE, Florence (1820-1910)	Mar 13, Jul 7, Aug 9, 27, Dec 1
NOBLE, Kenneth	Jan 16, Mar 28
NORWID, Cyprian	Dec 29
NUFFIELD, Viscount (1877-1963)	Sept 23
NUTTALL, Dr G F	Mar 9
NYEIN THA, Daw	Feb 19
O'CONNELL, Daniel (1775-1847)	Jun 12
OKOMU, Professor Washington	Apr 30
ORIGEN of Alexandia (c185-254)	Dec 10
ORTIZ, Jean	Oct 31
PACKER, J I	Jan 22, Aug 30
PALMER, Mrs Margaret	Mar 31
PARKHURST, Charles W	Sept 21
PASCAL, Blaise (1623-62)	Jan 20, Feb 10, Jun 29, Oct 11, Dec 9
PATRICK, St (c385-461)	May 12, Dec 22

SCHWEITZER, Dr Albert (1875-1965)	May 29
SCOFIELD, Rev C I	Feb 19
SCOTT, Sir Walter (1771-1832)	May 11
SCROGGIE, Dr Graham	Jan 23, Aug 11
SECRET, THE, authors of (Juliet Boobbyer, Sydney Cook, James Hore-Ruthven, John Lester, Graham and Jean Turner)	Mar 1, Jul 13,14, Sept 24, Oct 1,17
SEGESTRÅLE, Lennart	Sept 10
SHAKESPEARE, William (1564-1616)	Jan 19, Nov 10, 28, Dec 8
SHAW, G Bernard (1856-1950)	Aug 13
SHEEN, Archbishop Fulton J (d1979)	Feb 17, 26, Aug 10, Sept 12, Oct 10
SIBBES, Richard	Mar 4, Nov 9
SIDER, Ronald J	Jan 21
SIMPSON, Donald	Oct 12
SMUTS, J C (1870-1950)	Nov 24
SNELLMAN, Paula	Jan 25
SOLZHENITSYN, Alexander	Apr 5, Dec 12
SPINOZA, Baruch de (1632-77)	Sept 6
SPOERRI, Pierre	May 20, Nov 20
With Lester:	Mar 5, Oct 22, Nov 18
SPOERRI, Professor Theophil (1890-1975)	Jan 25, Mar 30, Apr 20, Aug 14
SPURGEON, Charles H (1834-92)	Jan 7, Mar 31, Apr 4, Jun 25, Aug 14, Nov 2,19
STAM, John	Jan 29
STEWART, James S (1843-1913)	Aug 5, Dec 16
STOTT, Rev John R W	Jan 27, Aug 28
STRAIT, Neil	Jan 2, Aug 29, Sept 26, Dec 21
STREETER, Canon B H (1874-1937)	Apr 28, Aug 19, 20, Sept 13
STUDD, C T (1862-1931)	Mar 7,27, Jul 26
STUDDERT-KENNEDY, G A (1883-1929)	Jan 9, Jul 17, Sept 2, Oct 29
SUENENS, Cardinal Leon J (1904-	Feb 14, Aug 14
SUNDAY, Bill (1863-1935)	Jun 20
SURUR Sheikh Ahmad	Mar 17
SWIFT, Jonathan (1667-1745)	Oct 31
TAULER, Johann (1301-1361)	Jan 11
TAYLOR, Bishop John	May 10
TAYLOR, Bishop Jeremy (1613-1667)	Feb 13, Apr 15
TAYLOR, Dr Hudson (1832-1903)	Jan 8, Mar7, May 8, Oct 3
TAYLOR, Sir Thomas	Jun 6
TEMPLE, Archbishop William (1881-1944)	Jan 14, Feb 25, Mar 3,27, Apr 15, May 3, Jun 1, Jul 15, Aug 16,30, Sept 11,24, Nov 12
TENNYSON, Alfred Lord (1809-92)	Jan 29, Dec 31
TERESA of AVILA (1815-82)	Jan 24, Mar 23, Jun 8, Sept 3

TERESA, Mother of Calcutta	May 13, Jun 12,15,20, Jul 7,27, Dec 23
TERSTEEGEN, Gerhard (1697-1769)	Jan 28, Jun 15
TERTULLIAN, Quintus (160-220)	Sept 14
THÉRÈSE, St of Lisieux (1873-1897)	Jun 28, Jul 9,24
THORNHILL, Rev Alan	Nov 13, Dec 9
TOLSTOY, Count Leo (1828-1910)	Sept 21
TOPLADY, Augustus M (1740-1778)	Jan 5,9, Oct 14
TOURNIER, Dr Paul	Jan 2, Jul 12, Nov 30
TOURVILLE, Abbé Henri de (1842-1903)	Jul 13
TOYNBEE, Arnold (1889-1975)	Feb 9
TOZER, A V (1897-1963)	Feb 29, Apr 6, May 8, Aug 21, Oct 30
TRAHERNE, Thomas (1638-74)	Sept 18
TRUMAN, President Harry S (1884-1972)	Mar 16
TUTTIET, L	Dec 30
TUTU, Archbishop Desmond	Mar 3, May 4
TWAIN, Mark (1835-1910)	Sept 22, Oct 6
TWITCHELL, Kenaston	Mar 17, Aug 21, Dec 11
ULLATHORNE, Archbishop William (1806-89)	May 22, Aug 18
UNDERHILL, Evelyn (1875-1941)	Jan 2, 27, May 24, Jun 21
UPHAM, T C	Nov 14
URQUHART, Colin	Oct 7, Nov 13,16
VÉNARD, Blessed Théophane (1829-61)	Jul 15
VIANNEY, Jean-Baptiste (1786-1859)	Jul 15
VICKERS, John	Sept 19
VINCENT de Paul, St (1581-1660)	Jun 29, Nov 21
VINEY, Rev Hallen	Feb 8, 18, 22, Mar 26
WALTER, H A (1883-1918)	May 25
WARD, Barbara (1914-81)	Sept 20
WARD, William A (1812-1882)	Mar 16
WARING, Anne Letitia (1820-1910)	Dec 14
WASHINGTON, President George (1732-1799)	Feb 23, Apr 29, Dec 2
WATSON, Canon David	Jan 4,13, Feb 15, Mar 30, Apr 11,17, Jun 6,29, Jul 10, Aug 6, 8, Oct 16, Nov 20, Dec 18, 22
WATSON, Dr John	Jul 18
WATSON, Thomas	Jan 18, Sept 6
WATTS, Isaac (1674-1748)	Apr 16
WATTS, Malcolm	Aug 31
WEBSTER, Daniel (1782-1852)	Dec 12
WELLS, H G (1866-1946)	Jan 17, Aug 27
WESLEY, Charles (1707-88)	Mar 8,11, Jun 25, Oct 30, Dec 16
WESLEY, John (1703-91)	Feb 19, Apr 19, Jun 24, Oct 13

270

WHITEFIELD, George (1714-70)	Mar 23, Oct 6, Nov 19, Dec 16
WHITTIER, John Greenleaf (1807-1892)	Sept 6, Oct 18
WIESBE, Warren	Jul 24
WILBERFORCE, William (1759-1833)	Jan 1, Apr 13, Oct 6,12
WILHELMSEN, Jens-J	Oct 10
WILLIAMS, J (1802-65)	Jun 25
WILLIS, L M	Oct 10
WILSON, Sir Harold (1916-95)	Sept 21
WILSON, Rev Roland	Nov 6
WILSON, Bishop Thomas (1663-1755)	Apr 20, Dec 12
WILSON, President Woodrow (1854-1924)	May 23
WINSLOW Rev Jack	Jun 19
WISE, Gordon	Mar 18
WOOD Frederick P	Mar 10, May 7, Dec 2
WORDSWORTH, Bishop Christopher (1807-85)	Sept 7
WORDSWORTH, William (1771-1856)	May 2, Jul 15
WOTTON, Sir Henry (1568-1639)	Jun 23
WRIGHT, Professor Henry B	Apr 14, May 26, Nov 25, Dec 6
WURMBRAND, Pastor Richard	Feb 20, Mar 11, Apr 4,12, Jul 1, 19, 27, 29
XENOPHON (BC430-355)	Feb 19
ZWINGLI, Ulrich (1484-1531)	Jun 14

Bible Source Index

278

Acknowledgements

The authors acknowledge with great appreciation the wide range of literature from which they have been able to draw their quotations. Their aim is to make available for the next generation the riches that have strengthened their own faith over a lifetime.

Where possible permission to reproduce these quotations has been sought from the appropriate publishers and trusts for this limited edition, but we regret that this has not been possible in every case. In the event of anyone wanting to reproduce a quotation not acknowledged below, which is still in copyright, please write to the publisher enclosing a stamped addressed envelope and we will do our best to advise the copyright holder.

Extracts from the Authorised Version of the Bible (The King James Bible), the rights of which are invested in the Crown, are reproduced by permission of the Crown's Patentee, Cambridge University Press.

Scriptures quoted from the Good News Bible, published by The Bible Societies / Harper Collins Publishers Ltd., UK, © American Bible Society, 1966, 1971, 1976, 1992.

The Revised Standard Version of The Bible, © 1946, 1952, 1971 by the Division of Christian Education of the National Council of Churches of Christ in the USA. Used by permission.

New English Bible © Oxford University Press and Cambridge University, 1961, 1970.

Quotations from the New Testament translation by J B Phillips are quoted by permission of Harper Collins Publishers Ltd.

Quotations from Michel Quoist's *Prayers of Life* are published by permission of Gill and Macmillan.